Crises of the Sentence

Crises of the Sentence

Jan Mieszkowski

The University of Chicago Press CHICAGO & LONDON

The University of Chicago Press, Chicago 60637
The University of Chicago Press, Ltd., London

Published 2019
Printed in the United States of America

28 27 26 25 24 23 22 21 20 19 1 2 3 4 5

ISBN-13: 978-0-226-61705-3 (cloth)
ISBN-13: 978-0-226-61719-0 (paper)
ISBN-13: 978-0-226-61722-0 (e-book)
DOI: https://doi.org/10.7208/chicago/9780226617220.001.0001

Library of Congress Cataloging-in-Publication Data

Names: Mieszkowski, Jan, 1968– author.
Title: Crises of the sentence / Jan Mieszkowski.
Description: Chicago : The University of Chicago Press, 2019. | Includes bibliographical references and index.
Identifiers: LCCN 2018036445 | ISBN 9780226617053 (cloth : alk. paper) | ISBN 9780226617190 (pbk. : alk. paper) | ISBN 9780226617220 (e-book)
Subjects: LCSH: Grammar, Comparative and general—Sentences—Philosophy.
Classification: LCC P295 .M54 2019 | DDC 415.01—dc23
LC record available at https://lccn.loc.gov/2018036445

♾ This paper meets the requirements of ANSI/NISO Z39.48–1992 (Permanence of Paper).

CONTENTS

ACKNOWLEDGMENTS

I first tried out the idea of "a book about the sentence" on Hugh Hochman. His enthusiasm for the project convinced me that it was something I should pursue. Many other friends and colleagues provided advice and inspiration, sometimes in the form of their own elegant or witty sentences. I especially want to thank Eyal Amiran, Ian Balfour, Kris Cohen, Rebecca Comay, Troy Cross, Elena Epaneshnik, Katja Garloff, Markus Hardtmann, Daniel Hoffman-Schwartz, Paul Hovda, Eric Jarosinski a.k.a. @NeinQuarterly, Anna Kornbluh, Brian McGrath, Kristina Mendicino, Julia Ng, Katrin Pahl, Thomas Pfau, Marc Redfield, Avital Ronell, Morgan Ross a.k.a. @tinynietzsche, Haun Saussy, Thomas Schestag, Zachary Sng, Rei Terada, and Catherine Witt. Continuing a conversation we began over thirty years ago, John Stewart valiantly fielded my linguistics questions and managed to keep his sense of humor when even his wise counsel couldn't prevent me from going astray. My mother, Gretchen Mieszkowski, read the first draft of the manuscript and offered her usual illuminating commentary. Her sense of what was and was not working gave me confidence that the finish line was in sight.

I received valuable feedback on some of the book's major arguments from audiences at Brown University, Duke University, Goldsmiths (University of London), Indiana University, Johns Hopkins University, and New York University. Early drafts of a few sections of chapter 1 appeared in "Romancing the Slogan," *European Romantic Review* 28, no. 3 (May 2017), and "What's in a Slogan?," *Mediations* 29, no. 2 (Spring 2016); some passages in chapter 3 appeared in "The Romantic Sentence," *Romantic Circles Praxis Series* (December 2016).

At the University of Chicago Press, Alan Thomas expressed great enthusiasm for this project at a formative stage, enabling me to broaden its scope without losing the original focus. The anonymous readers he commissioned offered new perspectives on my analyses that proved extremely helpful in finalizing the manuscript. The expertise of Jo Ann Kiser, Randolph Petilos, and the rest of the Press's staff made for an exemplary editorial and production process.

Sarah Roff has long brought her unique combination of stylistic exactingness and wry humor to bear on my sentences, always to their benefit, if not infrequently to their peril. Hopefully she won't get tired of reading them anytime soon.

Introduction: What Is a Sentence?

The sentence is the greatest invention of civilization.

JOHN BANVILLE

I really do not know that anything has ever been more exciting than diagramming sentences.

GERTRUDE STEIN

All grammars leak.

EDWARD SAPIR

What is a sentence? Surely we have all known the answer for as long as we can remember. Save perhaps the word, no other concept has so profoundly shaped our existence as linguistic beings. In early childhood, we reached a milestone the first time we conjugated a verb and aligned it, whether implicitly or explicitly, with a subject or object. Soon thereafter we were producing hundreds and then thousands of subject-predicate constructions on a daily basis, for the most part without great effort or concentration. In elementary school, we learned that a sentence is a "complete thought" and that it "stands alone," which is to say that it is a group of words that articulates a proposition, question, or command. Working from this first principle, we were taught to create simple, compound, and complex sentences while avoiding fragments and run-ons. By high school, we were well versed in the trials and tribulations of producing lively or elegant prose. When we reached college, our professors cautioned us that we would never know how well worked out our thoughts were until they were set down as complete statements on the page. Whatever the context, whatever the concern, sentences are on the job, forever signifying, referring, and performing, their beginnings and endings clearly delineated in speech by rhythms of intonations, stresses, and pauses, and in writing by capitalized words and terminal punctuation marks. Tastes, genres, and conventions may change, styles come and go, new media emerge, but it is to the sentence—or to an ellipsed version thereof—that we turn countless times a day when we want, in J. L. Austin's famous phrase, to do things with words.

Thanks to the sentence, we are always ready to propose or command, entreat or cajole, wish or promise at a moment's notice. This overwhelming evidence of the sentence's utility may disincline us to treat it as a source of conceptual complexity or confusion. As Sisyphean as the labors of our writing may be, we tend to regard our inability to get a particular phrase or clause "just right" as a symptom of our own subjective failings rather than an indication that grammar is intrinsically flawed. More generally, this appears to be an area in which praxis decidedly has the upper hand over theory. Any abstract account—or critique—of the sentence is bound to seem schematic or impoverished when measured against the wealth of clever, elegant, and imaginative formulations that surround us all the time.

The sentence's impressive track record notwithstanding, there is a long history of efforts to improve on or outright replace it. Fiction and nonfiction writers alike have suspected that their inability to perfect their texts may be less a sign of a dearth of talent or dedication to their craft than an indication that the traditional sentence is too restrictive in the limits it imposes on expression or, more insidiously, that it creates expectations for the coordination of thought and representation that simply cannot be met. In the resulting challenges to the authority of grammar, punctuation, and more informal conventions, linguistic norms are often loudly condemned, particularly the assumption that relatively short strings of words neatly separated by full stops are the "natural" units of expression. Other authors have tried to pen prose or verse that cannot be read without calling into question the presumed hierarchies that obtain between different parts of speech, between dependent and independent clauses, or between individual sentences—assuming they are still identifiable as such—and the texts in which they appear.

Some philosophers have been even more strident in their indictment of the sentence. G. W. Leibniz envisioned a *characteristica universalis*, a rational system of signs and operations that would function with mathematical rigor, making it impossible to craft vague or false propositions. More recently, Gottlob Frege and Bertrand Russell endeavored to develop formal symbolic systems no longer plagued by the inherent imprecision and ambiguity of so-called "natural" languages. Variations on these projects are still pursued by countless logicians who take it as a matter of course that the inadequacies of ordinary sentences severely limit the rigor of discourse.

Calling on us to "rise above [our] faith in grammar," Friedrich Nietzsche famously deplored our unquestioning reliance on sentences and strove to highlight the degree to which this central verbal form organizes our ideas about virtually everything.[1] Most technical accounts of the sentence invoke some version of a subject-predicate construct (noun phrase and verb phrase; subject-verb-object; actor-act-goal) or describe it as a unit organized around one or more finite verbs specifying tense or modality. Assessing the hegemony of this paradigm, Nietzsche asks: "Might not this belief in the concept of subject and predicate be a great stupidity?"[2] His claim is that our convictions that events are the "effects" of "causes" and that "deeds" are the products of a "doer" are evidence of the "seduction of language (and the basic errors of reason petrified in it)."[3] In a frequently cited example, he proposes that grammar errs in presenting an occurrence, a flash of lightning, as a relationship between an agent and its action, transforming a single happening, the flashing, into a subject, "lightning," and a verb, "flashes." The "doer," Nietzsche insists, "is merely tacked on as a fiction to the doing."[4]

Everything we believe about events and praxis, and hence about history, politics, and even the priority of being over becoming, is shaped by this blind allegiance to subject-predicate thinking. Anything but an abstract philosophical concern, our investment in this conception of language makes its influence felt in eminently pragmatic contexts, for example when writing manuals explain that "people tend to perceive a sentence as clear when its narrative—generally, the story it tells or the relationship it describes—corresponds to its grammatical structure. In other words, if you wish to write clearly, begin by making your narrative's characters the subjects of sentences, and their actions and identities the predicates."[5] Unfortunately, having characterized us as trapped within this linguistic ideology, Nietzsche offers little encouragement about our prospects of escaping from it.

Nietzsche is hardly the only author to have suspected that our ethico-political fate is inextricably bound up with the standing of the sentence. Karl Marx identified a critique of the classical proposition as a crucial feature of resistance to the ruling order, while his contemporary Walt Whitman attempted

1. Friedrich Nietzsche, *Beyond Good and Evil/On the Genealogy of Morality*, *The Complete Works of Friedrich Nietzsche*, vol. 8, trans. Adrian Del Caro (Stanford, CA: Stanford University Press, 2014), 38.

2. Friedrich Nietzsche, *Writings from the Late Notebooks*, trans. Kate Surge (New York: Cambridge University Press, 2003), 74.

3. Nietzsche, *Beyond Good and Evil/On the Genealogy of Morality*, 74.

4. Nietzsche, *Beyond Good and Evil/On the Genealogy of Morality*, 236.

5. Michael Harvey, *The Nuts and Bolts of College Writing* (Indianapolis: Hackett Publishing, 2003), 10.

to write sentences that would embody an irreducibly democratic spirit. In the twentieth century, Gertrude Stein linked the decline of the literary sentence with the rise of imperialism, and Karl Kraus suggested that a flawed syntactic formation could be a tragedy of world-historical proportions. More recently, a wide range of critical projects have proceeded on the assumption that to articulate the specificities of ethnic and cultural hybridities, we must embrace discursive modes that escape the petrification of action and becoming that is effected by the subject-predicate language Nietzsche attacked.

These many different reflections on the powers and limits of the sentence form have rarely been treated as parts of a common discussion. This book will attempt to tell the story of the sentence in the modern era, beginning at the turn of the nineteenth century, which saw broad challenges to the traditional philosophical proposition and neoclassical models of clarity, and working forward to the present day, when the celebration of great books has been replaced by a celebration of great sentences. As we start to connect the dots and see the outline of an intellectual history of the sentence emerge, we may be struck that this concept has played such a muted role in literary theory and criticism. This may sound implausible, since scholars of literature study sentences for a living and are constantly hunting for choice specimens. Numerous academic works discuss the styles and forms of the sentences peculiar to a given work or author, aesthetic movement, or era—indeed, one could argue that any study of prose has something to say, if only implicitly, about its sentential structures and rhythms. Nonetheless, the sentence as such has rarely been an object of explicit reflection. Analyzing particular sentences, identifying different kinds of sentences, explaining how a given sentence does or does not produce its intended effect—all of this can be accomplished without ever treating the sentence as a dynamic to be considered in its own right. We routinely assume that we understand the sentence's nuances, if it has any, and take for granted that it is the building block of larger formations (paragraphs, arguments, essays) without feeling any need to detail precisely what the sentence is and how it works, as if it were of no more interest than the conventions of orthography.

If literary studies has largely kept the concept of the sentence in the background, this has in part been due to the preeminence of close reading practices in which signification is treated primarily as an interplay of grammatical and rhetorical relationships at the level of the word or phrase rather than in terms of predicative structures. Equally significant has been the widespread embrace of semiotic and structuralist models of language that have on the one hand focused attention on the smallest of verbal elements—words, syllables, and letters—and on the other hand have prompted the elaboration of more abstract models of representation that reject the organizational priority of the grammatical structure or "surface level" of a text. Lying just outside the purview of the prevailing microscopic and macroscopic paradigms of analysis, the sentence has been left alone. The institutional bifurcation of the teaching of literature and writing has helped to solidify this state of affairs. As professors of literature have contented themselves with studying the peculiarities of individual sentences and authorial styles, more general considerations of the sentence have either been delegated to those engaged in teaching composition or else outright ignored, with the tacit assumption that linguists and possibly philosophers will pick up the slack.

The consequence is that students of literature study Aristotle's metaphor, Coleridge's symbol, or Kristeva's chora, whereas theories of the sentence have no comparable place in the curriculum. Despite its affinities with the classical units of discourse such as the *periodus* or the *oratio*, the sentence has no entry in any glossary of literary-critical, poetic, or rhetorical terms, nor is it a topic of any of the various essays in the standard anthologies of literary criticism, not warranting a single entry in their subject indexes. Even in studies of verse, where the potential clash between the line and the sentence is often overt—to the point that some scholars have gone so far as to argue that the tension between them defines the genre—there is a tendency to treat enjambment as one more rhetorical maneuver in the poet's bag of tricks rather than as an indication of how poetry can alter our conception of discourse. When these problems are posed in formal terms, they are prone to devolve into debates about the distinction between poetry and prose rather than prompting reflections on the differences between sentential and nonsentential language.

We should not rush to conclude that this "neglect" of the sentence necessarily constitutes a missed opportunity or a mistake. There may be perfectly good reasons for not according the sentence a prominent role in the conceptualization of literary language or designating it as a central parameter of our interpretative labors. Alternatively, we might consider whether the sentence has always been a preoccupation of literary studies, albeit one that is kept implicit or goes by other names. In either case, the first step will be to convince ourselves that we do not already know everything that there is to know about the sentence and that there is some rationale for searching for complexity where there appears to be none. Sentences constantly do so much work for us that we could be excused for wanting to let well enough alone.

How difficult is it to explain why one group of words constitutes a self-standing proposition or query or otherwise presents itself as "complete" while another does not? Most morphology textbooks begin by acknowledging that there is no single definition of the word on the basis of which we can rigorously distinguish words from nonwords, and one might say the same thing about the sentence, with the additional complication that the very ambition to define a sentence is potentially already a challenge to its authority, since dictionary entries are one of the few places where sentences are not the dominant verbal form. Examining definitions of the term, we find that each has several facets whose interrelationships are not entirely clear. We are told what a sentence does ("it expresses a statement, question, command, or wish" or, more colloquially, "expresses a complete thought"); what it comprises ("it typically contains a subject and a verb"); and where it starts (with a capitalized word) and ends (with a period, exclamation point, or question mark).[6] We are not told whether a particular characteristic is a necessary or a necessary and sufficient condition of the sentence, or whether any of these features is unique to sentences. Is the sentence the only verbal formation that can express a statement, command, or wish? What about the many different strings of words that begin with a capital letter and end with a period without meeting many of the other criteria for a complete sentence? Further complicating matters, definitions of the sentence tend to rely on concepts that either raise a host of metaphysical or psychological issues (What is a complete thought? What does it mean for an utterance to stand alone?) or betray more than a hint of circularity, as when we are told that a sentence is a set of words that respects the rules of grammar in virtue of which a given set of words constitutes a sentence. Attempting to distinguish and prioritize these different versions of the term "sentence," we find ourselves shuttling between philosophy, psychology, and rhetoric, mixing logic and communicative pragmatics with no clear sense of which paradigm can or should anchor the discussion.

As we review the salient features of the sentence, we begin to realize that substantial complexities lurk beneath many of our intuitions and assumptions about it. The sentence is a unit of discourse, a clearly delineated part of a larger whole, be that a paragraph, a casual exchange of remarks on the street, or a warning label on a cleaning product. At the same time, the sentence is only one of a number of such units. Viewed as a collection of constituent parts, language can be characterized as a series of elements of ever-greater length or scale that occur sequentially but are not contained within one another, moving

6. For representative definitions, see "sentence" in the *American Heritage Dictionary of the English Language*, 4th ed. (Boston: Houghton Mifflin, 2000); *Oxford English Dictionary*, 2nd ed., 20 vols. (Oxford: Oxford University Press, 1989); and *Webster's Third New International Dictionary of the English Language, Unabridged* (Springfield, MA: Merriam-Webster, 1993).

from letters and syllables (graphemes and phonemes) to words, phrases, and clauses, and then on to sentences, paragraphs, and beyond.[7] There are, however, fundamental differences between these various units and the ways in which they interact. The relationship between letters and words is not structurally reproduced in the relationship between words and sentences, just as the relationship between words and sentences is not formally or semantically identical to the relationship between sentences and paragraphs.

Once we open this can of worms, it becomes difficult to distinguish between compositional forms that are products of convention and those that are integral to the substance of an argument. Even customarily unremarkable terms such as "paragraph" or "chapter" start to seem like mysterious constructs whose internal structure and authority are not nearly as self-evident as we assume. On this uncertain terrain, the sentence holds out hope of some order and stability, since it marks a crucial frontier within the hierarchy of verbal units. The borders of the sentence are the point at which grammar's stipulations for how we should arrange words and phrases reach, or nearly reach, their limit.[8] Each sentence is a grammatical system unto itself, but whatever governs the relations between sentences, it is not the legislations of grammar.[9] Move beyond the sentence and we find ourselves in the domain of style, as hard and fast rules give way to taste and custom, and our freedom of expression becomes less constrained by objective guidelines than when we are operating at the level of the phrase, clause, or word.

Naturally, conventions exist at every level of composition. Teachers often offer templates for their students' paragraphs or essays that seem as rigid as grammar or spelling rules, and rhetoricians and narratologists have long sought to identify less explicitly codified but no less significant patterns, rhythms, and structures of language that may enjoy the same, or nearly the same, authority as grammar. Nevertheless, it is in the sentence that the tension

7. On the sentence as a unit not contained within another similar unit, see Rodney Huddleston and Geoffrey K. Pullum, *The Cambridge Grammar of the English Language* (New York: Cambridge University Press, 2002), 44.

8. There are trans-sentential features of grammar. As the example of pronouns and their antecedents readily makes clear, "reference and substitution often operate over stretches of discourse larger than the sentence." Bas Aarts, Sylvia Chalker, and Edmund Weiner, *The Oxford Dictionary of English Grammar* (New York: Oxford University Press, 2014), 359.

9. The influential American linguist Leonard Bloomfield defined the sentence as "an independent linguistic form, not included *by virtue of any grammatical construction* in any larger form." Leonard Bloomfield, *Language* (Chicago: University of Chicago Press, 1933), 170 (my emphasis).

between writerly freedom and linguistic necessity is most acutely played out, since there the guidelines for when we are following the rules and when we are wittingly or unwittingly breaking them are clearer than anywhere else. To compose sentences, arguably the defining act of self-expression, is to engage with the limits of our own aims and tastes, exposing ourselves to directives whose function we may not always understand, because much of our experience of grammaticality takes the form of intuitions about what "sounds right," the logic of which we would find ourselves hard-pressed to articulate. Writers do routinely bend or break the rules, whether by coining words or egregiously violating narrative conventions, but tinkering with the mechanics of the sentence brings with it added risks insofar as we are playing around with the very means by which language allows us to say anything about anything.

Of all the conventions surrounding the sentence, none is as familiar, or as ostensibly straightforward, as the rule that a sentence begins with a capital letter and ends with a terminal punctuation mark. Precisely what, however, is punctuation? The rules of grammar govern sentences, but punctuation, ostensibly as rule-bound as anything else, is not part of this system in the same way that syntax or morphology are. Punctuation is sometimes assumed to be an attempt to transcribe the patterns of intonation and stress that occur in oral discourse. Speakers of English, for example, are often taught that commas go "wherever there should be a pause." Of course, let a class of middle-school students follow this guideline in punctuating a text, and no two of them are likely to make the same set of decisions about where the sentences are to be briefly interrupted; and there is scant evidence that age and experience will ameliorate the sense that such judgments are thoroughly subjective.[10]

Beginning with the Hellenic grammarians' efforts to explain the differences between individual punctuation marks, it has proven extremely difficult to decide whether such written symbols represent distinct auditory phenomena, create rhythms and patterns that auditory phenomena in turn seek to imitate, or reveal the presence of differential dynamics that shape both speech and writing. We hold fast to the rules we are taught, which quickly acquire the status of self-evidence, as we come to believe, for example, that we put commas after adverbial phrases at the beginning of sentences because they should "naturally" be there. This is all well and good until a copy editor who has been encouraged to cut down on characters informs us that these punctuation

10. "No two people," writes William H. Gass, "are likely to scan a line or a sentence in the same way, except by mischance." William H. Gass, *Life Sentences: Literary Judgments and Accounts* (New York: Knopf, 2012), 338.

marks are in many cases optional, after which we may begin to wonder why we ever thought we needed them in the first place. In the same vein, we are certain to be taken aback by the placement of commas, semicolons, and even periods in a book fifty or a hundred years old, although we would have been no less confused if someone had told us twenty years ago that in 2018 billions of electronic messages rife with acronyms, images, and icons would be sent every day, frequently with little or no context to aid in deciphering them, yet with scarcely any complaint about the near absence of capitalization or what would traditionally be regarded as punctuation.

The uncertain status of punctuation conventions comes further into relief when we consider how changes in them greatly complicate comparisons of style across eras. As Morris W. Croll notes, one school of thought has maintained that the "long" sentences of Michel de Montaigne or Francis Bacon were crude imitations of the Ciceronian sentence, and if one were to replace their semicolons and colons with commas, one would immediately recognize them as "quaint failures in the attempt to achieve sentence unity."[11] An opposite view maintains that if we simply replace the semicolons and colons with periods, "we should then see that what look like long sentences are really brief and aphoristic ones."[12] In other words, what appear to be two completely different modes of written expression are potentially just a few punctuation marks away from becoming virtually indistinguishable from one another. Croll's observation may confirm the significance of punctuation for our understanding of composition, or it may expose the superficiality of our concepts of style when it comes to characterizing the form and content of a piece of writing.

Another narrative about punctuation holds that its importance increased over time with the rise of secular private reading, as larger numbers of people were individually consuming texts with which they had no prior familiarity. In this account, the *scriptio continua* of classical Greek or Latin, in which there were no spaces between words, gradually gave way to increased punctuation in handwritten manuscripts and finally to a standardized set of symbols with the emergence of the printing press.[13] This story is less compelling when we realize that the very notion that punctuation is a question of rules rather than style

11. Morris W. Croll, *Style, Rhetoric and Rhythm: Essays by Morris W. Croll*, ed. J. Max Patrick et al. (Princeton, NJ: Princeton University Press, 1966), 230.

12. Croll, *Style, Rhetoric and Rhythm*, 230.

13. Such a story of punctuation's development is told by M. B. Parkes, *Pause and Effect: An Introduction to the History of Punctuation in the West* (Berkeley: University of California Press, 1993).

is itself of relatively recent vintage. As Cecelia Watson has proposed, "prior to the 1800s, the majority of grammarians and scholars advocated taste and judgment as a guide to pointing a text."[14] Indeed, she adds, "the Italian humanists, who invented the semicolon and the parenthesis, believed that each writer should work out his punctuation for himself."[15]

Perhaps it is not surprising, then, that punctuation marks, ostensibly designed to defend against vagueness or ambiguity, are frequently as much a source of confusion as words and phrases and in many cases threaten to turn the tables entirely, becoming the elements in a sentence that cry out for clarification. Punctuation's role as a clarifying supplement may even seem like a symptom of larger structural failings, as if it might prove unnecessary to punctuate one's writing if one's sentences were better designed. Sadly, the harder we look at punctuation, the less we understand it. Jennifer DeVere Brody scarcely exaggerates when she observes, "Punctuation's aspirations are problematic. Punctuation is not a proper object: it is neither speech nor writing; art nor craft; sound nor silence. It may be neither here nor there and yet somehow it is everywhere."[16]

While the sentence is the domain of language in which grammar and punctuation are said to hold sway, we tend to disregard their authority when characterizing a sentence's representational or semantic functions. We speak of sentences "unfolding" in a linear fashion, moving from start to finish like a short speech or a brief short story, and most contemporary style manuals recommend that we close our sentences with the "payoff," the new information being imparted to the reader, like the conclusion of a joke. This sounds uncontroversial, since a given sentence's effectiveness clearly has a great deal to do with how its speaker or writer highlights specific elements by situating them at the beginning, middle, or end. A sentence, however, is not simply a sequence of terms that follow one another chronologically, like items in a ranked list. It is also a hierarchical structure of phrases and clauses, and its various parts function only insofar as their respective authority over or subordination to one another is clear, which is to say that a sentence necessarily

14. Cecelia Watson, "Points of Contention: Rethinking the Past, Present, and Future of Punctuation," *Critical Inquiry* 38, no. 3 (Spring 2012): 650. Watson observes that at the end of the eighteenth century "grammar books began to espouse systems of rules that were purportedly derived from logic," at which point the punctuation practices of the canonical writers of yore started to be lambasted for their gross errors (650).

15. Watson, "Points of Contention," 651.

16. Jennifer DeVere Brody, *Punctuation: Art, Politics, and Play* (Durham, NC: Duke University Press, 2008), 3.

articulates relationships that are not determined by ordinal placement. The fact that a word or phrase comes "first" or "last" may not, from a grammatical perspective, have anything like the significance we accord it when we consider it from a rhetorical or narratological perspective. We know that we do not read in a purely linear manner and that sentence processing is a matter of scanning back and forth, assessing and reassessing based on the new information one acquires with each additional phrase and clause. Nonetheless, the temptation to treat the sentence as a unidirectional series of terms remains profound.

To be sure, it would be equally misleading to imagine that we ever engage with all the parts of a sentence simultaneously, however flexible or multidirectional its organizing patterns may be. Linguists maintain that we process sentences section by section and that no matter what surprises await us at the end of one, we can only reevaluate what we have already read to a degree.[17] One of the few contemporary literary critics who have written at length about what a sentence actually is, Stanley Fish offers a different account of the inexorable forward progress of sentential dynamics, arguing that "sentences move in time and promise to deliver us somewhere at their conclusion" and that "the deferral of meaning—the sense of building toward a completed thought—is the very nature of a sentence."[18] In these terms, the unidirectional quality of a sentence, or at least the semblance of unidirectionality, is essential because a sentence is like a mini-drama, turning its inability to do everything at once into a means of holding its reader or listener's attention and proving its value by virtue of its very capacity to get its audience to follow from A to Z. Like Scheherazade, who stays alive by telling one story after another, the sentence has us as long as it has not yet reached its conclusion—it keeps us hanging, for as long as it dares. Reaching the end of a sentence thus becomes a sign of progress in its own right. Simply by virtue of having proceeded from start to finish, we can be confident that something has happened, that is, the story or argument has advanced, or at least that we have garnered some insight or information that we did not possess when we were back at the opening word.

If it intuitively makes sense to us to treat individual sentences as miniature stories or demonstrations unto themselves, this is because we were taught as children that a sentence "stands alone." What we were not taught is that what

17. See Noam Chomsky, "On Phases," September 26, 2005; available online at http://www.fosssil.in/Chomsky_Phases.pdf.

18. Stanley Fish, *How to Write a Sentence: And How to Read One* (New York: HarperCollins, 2011), 70. It is notable that Fish tackled this topic in a book intended for a mass audience (it did in fact become a *New York Times* best-seller) rather than in a more scholarly venue.

this means has changed drastically over time. In Greek and Roman philosophy and for more than a millennium afterward, the autonomy of the sentence was a factor of logical or rhetorical considerations and not grammatical ones. The modern English word *sentence* comes from the Latin *sententia*, in turn a translation of Aristotle's *gnomê*: "a maxim, judgment or opinion, especially of the wise."[19] Aristotle worried that such maxims smacked of the pseudo- or quasi-logical, because their persuasiveness was not entirely a factor of what they said but also of how they did it. He deemed them enthymemes: powerful gestures perched uneasily on the border between sound syllogistic reasoning and "mere" rhetoric.[20] In the middle ages, a *sententia* was regarded as autonomous in the sense that it could constitute an independent intervention in an argument. Frequently a moral saying or apothegm drawn from classical literature or the Bible, it had the air of a quotation one was expected to know, although no explicit citation was necessary, since the formulation's apodictic compactness was regarded as autolegitimating.[21] Not unlike what we know as the aphorism, the appearance of a *sententia* was somewhat ambiguous, at once summing up the argument that had preceded it and threatening to take things in a new direction.

The English word "sentence" subsequently came to designate a finished thought, verdict, or judgment, and it also began to acquire the sense of an indefinite portion of discourse, but in all cases, it remained first and foremost a semantic category and had nothing to do with the independence of a given syntactic structure.[22] Today the situation is quite different. The notion that a sentence expresses a complete thought is regarded as an elementary-school truism that should ultimately cede ground to the more technical claim that a sentence stands alone insofar as it is not grammatically dependent on other

19. The meaning of the Latin *sententia* survives in the modern English *sententious*: "given to or abounding in aphoristic expression or excessive moralizing." *Gnomê* is the root of our words *gnomic* and *gnostic*.

20. See Aristotle, *On Rhetoric*, trans. George A. Kennedy (New York: Oxford University Press, 1991), 1394a19ff.

21. As James Herrick explains: "Scholasticism developed around the medieval tendency to treat ancient sources—both the Bible and certain texts of classical antiquity—as authoritative. So strong was this tendency that individual sentences from a respected source, even when taken out of context, could be employed to secure a point in debate. These isolated statements from ancient sources were called sententiae." James Herrick, *The History and Theory of Rhetoric* (Boston: Allyn & Bacon, 1997), 124.

22. See "sentence," the *Oxford English Dictionary*.

formations and constitutes an instance of predication in its own right, irrespective of whether or not what it says makes any sense.[23]

This is not to suggest that the ideal of the sentence as a perfect coordination of logic and grammar has entirely eclipsed other ambitions for it.[24] The aim of the Latin *periodus* to realize a "perfectly rhythmic pattern" survives as well—authors of all ages and stages continue to have strong opinions about whether a given string of phrases and clauses "sounds" right. The problem is that classical models of expression as words in motion sit poorly with attempts to codify forms of predication, to treat language as the object of empirical scientific inquiry, or most simply to proceed as if there were a decidedly right and wrong way to do things when it comes to trying to say what one thinks one wants to say. In exploring the modern "sentence," one of our principal tasks will be to describe how the semantic, rhythmic, and grammatical meanings of the word coexist or clash and how and why one of them periodically takes priority over the others in various aesthetic—and political—paradigms.

As the history of the term *sententia* suggests, one of the problems in highlighting the grammatical autonomy of a sentence is that from virtually all other perspectives, no sentence is an island and no sentence wants to be treated as one. Monological or dialogical as the discourse in which it appears may be, a sentence aims to be part of a larger dynamic and betrays relationships with the utterances it implicitly or explicitly precedes or follows by referencing, addressing, or calling out to or for them. By definition, a sentence is finite—it starts and stops—and it may well gain much of its logical and rhetorical force precisely from the sense of predictability and closure that comes from having

23. There is some scholarly disagreement about precisely when an explicitly syntactic model of the sentence first emerges. Ian Robinson has argued that prior to the fourteenth century, if not until later, there is no "specifically syntactic definition of the unit of sense." Ian Robinson, *The Establishment of Modern English Prose in the Reformation and the Enlightenment* (New York: Cambridge University Press, 1999), 18. Robinson emphasizes that in Middle English the word *sententia* did not mean "grammatical sentence," and he challenges the *Oxford English Dictionary's* fifteenth- and sixteenth-century examples of "sentence" as a grammatical concept. G. A. Padley comes to a similar conclusion, and he stresses that no one in classical letters "treats the sentence simply as a structure which does not form part of another linguistic structure." G. A. Padley, *Grammatical Theory in Western Europe 1500–1700: The Latin Tradition* (London: Cambridge University Press, 1976), 32. For a discussion of how *oratio*, *periodus*, and other classical units of discourse differ from the modern notion of the sentence, see H. C. Gotoff, "The Concept of Periodicity in the *Ad Herennium*," *Harvard Studies in Classical Philology* 77 (1973): 217–23; and Parkes, *Pause and Effect*, 4ff.

24. Croll, *Style, Rhetoric and Rhythm*, 231.

a clearly defined beginning and end. At the same time, these beginnings and endings must reveal themselves as to some degree provisional, or a sentence is at risk of seeming unprovocative, static, or outright irrelevant, a stray fragment of uncertain provenance and authority.

For the writer, nothing is more nerve-wracking than the question of whether one's sentences are convincingly coordinated with one another. The connection between a "complete thought" and the one that follows may feel rock solid at one moment and utterly tenuous the next. Scanning a paragraph we have just written, we may find that transitions that at first appeared to effect an inexorable forward march now look like gross gaps framing a string of *non sequiturs*. In such instances, the temptation may be to insert adverbial expressions—"thus," "accordingly," "as a result"—as if this will help to express connection and consequence more definitively. Alternatively, repetition of one form or another may be deployed in an effort to link our sentences by ensuring that they literally contain parts of one another. Contemporary English-language style manuals are all but unanimous in their recommendation that we begin a sentence with information to which the reader has already been exposed as a lead-in to the introduction of new material at the end. In other words, we should craft our sentences less with an eye to their status as stand-alone formations than with an interest in perfecting the modulations between them. If things still feel insufficiently motivated, we may find ourselves casting an envious glance at formal logicians or computer programmers, who can lend their texts an even greater sense of cohesion by numbering the lines.

As much as we want the relationships between our sentences to be clear, we also aspire to write individual formulations that people will remember, quote, and even imitate. The problem is that the harder we work on any given utterance, the less certain we will be that it links up with its brethren; correspondingly, the more flawlessly our sentences flow together, the less likely any one of them is to be memorable. In its most authoritarian form as the pronouncement of a tyrant, the sentence is an incontestable decree: *I sentence you to life in prison!* At the opposite end of the spectrum, any given sentence is just one small part of a description or a proof, in which case its authority resides either in the fact that it contributes to a growing stock of information or that it constitutes a link in a long chain of reasoning.

What, if anything, "happens" in the space between a period, exclamation point, or question mark and the next capitalized word? What should happen? Ideally a sentence is supposed to offer a sound coordination of grammar and logic. If all goes well, the rules governing language's capacity to articulate statements that can be judged as true or false will not clash with the rules for properly arranging a collection of words around a finite verb to show tense, number, and/or mood, and thereby make some claim to predication. The problem is that even the tidiest complete sentence may never prove complete enough. Logically speaking, a single proposition cannot stand alone, because what is at stake in any particular statement is what can reliably be inferred or deduced from it. From this perspective, the power of a sentence is a factor of its status as an impetus for and influence on the sentences that follow. If it is grammatically autonomous, it is substantively heteronomous.

What is a sentence? In trying to answer this question, we have described less a stable grammatical or stylistic category than a set of ideas about what sort of unit or units of discourse can or should exist, how different units should interact, and what kinds of relationships between grammar and representation should be exemplified by them. It may be that what we customarily refer to as the sentence is a jumble of different, potentially incompatible, linguistic paradigms. Perhaps the word "sentence" is simply being asked to do too much.

This is not to say that it is in our power to put the authority of the sentence aside, as if the rules and conventions governing its uses and abuses could be casually turned on and off. The ability to use language "properly" is essential to function successfully in virtually any communal domain, for to be a citizen in good standing is first and foremost to be a producer and consumer of correct sentences. Put more negatively, the sentence can be regarded as part of a system designed to ensure the cohesiveness of a particular group by legislating the manner in which we can participate in it as discursive agents, whether this means making propositions worthy of consideration as true or false, posing questions deserving of answers, or giving orders and making requests worthy of respect.[25]

From this perspective, investments in different sentence styles can never be innocent. Upon examination, even the most ostensibly straightforward of recommendations—to write clearly and concisely—will betray ideological commitments, resting as it must on specific ideas about the relationships between thought, representation, and material praxis. Individual communities and institutions have their own methods of regulating clarity, articulating the distinction between vague and precise writing, and deciding who is to be afforded the luxury of being brief or verbose. In all such cases, however, any claim to lucidity and eloquence can only be made by producers of valid sentences. In

25. On the notion of the sentence as a form of social control, see Julia Kristeva, "The Ethics of Linguistics," *Desire in Language*, ed. Leon S. Roudiez (New York: Columbia University Press, 1980), esp. 23–24.

this vein, Roland Barthes describes the sentence as a cultural artifact "created by rhetors, grammarians, linguists, teachers, writers, [and] parents."[26] We can play with this object, happily or unhappily, we can abuse it, or we can ignore it; but in the end, we seem fated to confirm its authority as the sanctioned verbal form. To say, then, that the sentence is a set of injunctions about how to speak or write is to underestimate its reach. The sentence's prescriptions shape our understanding of what it means to think and act meaningfully as social and historical entities. Its dictates legislate what will count as authentic or consequential experience to such a degree that we may wonder whether true political change is conceivable without some change in the hegemonic sentential order.

Having characterized the sentence as the cornerstone of social and political discourse, we must now ask whether it is really as dominant a verbal force as this account suggests. Are the rules of the sentence universally acknowledged and respected, and if not, is this because the sentence constitutes an ideal that is rarely in force, or because the sentence is merely one form that meaningful utterances can take, and far from the only one? That this may be a case in which the rules were made to be broken is nowhere more apparent than with the injunction to write complete sentences. As fundamental as the imperative to avoid authoring sentence fragments was in our early education, such constructions abound in countless documents that have been scrupulously examined by copy editors. Journalists routinely use fragments, from allowing subordinate clauses to stand alone for emphasis to breaking up words in lists.[27] (*She told a grim story. A story with many twists. And turns.*) Such writing is ubiquitous, although no schoolteacher would ever sanction it. Crucially, we should not make the mistake of assuming that this is a nascent practice spawned by new forms of communication technology or by the ever-shifting mores of social media. In the same classrooms in which children are taught to write in complete sentences, they are asked to memorize selections from famous texts in which fragments play an important role, from the *Declaration of Independence* to the essays of Ralph Waldo Emerson, Henry David Thoreau, and H. L. Mencken.

These kinds of stylistic gestures are by no means self-evidently "transgressive." When newspaper or magazine writers set off a dependent clause with a

26. Roland Barthes, *The Pleasure of the Text*, trans. Richard Miller (New York: Hill & Wang, 1975), 51.

27. See Edgar H. Schuster, "A Fresh Look at Sentence Fragments," *English Journal* 95, no. 5 (May 2006): 78–83; and Charles R. Kline Jr. and W. Dean Memering, "The English Minor Sentence," *Research in the Teaching of English* 11, no. 2 (Fall 1997): 97–110.

capital letter and a period for emphasis, they are respecting standard syntactic patterns as they extend a single, "proper" sentence across more than one terminal punctuation mark. If anything, breaking the rules of grammar for rhetorical effect implicitly confirms their authority. A different limit to the reach of the sentence may become more apparent if we move from written to spoken language. A common practice in oral discourses that is routinely replicated in informal media such as text messaging or online chat threads is situational ellipsis. As the *Oxford English Dictionary* is quick to remind us, a sentence, "the verbal expression of a proposition, question, command, or request," will normally contain a subject and a predicate, but "either of these may be omitted by ellipsis"; and there are many situations in which not to ellipse one's remarks would be arrestingly uncolloquial: What are you doing? *Nothing*. When are you arriving? *Tomorrow*. I may be late. *No problem.*[28] In these exchanges, the curt responses are readily comprehensible, and we can easily explain how each is standing in for a complete sentence. This is not, however, evidence of the degree to which speech is "more casual" than writing. We might just as well argue that such examples demonstrate how completely the power of the sentence form governs both spoken and written language, providing syntactic templates that are in force whether or not they are explicitly articulated.

Is there a point at which the sentence form has become so "implicit" that it has genuinely yielded to other organizational patterns of language? Based on empirical studies of oral conversations, some linguists have proposed that sentence grammar does not enjoy the same authority in spoken as in written discourse, going so far as to argue that "it is difficult to give a good linguistic definition of a sentence which applies equally well to writing and spontaneous speech," and that speech therefore demands to be analyzed in terms of both clausal and nonclausal units.[29] Others are more skeptical that we can rigorously distinguish between speech and writing on such grounds. It is easy enough to show that written language is also characterized by an interplay of clausal and

28. "Sentence," *Oxford English Dictionary*. On incomplete and elliptical sentences, see Sidney Greenbaum, *The Oxford English Grammar* (Oxford: Oxford University Press, 1996), esp. 309; and Randolph Quirk et al., *A Comprehensive Grammar of the English Language* (New York: Longman, 1985), esp. 838, 849.

29. Douglas Biber et al., *Longman Grammar of Spoken and Written English* (Harlow, Essex: Pearson, 1999), 202. Supporters of this position argue that "whereas the sentence has been treated, traditionally and in modern theory, as the fundamental structural unit of grammar, such a unit does not realistically exist in conversational language," and that "in reality, conversation has no generally recognizable sentence-delimiting marks such as the initial capital and final period of written language" (Biber et al., *Longman Grammar,* 1039).

nonclausal forms, because the sentence is hardly the only structure, spoken or written, in which grammatically coherent formulations manifest themselves.[30] Take the first "sentences" of Charles Dickens's *Bleak House*:

> London. Michaelmas term lately over, and the Lord Chancellor sitting in Lincoln's Inn Hall. Implacable November weather. As much mud in the streets as if the waters had but newly retired from the face of the earth, and it would not be wonderful to meet a Megalosaurus, forty feet long or so, waddling like an elephantine lizard up Holborn Hill. Smoke lowering down from chimney-pots, making a soft black drizzle, with flakes of soot in it as big as full-grown snowflakes—gone into mourning, one might imagine, for the death of the sun. Dogs, undistinguishable in mire. Horses, scarcely better; splashed to their very blinkers.[31]

The opening lines of Dickens's novel read like a set of stage directions. The parameters of the setting are transmitted via increasingly complex metaphors and similes that evolve into conceits. The temporality of the "action" is organized by an unusual hierarchy in which past and present participles play a central role while conventional alignments of subjects and verbs enter as afterthoughts. To deem the style "elliptical" would scarcely do justice to the rhythm, order, and balance of the language, which in no way calls out to be expanded to some more complete "original" text of non-ellipsed sentences. This is certainly not an effort to replicate the patterns of speech. At the same time, the passage is anything but lawless. While the series of words framed by capital letters and periods is unquestionably a string of sentence fragments, numerous rules are respected when it comes to word order; the formation of singulars and plurals; and the relations between nouns, prepositions, adverbs, coordinators, articles, and determinatives. Despite the paucity of finite verbs, grammar is very much at work.

If Dickens's reliance on phrases in place of conventional predicate utterances is striking, we should not assume that it illustrates a rare practice, much less a style peculiar to or characteristic of literary language. Grammarians use

30. One study of English "found that speakers in conversation use a number of relatively complex and sophisticated grammatical constructions, contradicting the widely held belief that conversation is grammatically simple. . . . Conversely, supposedly colloquial, inexplicit grammatical features sometimes turn out to be common in formal academic writing" (Biber et al., *Longman Grammar*, 7).

31. Charles Dickens, *Bleak House* (New York: Penguin Classics, 2003), 13.

the term "nonsentences" for formulations that appear to resemble instances of situational ellipses but that cannot be unambiguously resolved into longer "originals."[32] One common example is the *Exit* sign hovering above countless doorways, which could be expanded to "This is the exit" or "You can/should/may exit here." (A similar point could be made about the first word of *Bleak House*: "London.") If someone barks "The door!" they may mean "Shut the door!" or "Get the door!" or "Watch the door!" or "Leave the room!"[33] In this vein, one can identify exclamatory noun phrases ("The fuss they made!" "The things he said!" "You and your emojis!") or prepositional phrases ("Of all the things to say!") that "stand alone" even though they cannot be unambiguously expanded into a single "complete" sentence.[34] To call such instances of signification "fragments" would be an injustice because they are not defined by, or by their divergence from, a logico-grammatical paradigm in which a finite verb takes center stage as the semantic core—a point that becomes even clearer in irregular forms such as "Off with their heads!" or "On with the show!" or in similar nonclausal units such as "My turn?" or "Good for you."

In none of these examples is it a matter of opposing the orderly, predictable sentence to some mélange of ambiguous fragments or chaotic concatenation of brief expostulations. Nor are these examples particularly unusual. The list of forums in which sentences play little or no role—news headlines, weather reports, crossword puzzles—can be expanded so easily that we may begin to wonder whether we need such clunky formations at all given how functional other linguistic dynamics appear to be. Ads, posters, and timetables get by very well without sentences, just like many of the signs—*For Sale, Going Out of Business, No GMO*—that we see on a daily basis. The live commentary of sporting events often proceeds in a verbal shorthand with no finite verbs, as do auctions, stock and commodity transactions, and card games. Far from offering the hegemonic paradigm from which all ellipsed utterances or creative modifications deviate, the sentence appears to be only one kind of grammatical utterance among others, merely one of the many different semantic units that a properly functioning syntax is capable of generating.

Rejecting the notion that the sentence is the defining semantic quantum, the linguist David Crystal argues that "there is [simply] no fixed grammatical rule which tells us what a unit of sense is. Traditional grammars were desperate to find one, and would insist on such 'rules' as 'a sentence must have a verb'

32. Quirk et al., *A Comprehensive Grammar of the English Language*, 838.

33. Quirk et al., *A Comprehensive Grammar*, 838, 850.

34. Quirk et al., *A Comprehensive Grammar*, 849–50.

or 'a sentence must have a subject and a predicate.'"[35] According to Crystal, sub- or presentential forms are not one-off interjections that are entirely context dependent and can only function insofar as they emerge in the midst of conventional sentences. On the contrary, he stresses that entire exchanges can take place in which none of the utterances are governed by complete subject-predicate forms, citing as an example a passage from Samuel Beckett's *Waiting for Godot* in which Estragon inquires whether Vladimir can remember what they asked Godot for:

> VLADIMIR: Oh . . . nothing very definite.
> ESTRAGON: A kind of prayer.
> VLADIMIR: Precisely.
> ESTRAGON: A vague supplication.
> VLADIMIR: Exactly.[36]

Crystal proposes "that the units of sense are clear, thanks to the use of the period, even though the grammatical structures are various and (in the last example) Vladimir's responses are grammatically autonomous, unconnected to any 'fuller' previous sentence."[37] The phrase "grammatically autonomous" calls attention to the fact that Vladimir's two responses—"Precisely." "Exactly."—cannot be understood to be grammatically dependent on what precedes them because they are adverbs rather than adjectives and therefore cannot modify the noun phrases "a kind of prayer" and "a vague supplication." In context, Vladimir's remarks "follow" what has come before them, each modifying the speech act that precedes it, but they do not do so because of any implicit or explicit sentence structure that links the utterances across speakers, as was the case with our earlier examples, for instance, When are you arriving? *[I'm arriving] Tomorrow*.

Just when we are seemingly well outside the authority of the sentence, it has a way of reasserting itself. Vladimir's responses to Estragon could also be characterized as ellipsed versions of: "What you said is precisely/exactly right." The question thus remains: Is this exchange from *Waiting for Godot* an illustration of the limits of sentential dynamics, or does the sentence form implicitly persist, regardless of how far it may have receded into the background?

35. David Crystal, *Making a Point: The Persnickety Story of English Punctuation* (New York: St. Martin's Press, 2015), 139.

36. Cited in Crystal, *Making a Point*, 140.

37. Crystal, *Making a Point*, 140.

Perhaps even a grocery list, an a-syntactic string of nouns semantically indifferent to one another's particularities, has to be thought of as headed by a phantom imperative: *Purchase the following items . . .*

The example from Beckett's play may be unusual because adverbs are peculiarly flexible modifiers, capable of impacting one word or an entire sentence. There are, however, forms of adverbial interventions that appear "in" or "next to" sentences but which do not enter into any sort of syntactic relationship with the words around them, most notoriously "yes" and "no." Linguists hesitate to call such brief expostulations words, deeming them "gestures" or "pragmatic interventions" and likening them to other subclausal units such as interjections, exclamations, and expletives, which are frequently no more than a syllable long (*Hi! Wow! Oops! Zing! Drat!*).[38] Genuine alternatives to predicative semantics, these verbal phenomena are indifferent to their placement within any hierarchy of phrases or clauses and betray the presence of semantic dynamics whose structure and function can scarcely be analogized with, much less be said to be based on, sentential patterns.

We have moved from an account of the sentence as the preeminent verbal form—the medium of substantive discourse, the standard of correct expression against which all utterances must be measured—to a description of a linguistic landscape in which proto- or nonsentential elements abound, at times complemented by one-word interventions that test the very limits of syntax as a characterization of how phonemes and graphemes relate. If the sentence is only one of many different referential and signifying dynamics, modern literary scholars may have been wise in not according it unquestioned conceptual priority, recognizing that to privilege subject-predicate grammar in this way is a gross simplification and does great injustice to the richness of discursive forms. The very desire to cling to the authority of the sentence may bespeak a kind of intellectual or aesthetic, if not political, conservatism, or at the very least an unwillingness to acknowledge just how varied the linguistic processes of any verbal act can be, from snippets of everyday speech to a passage from a classic novel.

Of all the factors influencing the relative disregard for the sentence in literary studies, none have been as important as the work of Ferdinand de Saussure and the semiotic and structuralist linguistic traditions it inspired. In a brief line in the *Course in General Linguistics* that has proven extraordinarily consequential for scholars across the humanities, Saussure declares: "The sentence

38. On nonclausal units, see Biber et al., *Longman Grammar*, 1082.

belongs to *parole*, not to *langue*."[39] Denying the sentence any systemic or paradigmatic status for signification, Saussure relegates it to the realm of subjective expression, where its particularities are to be treated as the products of individual choices made by specific speakers or writers. As to why so many of our utterances should manifest themselves in sentence form, he has remarkably little to say.

In explaining his relegation of the sentence to the domain of *parole*, Saussure describes what he considers to be a common misconception about its salient import for linguistics. "A rather widely held theory," he writes, "makes sentences the concrete units of language: we speak only in sentences and subsequently single out the words."[40] Saussure begins his rebuttal of this position with the observation that when one views the totality of sentences, "their most striking characteristic is that in no way do they resemble each other."[41] Arguing that the only thing they do share is "the word," it is with it and its constituent elements—phonemes, morphemes—that he will work as he elaborates his account of differential signification.[42] The grammar of sentences will not be a primary or even a secondary concern.

Saussure's claim that in language there are only differences without positive terms is crucial for understanding the semiosis of letters and words and is routinely accepted as fact by contemporary linguists and literary scholars. Indeed, it would be hard to overstate just how formative this idea has proven to be for both the humanities and the social sciences. A focus on signifiers freed of their grammatical and logical shackles has allowed for the elaboration of new models of textuality and experience that have influenced the study of culture, history, and politics on all fronts.

It is less clear why Saussure's doctrine of differential signification has been treated as if it were a comprehensive theory of language. Starting with the morpheme and phoneme, Saussure moves to the word and even begins to discuss phrases, but he never attempts to explain the structure of the predicative clause. To the extent that he does discuss "terms in a series," it is merely to consider idiomatic phrases, for example, *la terre tourne* ("the world turns"), which he treats as one would any other element in a lexicon. Subject to "collective usage," Saussure proposes, such expressions are "language fact[s]" that

39. Ferdinand de Saussure, *Course in General Linguistics*, trans. Wade Baskin, ed. Perry Meisel and Haun Saussy (New York: Columbia University Press, 2011), 124.

40. Saussure, *Course in General Linguistics,* 106.

41. Saussure, *Course in General Linguistics,* 106.

42. Saussure, *Course in General Linguistics,* 106.

a speaker or writer may choose to employ as she might decide to use an individual word.[43] If Saussure comes close to stating that one combines phrases to create clauses, the *Course* offers nothing resembling a formal account of syntax.[44]

Saussurean linguistics is grounded in an atomic model of language in which the production of meaning is understood in terms of the interaction of the most elemental parts of a discourse or by analogy thereto. As a consequence, Saussure's work and the projects it has informed have an irreducibly taxonomic quality. Most structuralist and semiotic analyses begin by identifying the constituent units of a system and then explaining their interrelations, building up, as it were, from smaller to larger parts, as opposed to starting by examining the general parameters by virtue of which signifiers can interact (e.g., syntax). Assessing the first generation of Saussure's inheritors, the Soviet linguist V. N. Voloshinov diagnosed this limitation: "As the product of comparative phonetics and morphology, such [Saussurean] thought is incapable of viewing other phenomena of language except through the spectacles of phonetic and morphological forms. It attempts to view syntax in the same way, and this has led to the morphologization of syntactic problems."[45] For Voloshinov, Saussure and his followers have nothing to say about any aspect of language beyond the level of the phrase. Voloshinov also takes issue with the notion that morphological or phonological forms are somehow more concrete than syntactic ones. For him, Saussure's claim that signifiers are material whereas syntax is incorporeal is an ideological position, not a scientific one.

Modern literary theory and criticism have relied extensively on Saussurean linguistics and structuralism with surprisingly little reflection on their potentially incomplete character. The inheritors of Saussure who have had the biggest impact on literary and cultural studies do explicitly acknowledge the limits of differential logics when it comes to accounting for the dynamics of reference and signification, but none goes so far as to elaborate a full-fledged theory of sentential paradigms. Particularly influential in this regard

43. Saussure, *Course in General Linguistics,* 125.

44. Noam Chomsky maintains that his approach to the study of language was shaped by his conviction that Saussure's inheritors cannot account for the complexities of syntax and basically ignore the sentence: "In Saussurean structuralism, a language (*langue*) was taken to be a system of sounds and an associated system of concepts; the notion of sentence was left in a kind of limbo, perhaps to be accommodated within the study of language use." Noam Chomsky, *Knowledge of Language: Its Nature, Origin, and Use* (Westport, CT: Praeger, 1986), 19.

45. V. N. Volosinov, *Marxism and the Philosophy of Language*, trans. Ladislav Matejka and I. R. Titunik (Cambridge, MA: Harvard University Press, 2000), 109.

is Roman Jakobson, who shows a concern with sentence production that is absent in Saussure. In fact, Jakobson betrays reservations that sound strikingly similar to Voloshinov's: "Saussure understood the purely differential and negative character of phonemes perfectly well but . . . he overhastily generalized this characterization and sought to apply it to all linguistic entities."[46] Jakobson offers grammatical categories as an example of a feature of language not governed by a differential logic, insisting that some of them have a positive content, "whereas the opposition of two phonemes never has."[47] In his well-known essay on linguistic aphasia, he is even more explicit about what a purely Saussurean model is missing when he praises Hughling Jackson for the claim that "it is not enough to say that speech consists of words," for what is at issue is the "power to propositionize."[48] The two kinds of aphasia under consideration are distinguished by the fact that someone afflicted by the similarity disorder still speaks in sentences, whereas someone suffering from the contiguity disorder "loses the syntactical rules organizing words into higher units."[49] We might say—only partly in jest—that the implicit thesis of Jakobson's essay is that Saussurean thought itself suffers from contiguity disorder.

Acknowledging that without a theory of the arrangements that words can assume we will have at best a jumble of signs, Jakobson accords the study of syntax a far more central role than does Saussure, but the implications of this shift in emphasis are not pursued. Like arguably all the structuralists—who, in this sense, are not first and foremost concerned with the *structure* of language—Jakobson follows Saussure in taking the phoneme and the morpheme as the foundational atoms of signification that combine to produce higher-order constructions. In the passage from phrases to clauses, predication becomes an unavoidable issue, but phonology has nothing to say about it.

Émile Benveniste explicitly describes the impossibility of "building up" to sentences from the essential atoms of language, observing that while the word is composed of phonemes, "the relationships are less easy to define in the inverse situation, between the word and the higher level unit. . . . The sentence is realized in words, but the words are not simply segments of it. A sentence

46. Roman Jakobson, *Six Lectures on Sound and Meaning*, trans. John Mepham (Cambridge, MA: MIT Press, 1978), 65.

47. Jakobson, *Six Lectures*, 65.

48. Roman Jakobson, "Two Aspects of Language and Two Types of Aphasic Disturbances," *Language in Literature*, ed. Krystyna Pomorska and Stephen Rudy (Cambridge, MA: Harvard University Press, 1987), 106.

49. Jakobson, "Two Aspects," 106.

constitutes a whole which is not reducible to the sum of its parts."[50] On this basis, Benveniste gives predication, about which Saussure's theory of the sign has so little to say, pride of place, declaring that "the predicate is a fundamental property of the sentence; it is not a unit of the sentence," which is why "the sentence is fundamentally different from the other linguistic entities."[51] Like Jakobson, however, Benveniste does not take these observations as an impetus for moving in a new direction, instead rehashing a version of Saussure's distinction between *langue* and *parole*: "With the sentence we leave the domain of language as a system of signs and enter into another universe, that of language as an instrument of communication, whose expression is discourse."[52] Rather than attempting to elaborate a theory of syntax or of the relationship between grammar and logic, Benveniste treats the sentence in terms of its utility, emphasizing its status as a communicative tool. To the extent that it privileges the semantic over the formal, the resulting model of discourse will never approach the precision or detail of the system of signs it has left behind.

A similar ambivalence about the limits of differential signification as a model of language can be found in the work of Roland Barthes. Barthes insists on the need to progress beyond a mere semiosis of words if we are to develop an account of the sentence, bluntly declaring that "the sentence, being an order and not a series, cannot be reduced to the sum of the words which compose it and constitutes thereby a specific unit."[53] Like Jakobson and Benveniste before him, Barthes avers without qualification that if the parts make up the whole, they do not govern the dynamics that organize it, but once again, the consequences of this insight are minimal. Recalling Benveniste's distinction between sign system and discourse, Barthes adds that "the most reasonable thing is to posit a homological relationship between sentence and discourse insofar as it is likely that a similar formal organization orders all semiotic systems, whatever their substances and dimensions. A discourse [or narrative] is a long 'sentence' (the units of which are not necessarily sentences), just as a sentence, allowing for certain specifications, is a short 'discourse' [or narrative]."[54] Barthes feels licensed to posit a homology between the sentence and what he calls

50. Émile Benveniste, *Problems in General Linguistics*, trans. Mary Elizabeth Meek (Coral Gables, FL: University of Miami Press, 1971), 105.

51. Benveniste, *Problems in General Linguistics,* 109. As Benveniste puts it pithily: "The sentence contains signs but it is not itself a sign" (109).

52. Benveniste, *Problems in General Linguistics,* 110.

53. Roland Barthes, *Image, Music, Text*, trans. Stephen Heath (New York: HarperCollins, 1977), 82.

54. Barthes, *Image, Music, Text*, 83, 84.

"discourse" without saying anything about the sentence's structural nature, contenting himself with a vague reference to a "formal organization" whose precise relationship to semiotic dynamics he does not explain. In the move from signs to discourse, the sentence constitutes a crucial hinge, yet any scrutiny of its unique features is bypassed, despite the fact that it is ostensibly the main topic under consideration. The door is thereby opened for narratology and discourse analysis, which will subsume the sentence under more abstract semantic models, with little concern for the possibility that sentence grammar may not have any authority at the trans-sentential level.

With its reticence about the sentence, Saussurean thought puts itself squarely at odds with the work of the preeminent linguist of the latter half of the twentieth century, Noam Chomsky. From the outset, Chomsky is motivated by the same observation that Saussure makes about the extraordinary diversity of sentences and the perceived need to explain what is common to these radically different formations. In contrast to his predecessor, however, he concludes that sentences are characterized not just by the semiotic properties of their elements but by grammar. To describe how a language functions, one must be able to enumerate the finite number of rules that inform the processes by which all the grammatically correct sentences in it are generated.[55] Crucially, Chomsky insists that whether or not a given string of words is regarded as grammatical is not a factor of whether it is perceived to be a sensible utterance.[56] This commitment to understanding syntax without reference to semantics informs his broader antipragmatist leanings.[57] The question of

55. As Chomsky writes in the opening pages of his now canonical *Syntactic Structures*: "Syntax is the study of the principles and processes by which sentences are constructed in particular languages. Syntactic investigation of a given language has as its goal the construction of a grammar that can be viewed as a device of some sort for producing the sentences of the language under analysis." Noam Chomsky, *Syntactic Structures* (New York: Mouton de Gruyter, 2002 [1957]), 11. While Chomsky's theories may appear to have undergone substantial revisions over the decades, it can be debated how fundamental these changes have actually been.

56. To illustrate this point, Chomsky famously offers a comparison of two strings of words that he deems "equally nonsensical": "Colorless green ideas sleep furiously" and "Furiously sleep ideas green colorless" (*Syntactic Structures*, 15). Chomsky maintains that the English speaker will characterize the first as grammatical and the second as ungrammatical, because the former respects the rules of syntax, i.e., the noun comes before the verb, the adverbs and adjectives are acceptably situated, a plural noun goes with a plural verb, and so on.

57. In contemporary linguistics, syntax is not the only model for characterizing sentence dynamics. In some phonologically based paradigms, for example, intonation and other kinds of rhythmic patterns are accorded an authority that is not entirely comprehensible in classical Chomskyan terms. In general, scholars outside the discipline of linguistics are prone to

whether context, however conceived, contributes to the meaning of an utterance is simply of no interest to him and is left to the sociolinguists.[58]

While Chomsky's ideas about the linguistic faculties innate to the human mind and the ability of children to learn language with minimal environmental stimuli have been heralded as revolutionary, many aspects of his thought are quite traditional, particularly his reliance on a classical rationalist model of judgment and his basic account of sentences as alignments of noun phrases and verb phrases, subjects and predicates. More distinctive is his insistence that recursion is the defining feature of human language that distinguishes it both from the communicative acts we detect in other species and from abstract organizational systems grounded in the similarities and differences between their elements. Not to be confused with simple patterns of repetition, recursion, or the "nesting" of phrases within phrases or clauses within clauses, names the possibility for a particular linguistic unit or structure to be contained within another linguistic unit or structure of the same type, as in the familiar nursery rhyme: *This is the dog that worried the cat that killed the rat that ate the malt that lay in the house that Jack built.*

There is no clear limit to the number of units that can be embedded within a given sentence, so even without taking recourse to the nonrecursive form of an open-ended list (*they ate x, and y, and . . .*), we must, as the *Oxford Dictionary of English Grammar* acknowledges, "recognize the theoretical possibility of a sentence of infinite length containing an infinite number of clauses."[59] Like the

---

exaggerate the hegemony of Chomskyan thought within it. As Steven Pinker explains: "Contrary to the claim that Chomsky's theories are an orthodoxy, dominant approach, or consensus (which makes any challenger into a giant-slayer), they have never been anything close to the default in the sciences of language. I'd say that perhaps Chomsky's theory (at any time) has attracted a plurality of linguists, but probably never a majority, since there have always been rival theories (Generative Semantics, Cognitive Grammar, Relational Grammar, Lexical Functional Grammar, Generalized Phrase Structure Grammar, and, perhaps for most, just no commitment to any overarching theory at all)." Quoted in John Horgan, "Is Chomsky's Theory of Language Wrong?," *Scientific American*, November 28, 2016. https://blogs.scientificamerican.com/cross-check/is-chomskys-theory-of-language-wrong-pinker-weighs-in-on-debate/

58. In principle, Chomskyan linguistics is an empirical science. The field researcher uses the intuitions of the native speakers of a language about which formulations are "right" or "wrong" as the basis for drawing inferences about the rules of their language. Sociolinguists have questioned whether empirical judgments about grammaticality can be a basis for theoretical work, since so many different factors beyond grammar may influence a given person's conclusions about the legitimacy of any particular formulation, and in many instances, these judgments are tentative rather than decisive.

59. Aarts, Chalker, and Weiner, *The Oxford Dictionary of English Grammar*, 359.

Tower of Babel extending upward toward the heavens, the vision of an infinite sentence takes the notion of building an utterance out of words to the extreme, as the construction, ostensibly intended to be a "complete" thought, becomes an interminable project, a linguistic unit beyond units, a syntax that in virtue of its constitutively incomplete form threatens to turn against its own organizing hierarchy. Chomsky is untroubled by this idea. Maintaining that it is memory rather than the structure of language that limits the length of sentences, he is content to distinguish between language competence, which is the systemic mental capacity of humans to generate correct syntax, and language performance, the empirical examples of this praxis, which necessarily take the form of finite formations.[60]

Other linguists are less comfortable with the implications of a never-ending sentence, to the point that they are willing to rethink their commitment to the very concept of a sentence. Effecting a tidy inversion, they propose that instead of grappling with the *largest* structure capable of grammatical characterization, they will take as their object of inquiry the clause, "the *smallest* grammatical unit that can express a complete proposition."[61] With little fanfare, the effort to develop a science of the sentence reconciles potential tensions between theory and practice by redefining its subject matter. The illimitable quality of syntax, the fact that we can build endlessly complex forms with it, is displaced by a focus on the minimal structure required to articulate a complete statement. The question is whether other discourses would do well to follow suit and give up on trying to make the different facets of our cumbersome model of the sentence fit together, or if there are important reasons to hold onto the various—potentially incompatible—features of the concept, despite the conundrums they create.

Given Chomsky's stature in modern linguistics and his influence on numerous fields in the sciences and social sciences, not to mention the notoriety of his political views, one might assume that his work would have played some

60. Beginning with Saussure's opposition between *langue* and *parole*, one could argue that almost all modern linguistic models rely on some version of a distinction—however tenuous or unsustainable it may prove to be—between a language system and its empirical instantiations. In *Unspeakable Sentences*, the linguist Ann Banfield attempts to take advantage of the universality of this distinction by trying to develop "an idealization of the [literary] text," an account of the "language [in effect, the Saussurean *langue*] of narration or fiction," that corresponds to "Chomsky's idealization from the utterance to the sentence." Ann Banfield, *Unspeakable Sentences: Narration and Representation in the Language of Fiction* (New York: Routledge, 1982), 203.

61. P. Kroeger, *Analyzing Grammar: An Introduction* (Cambridge: Cambridge University Press, 2005), 32 (my emphasis).

role, if not a large one, in literary theory and criticism over the past fifty years. Such an assumption would be false. While virtually all Western intellectuals had at least a brush with the Chomskyan revolution in its heyday, the encounter left very little mark on literary studies.[62] It has periodically been asserted that Chomsky was important for structuralist narratology, but given that he explicitly critiques structuralism's conception of language, it is likely that his project is being conflated with earlier American structural linguistics. The late 1960s and early 1970s did see an interest in fashioning a literary stylistics based on the insights of transformational grammar, but such efforts rarely engaged systematically with Chomsky's doctrines and did not prove to have a lasting impact. One looks in vain for any excerpts from Chomsky in the standard anthologies of literary theory or introductions to literary analysis. When the phrase "generative grammar" is invoked in these contexts, it typically functions more as a metaphor than anything else, and many if not most humanists seem to operate on the assumption that Chomsky's principal claims have been debunked.

An obvious stumbling block for literary scholars who may be inclined to draw on Chomsky's work is his insistence on a stark opposition between the syntactic and semantic. In his view, meaning always rests on an a posteriori interpretation of a structure. There can be no "dialectic" of form and content, a position Chomsky has maintained in the face of considerable resistance from new generations of linguists committed to developing a generative semantics. As a consequence, it is not really possible to undertake a Chomskyan "reading" of a poem or a novel, whereas the semiotic analysis of literary texts has thrived, inspired by the more dynamic relationship between morphology, syntax, and lexicology in Saussure.

62. Barthes's flirtation with Chomskyan thought is typical. In 1966, he briefly speculated about the existence of a "literature faculty" of the human mind: "Corresponding to the *language faculty* postulated by Humboldt and Chomsky, there is perhaps in people a *literature faculty,* an energy of discourse, which has nothing to do with 'genius,' for it is made up not of inspiration or personal will-power but of rules built up by many people besides the author." Roland Barthes, *Criticism and Truth*, trans. and ed. Katrine Pilcher Keuneman (New York: Continuum, 2007 [1966]), 29. While Barthes does not go into much detail about this idea, one has to conclude that his use of the term "faculty" is starkly at odds with Chomsky's vision of the individual language user. Barthes makes this feature of the mind sound less like a genetically inherited feature of our cognitive faculties than a socially determined discourse that supersedes individual capacities entirely, something akin to a collective literary unconscious. This may be an implicit critique of Chomsky or simply evidence of Barthes's limited understanding of Chomsky's ideas.

Equally unsettling for many literary scholars are the ideological implications of Chomsky's doctrines. Linguists and anthropologists have long tried to show that the rules of grammar are not, as Chomsky insists, universal. This core claim of his project has also been a target of disapprobation for philosophers interested in the relationship between language and power. Insofar as a "correct" human being is someone with an innate mastery of grammatically correct expressions, Gilles Deleuze and Felix Guattari fear that those betraying linguistic ignorance will necessarily end up "in special institutions."[63] In their view, it is glaringly evident that Chomsky works with a simplistic model of discursive norms and deviations from them.[64] This speaks to a larger concern with the way in which he almost completely bifurcates individual and group dynamics, investing so absolutely in the paradigm of the solitary language learner that language itself paradoxically begins to seem as if it has nothing to do with communal interactions. As we mentioned earlier, the moment we start talking about language *and* politics, society, or history, we have left what Chomsky regards as the purview of his research. This is another important contrast with Saussure and his structuralist inheritors, since one of the main reasons for the abiding popularity of their thought is that it offers alternatives to political models in which the individual is the defining form of agency.[65]

63. Gilles Deleuze and Felix Guattari, *A Thousand Plateaus: Capitalism and Schizophrenia*, trans. Brian Massumi (Minneapolis: University of Minnesota Press, 1987), 101. In this context, Julia Kristeva wryly comments on "the Janus-like behavior of a prominent modern grammarian; in his linguistic theories he sets forth a logical, normative basis for the speaking subject, while in politics he claims to be an anarchist." Julia Kristeva, "The Ethics of Linguistics," *Desire in Language*, ed. Leon S. Roudiez (New York: Columbia University Press, 1980), 23. Chomsky's defenders would probably respond that these charges are misguided, because Chomsky is never concerned with what it means to speak "correctly," a topic he would relegate to sociolinguistics, and in fact, his privileging of the model of the individual language producer may be informed by the same skepticism about any sort of "top-down" theory that is characteristic of much anarchist thought.

64. Writing of a "linguistic imperialism," the French philosopher Jean-Jacques Lecercle makes a similar point, insisting that we must affirm the possibility of resisting the hegemonic dictates of grammar, in particular the notion that the rules of language are laws of nature, an idea that threatens to make political resistance impossible. Jean-Jacques Lecercle and Denis Riley, *The Force of Language* (New York: Palgrave Macmillan, 2005), 163. See also 86ff.

65. The philosophical underpinnings of Chomsky's work are problematic for literary critics accustomed to a high level of self-scrutiny about the intellectual history of their concepts. While Chomsky routinely sounds more like an eighteenth-century philosophe than an empirical lab scientist, explicitly characterizing his account of the genetic inheritance of language in terms of Platonic anamnesis and Port-Royal logic and grammar, he appears to have little sense that

While Chomskyan linguistics represents the most comprehensive modern effort to detail the intricacies of sentence mechanics, much of twentieth- and now twenty-first-century literary and cultural theory is invested in very different visions of language in which the sentence is decidedly not an idealized form or standard that serves as the arbiter of discursive norms. From this perspective, Chomsky's work serves as a warning that a study of language that takes sentence grammar as its focus is inherently limited in what it can say about history or politics. Once we wall ourselves up inside the sentence, it will be difficult to get out.

If the encounter between literary studies and Chomskyan linguistics has been a nonevent, literary scholars have had equally little use for the other influential modern conception of the sentence that emerges in Anglo-American philosophy, where the sentence is vigilantly distinguished from the proposition. The distinction is putatively derived from Aristotle, although he understands a proposition to be one type of sentence among others, whereas contemporary philosophers have in mind an opposition between metaphysical thoughts (propositions) and their physical expression in marks of ink, chalk, or pixels (sentences).[66] In these terms, a proposition is independent of the particular form it takes in conventionalized arrays of phonemes or graphemes; it is ideational, not linguistic.[67]

---

his metaphysical assumptions may have ramifications for his arguments. Jean-Jacques Lecercle has accused Chomsky of philosophical incoherence, describing his doctrines as on the one hand "an admixture of Platonic epistemology (the child speaker is like the slave in *Meno*—his discovery is recollection) and Leibnizian monadology (the share of the innate in linguistic activity is unduly extended), and, on the other [hand], a mechanistic materialism which reduces the phenomena of language to the physical, the individual, the a-historical." Jean-Jacques Lecercle, *A Marxist Philosophy of Language*, trans. Gregory Elliott (Boston: Brill, 2006), 44.

66. In *De Interpretatione*, Aristotle introduces a general category, the *logos semantikos*, a meaningful linguistic utterance, typically translated as "sentence," and then characterizes one of its subsets as the *logos apophantikos*, our "statement" or "proposition." Whereas the *logos apophantikos* can be evaluated as true or false, the *logos semantikos* includes other types of utterances—Aristotle's example is a prayer—and he quickly allows that reflection on these other kinds of language "belongs to the study of rhetoric or poetry." Aristotle, *De Interpretatione, The Complete Works of Aristotle: The Revised Oxford Translation*, vol. 1 (Princeton, NJ: Princeton University Press, 1984), 17a6–7.

67. This line of discussion opens up into debates about the relative merits of Platonic realism (according to which abstract entities—the notorious "forms"—exist in their own right, irrespective of who or what is "thinking" of or about them); conceptualism (in which abstract "entities" exist insofar as they are thought by humans); and nominalism, which rejects the existence of abstract entities entirely.

Such a dichotomy may strike us as difficult, if not impossible, to sustain. Many Anglo-American philosophers nonetheless insist on the importance of preserving it, because they regard it as self-evident that a given proposition can be expressed by different sentences. This claim is usually demonstrated by appealing to instances of synonymy (*Jack is a bachelor* and *Jack is not married*), active and passive formulations (*Jill ate the cake* and *the cake was eaten by Jill*), or a host of interlingual comparisons (*it's snowing, il neige, es schneit*; *two plus two equals four*, *zwei und zwei gleich vier*). Each of these examples is supposed to illustrate the relative independence of conceptual content from the particular verbal form it assumes insofar as different words and grammatical structures can impart the same information. For philosophers who treat utterances as intentions expressing a psychological content or "frame of mind," the distinction between propositions and sentences is also important because they want to maintain that the same sentence can be true or false depending on who says it and when and where it is said.[68]

The philosophical opposition between sentence and proposition reproduces Chomsky's sharp distinction between syntax and semantics while reversing the emphasis, inviting us to dwell on meaning without reference to structure rather than the other way around. Such a doctrine will be foreign, to say the least, to most scholars of literature. All the key interventions in modern poetics and hermeneutics speak against the tenability of such a stark dichotomy of form and content, medium and message, word and meaning. Similarly, the notion that "it's snowing" and "il neige" are semantically identical is as evidently false for anyone familiar with Saussure's distinction between linguistic signification and value as it is true for an analytic philosopher. To take the familiar example from the *Course in General Linguistics*, the relationships that the French word *chat* has with all of the other words and expressions in the French language are not the same as the relationships that the English word *cat* enjoys with other English words and expressions. The doctrine of differential signification suggests that both interlinguistic and intralinguistic synonymy

68. The philosopher David Lewis has argued that the word *proposition,* like the word *sentence,* is simply asked to do too many things: "The conception we associate with the word 'proposition' may be something of a jumble of conflicting *desiderata*." David K. Lewis. *On the Plurality of Worlds* (Oxford: Blackwell, 1986), 54. In particular, Lewis is concerned that propositions are supposed to be objective expressions of truth, indifferent to the time and place of their articulation (in contrast to sentences, which on this account are contingent expressions of subjective thoughts); but propositions are also supposed to be what individual people think about, that is, they are the products of singular beliefs and desires, which necessarily vary depending on time and circumstance.

are impossible, forcing us to conclude that there can be no simple opposition between thought and language or content and vehicle, as if a stable "meaning," a *signifié*, could be indifferently plugged into multiple signifiers.

Do the doctrines of modern linguistics and philosophy reveal that any general theory of the sentence is bound to betray profound limitations, if not to lapse into idealizations that will necessarily fail to account for the singular dynamics of individual linguistic formations? Is the very notion that we can move from an abstract characterization of syntax to a rich description of actual verbal events fundamentally misguided? Here the fate of the sentence in the work of J. L. Austin proves instructive. At the beginning of *How To Do Things With Words*, Austin highlights the difference between saying that a sentence is a statement and saying that it is used to make a statement, stressing that the latter formulation, which rests on a traditional neo-Aristotelian distinction between sentences and propositions, is preferable. He is quick to acknowledge, however, that no one has yet offered a satisfactory definition of the class of utterances we call "sentences," and that he has no intention of attempting to do so.[69] To the contrary, as the lectures proceed Austin seems to be concerned to distance himself from the concept of the sentence as much as possible, the first step being his decision to speak about performative utterances rather than performative sentences, a move that prefigures his conclusion that to understand the performative powers of language, "what we have to study is *not* the sentence but the issuing of an utterance in a speech situation."[70] Just as linguists trade in "sentence" for "clause," so Austin gives up on the term "sentence," although for the opposite reason, that is, because its formal structure—in particular the homology it posits between grammar and logic—threatens to elide the dynamism, and volatility, of the linguistic performativity he seeks to analyze. For Austin, neither Chomskyan thought, with its distinction between competence and performance, nor Saussurean thought, with its distinction between *langue* and *parole*, can pass muster. If these two discourses hold diametrically opposed positions on the centrality of the sentence for the study of language, the difference between them is far less important for Austin than their common failure to articulate a notion of linguistic action. In this respect, he offers encouragement to contemporary literary scholars who are inclined to

69. See J. L. Austin, *How To Do Things with Words* (London: Oxford University Press, 1962), 6 n.2. Austin allows that if someone is one day to formulate a successful definition of the sentence, it will probably be a grammarian, although he does not explain why he believes this to be the case.

70. Austin, *How to Do Things*, 138.

keep studying the specificity of individual verbal formations while leaving top-down theories of the sentence to the analytic philosophers and syntacticians.

What is a sentence? Having shown how deceptively simple a question this may be, this book will explore the ways in which this and related queries impose themselves in modern European and American letters—sometimes in entirely predictable ways, at other points quite unexpectedly. In the course of the discussion, the rules of grammar will reveal themselves to be a site of ideological struggle. To take a position on what a sentence is or should be means committing oneself to one or more ideas about the power of language to shape individual and collective agency. The rationalist conviction that orderly syntax reflects the orderly working of the mind notwithstanding, compositional conventions necessarily fall under suspicion of being coercive or even outright oppressive. For every author who believes that success lies in playing within the rules, there is another who maintains that pushing formal dicta to their limits opens up new possibilities for resistance to the status quo, if not for revolution.

As we have already seen, a book about the sentence must inevitably grapple with questions of sentence style, but it is one of the ambitions of this study to illustrate the ways in which traditional understandings of style do as much to obscure as to highlight the issues we hope to address. If sentence style is only one facet of writing style, it is also only one facet of the sentence. As much as grammar offers writers the freedom to experiment with different modes of expression, it also confronts them with decisions that they did not and cannot make. If style can never be dismissed as "just" style, neither can the sentence be dismissed as "just" a stylistic concern. In this respect, our reflections on the sentence will be a testament to both the power and the inherent limitations of style as an organizational category.[71]

In his 1973 *The Pleasure of the Text*, Roland Barthes describes being semi-awake in a bar and finding himself surrounded by a mix of noises—music, stray voices, the sounds of moving furniture—that meandered in and out of his consciousness. In this way, he says, he became the site through which passed "words, tiny syntagms, bits of formulae, and *no sentence formed*."[72] Sporadic and discontinuous, "this *non-sentence* was in no way something that was incapable of ascending to the status of sentence, that might have been *before* the

71. For a fascinating study of the problems that arise in traditional accounts of literary style, see Jeff Dolven, *Senses of Style: Poetry before Interpretation* (Chicago: University of Chicago Press, 2017).

72. Barthes, *The Pleasure of the Text*, 49 (my emphasis).

sentence; it was what is eternally, splendidly, *outside the sentence*."[73] Informed by Saussure's focus on the autonomy and spontaneity of the signifier, literary and cultural theory has been enchanted by visions of a-sentential discourses that do not pit themselves against subject-predicate logics so much as they strive to escape their influence or reveal themselves to be thoroughly indifferent to them. In some cases, the need to recognize the limits of the sentence as a model of discourse is explicitly cast as a political imperative. Homi K. Bhabha argues that "if you seek simply the sententious or the exegetical, you will not grasp the hybrid moment outside the sentence—not quite experience, not yet concept; part dream, part analysis; neither signifier nor signified."[74] No less than Nietzsche, he enjoins us to push back against the dominance of the sentence form. In particular, he insists that some insight into "the antagonism between the sentence of predicative syntax and the discontinuous subject of discourse" is essential for critical projects concerned with ethnic and cultural hybridity and the relations of power that organize international dynamics of exploitation.[75]

At the same time, we can never simply abandon the sentence. As much as revolutionary action has always challenged the dominant discursive paradigms, it has also lived off those paradigms. If we do conclude that our task is to resist the sentence in one fashion or another, we will first have to determine the extent to which it competes with other forms of language. Initially, this will be less a matter of identifying alternative ways of writing or speaking than of learning how to read sentences in a different light, treating them not simply as ordered arrangements of elements but as patterns or rhythms not reducible to the sum of their logical or grammatical parts.

Chapter 1 of this book opens with a question that plagued authors at the turn of the nineteenth century: How powerful can a single sentence be? According to G. W. F. Hegel's doctrine of the speculative sentence, the significance of any proposition derives from the way in which its inherent instability inexorably generates inferences that may conflict with its overt claims. Truth lies not in the accuracy and forcefulness of a given statement, but in the transformations that take place within sentences and the clashes that take place between them. In contrast, Hegel's Romantic contemporaries suggest that aphorisms, fragments, and other so-called "minor" forms gain their authority from their brevity and their—often ironic—attempt to have the first and last word. These reflections

73. Barthes, *The Pleasure of the Text*, 49 (translation modified).

74. Homi K. Bhabha, *The Location of Culture* (New York: Routledge, 1994), 260.

75. Bhabha, *Location of Culture*, 259.

on the powers of stand-alone sentences prove influential for later authors who achieve notoriety for their witticisms and *bons mots*, including Friedrich Nietzsche, Karl Kraus, and Paul Valéry. They also influence the discourse on political language elaborated by Karl Marx and his inheritors. A mix of Hegelian and Romantic arguments shapes Marx's claim that to know someone's politics is to understand what kind of sentences they are trying to write. Ultimately, he maintains that a truly revolutionary praxis must embrace the slogan, a battle cry that aspires to be simultaneously a shibboleth, a wish, and a command. Inherently unstable, slogans are not without risks, since deploying them sets in motion a signifying dynamic over which we may have little, if any, control.

Chapter 2 considers whether verse texts by their nature challenge the authority of sentence grammar. In different but equally consequential ways, Walt Whitman and Emily Dickinson test our understanding of lineation and its relationship to syntax. Celebrated as the father of free verse, Whitman writes sprawling paratactic formations that wreak havoc with conventional grammatical relationships, as the phrase threatens to usurp the clause, and finite verbs become almost superfluous. The result may be an egalitarian—or as Whitman himself would have it, "democratic"—discourse of nonhierarchical sentences or simply an a-syntactic maelstrom in which there are no longer any sentences at all. Dickinson's minimalist poems contrast starkly with Whitman's maximalism, and her reliance on traditional quatrains and ballad meters scarcely seems disruptive on a formal level. Nonetheless, her short lines of verse graphically isolate individual phrases and clauses, almost as if her texts were diagramming themselves. Each of her poems thus becomes a miniature treatise about what is and is not possible when we try to put words together in meaningful ways. In some cases, the authority of individual words, their ability to function extrasyntactically, is pitted against the predicative powers of the sentence. In others, we see outright collisions between versification and the grammatical patterns that should ostensibly hold sway. Together, these two poets offer us a glimpse of what it means to denaturalize the sentence and to read without the assumption that it is the dominant linguistic paradigm.

Chapter 3 explores the clashing doctrines of genius and method that shaped nineteenth-century theories of composition and led a range of authors to conclude that there is no guarantee that we can ever be done with a sentence once we have begun it. Read as experiments in narrative forms rather than as Gothic tales of horror, Edgar Allan Poe's short stories are characterized by extreme inversions of part and whole, as entire texts are crafted for the sake of a single sentence, whether to demonstrate the power of a seemingly banal subject-predicate construction or to counter a given statement's claim to serve as the model for all sentences. A similar tension is encountered in Stéphane Mallarmé's prose poems, where the poet's ability to affirm the power of his sentences turns out to be inversely proportional to his ability to recognize the sentences he writes as his own. For Gustave Flaubert, writing is less a process of creation than one of potentially interminable revision. Articulating a conception of the sentence as both a physical object and a metaphysical ideal, neither of which enjoy a stable existence, his work paves the way for our modern conviction that to write well is above all to write good sentences. The final section of the chapter examines an unlikely inheritor of Flaubert, the schizophrenic Daniel Paul Schreber, made famous by Sigmund Freud. Schreber's struggles with his prose are a powerful illustration of the inherently problematic, if not psychotic, nature of the ambition to exercise sovereignty over one's sentences, especially by finishing them.

Nineteenth-century reflections on the sentence expose its powers and limits, as well as the dangers it may present. At first glance, early twentieth-century authors seem to embrace these maverick impulses, pushing the conventional sentence form to its breaking point, if not casting it aside altogether. Whether in haiku-like poems without verbs, stream-of-consciousness constructions in which pages go by without any terminal punctuation, or typographic experiments that eschew horizontal lines of text almost entirely, the literary innovations of modernism appear to challenge every rule and norm of the sentence. At the same time, the first decades of the twentieth century also witness rather conservative aesthetic impulses, including Fordist calls for verbal efficiency and an emphasis on precisely controlled diction. Chapter 4 explores these contradictions in an effort to assess just how disruptive transgressions of grammar and stylistic conventions really are. The first section examines the work of Virginia Woolf, Ezra Pound, and Ernest Hemingway, asking how far these modernists were willing to go in redesigning language, and the world, to ensure that their sentences would do what they wanted. The second section considers Gertrude Stein's attempt to develop a theory of writing not predicated on the assumption that we know what a sentence is. Following Hemingway in attempting to craft texts that make their own process of composition legible, she calls on us to conceive of a discourse in which every part is as important as every other part because nothing, as she puts it, is part of anything else. This conception of a language of radical equality becomes the centerpiece of her history of English imperialism and the rise of modernism.

In the Conclusion, I argue that the sentence has become such a fetishized object that the goal for many writers is less to produce exceptional texts than to be sure that their texts contain at least a few stellar sentences. Unable to reconcile aesthetic and utilitarian accounts of style and composition, we increasingly tend to base our judgments of form on content. Until we begin taking seriously the basic question of what a sentence is, we will find ourselves torn between celebrating it as humanity's most powerful tool and fearing it as a force we can never hope to control.

CHAPTER 1

Slogans and Other One-Liners

The real is the rational.

G. W. F. HEGEL

All Power to the Soviets!

BOLSHEVIKS

Impossible is nothing.

ADIDAS®

Any sentence, no matter how tentative or provisional, has at least some chance of turning out to be of great consequence. If it helps advance a crucial argument, it may be embraced as a foundational insight. As the pivotal line of a treaty or contract, it may change the course of history. At the same time, any sentence, no matter how ambitious or penetrating, can be sharply qualified, if not categorically refuted, by the next one. Alternatively, it may suffer the ignominy of being forgotten the very moment it has been heard or read. In this chapter, we will consider how sentences are shaped by their potential to be either lapidary or ephemeral, and in some cases both.

What can or should a single sentence hope to accomplish? Grammatical independence is not equivalent to logical or rhetorical autonomy, although many sentences nonetheless do appear to aspire to self-sovereignty. Wherever we go, we encounter persuasive, evocative, or transformative utterances that are ostensibly complete in and of themselves. Indeed, the strength of many of the formulations we regard as insightful, moving, or witty stems from their indifference to their own reception and their implicit suggestion that they have no need of external affirmation, much less clarification or revision. This freedom is a mixed blessing. A putatively definitive comment always risks falling victim to its own claim to finality and may well prove to be a voice in the wilderness rather than a guiding dictum. Perhaps it is precisely the sentences that demand a response—be it praise, revision, or rebuttal—that are the most consequential, their significance measured by the richness of the statements to which they give rise rather than by their ability to have the last word.

At the beginning of the nineteenth century, questions about the powers and limits of individual sentences and the kinds of relationships that could be established between them played an important role in efforts to rethink the classical model of the propositional judgment. In some cases, this meant asking if and how a sentence could be integrally connected with the sentences that preceded or followed it, whether the organizing link was understood to be logical, narratological, or simply the brute force of sequence. In other cases, a sentence's authority was tested by revising, reversing, or simply repeating it, either in the hopes that subsequent iterations would confirm its essential power or in an effort to neutralize it by tearing it out of context.

For this generation, the specter of Hegelian thought loomed large. In the preface to the *Phenomenology of Spirit*, Hegel enjoins philosophical thinking to transcend the traditional understanding of the propositional statement and embrace the "speculative" sentence. First and foremost, this will require us to give up on the conventional notion that either the subject or the predicate of a statement is a fixed reference point anchoring its semantic structure. Customarily, the subject is treated as the primary term, a sort of passive frame, while the predicates affixed to it are considered its accidents or contingent properties: a chair may be made of wood or metal; a rose may be red, white, or yellow. Conversely, the subject can be treated as the contingent entity—a particular rose, a particular chair—while the predicates are considered the stable universal terms: this rose is red and expensive; this chair is also red and expensive. In either case, the linearity of the sequence of words forming the judgment—*x is y*—is taken as a figure of development. Whatever we may think about the truth or falsehood of any particular alignment of subject and predicate, we know that their articulation signals that the discussion is going forward because something has been said.

In undermining such assumptions, Hegel enjoins us to consider the interactions of the parts of a sentence as primary and the terms that interact as secondary. This means thinking about the relationships between the relating elements as giving rise to them, and not the other way around. Instead of being treated as modular units that exist independently of the formulations in which they appear, individual subjects and predicates become constitutively transitional moments of an expressive dynamic in which the substance of what is being articulated is the interplay that unfolds between them rather than the meaning of any specific verbal formation. Understood speculatively, the "subject" of a sentence is no longer its grammatical subject, but the changes the sentence undergoes in the course of being read and reread.

As an example, Hegel offers an analysis of a proposition as philosophically (and theologically) complex as it is syntactically straightforward: *God is being*.[1] At first glance, he explains, we do not believe the statement to be enumerating one of God's traits among others; rather, we regard it as a claim about the essential nature, the essence, of God. This proposition identifies God with being, to the point that the grammatical subject of the sentence all but disappears in its predicate. The sentence thus threatens to reverse itself and read *Being is God*, although this never quite occurs. Disturbed by the potential loss of the original subject, by the possibility that God has been replaced by something else, we turn back to the original subject of the sentence, seeking reassurance that it still means what it meant when we first began. The problem is that our conception of God now looks different, as if by being articulated with *being* and almost replaced by it, God has changed. The sentence *God is being* is no longer what we read the first time, which is to say that we now have the intimation of yet another sentence—*God is not being*—that will ultimately resolve into *God is and is not being*, and so on. Dialectical thinking is this movement of the loss and rediscovery of a formulation that is at once the same and yet different, a constant reading and rereading of sentences that will never parse the same way twice. As the emphasis of the claim repeatedly shifts, the series of alignments and reversals becomes a rhythmic dynamic in which the ever-changing subject and predicate are identified with and distinguished from one another, fused and polarized. Instead of *a* syntax with *a* hierarchy, we have a fluid interplay of elements that flirts with many hierarchies.

As vigilantly as speculative philosophy works to unbalance the classical subject-predicate schema, the traditional sentence continues to haunt us. The most rigorous discourse is perpetually in danger of lapsing back into propositional thinking and presenting its insights as self-standing statements whose authority stems from their fixity and stability rather than their mercurial character. Even Hegel's exposition of *God is being* may be something of a simplification. As a challenge to the hegemony of traditional predication, it may not be radical enough.

Hegel's doctrines are notoriously difficult to summarize because his "position" is precisely that substantive positions cannot be encapsulated in individual statements and that no single proposition can lay claim to being truly consequential. If speculative thinking never produces a codified method, this is because it never takes for granted that it knows what a sentence is. With

1. G. W. F. Hegel, *Phenomenology of Spirit*, trans. A. V. Miller (New York: Oxford University Press, 1977), 38.

each verbal formation we encounter, we must reflect anew on the assumptions we are making about the relationships between its semantic, syntactic, and rhythmic features, remaining forever on the lookout for more extreme sentential dynamics that may confound our preconceptions of what language is and does. A striking example of the latter is what Hegel terms the "negative infinite judgment," which emerges in the course of his discussion of judgments of existence in the *Science of Logic*. Such judgments are relatively preliminary forms in which the subject is an abstract individual that simply *is*, and the predicate is a property of the subject, an abstract universal. Hegel begins with the positive judgment ("the rose is red"), which is followed by the negative judgment ("the rose is not red"), and then by the negative infinite judgment: "the rose is not an elephant."[2] Although the negative infinite judgment aligns a subject and a predicate, the relationship is less than nominal. Hegel struggles to characterize this broken, borderline impossible sentence in which "there is no longer any positive connection between [the predicate] and the subject."[3] The juxtaposition of the one with the other somehow links them, and yet that very link "ought not," writes Hegel, "to be there."[4] Such judgments are in a sense "correct or true"—the rose is not an elephant—but they are equally "nonsensical and fatuous"; or "more to the point," adds Hegel, "they are *not judgments at all*."[5] Arranged "anatactically" rather than syntactically, the words are placed together only to fall apart.

As extreme a transformation of propositional language as the negative infinite judgment appears to be, it still respects Hegel's privileging of nouns and verbs as the mainstays of the expression of thought and his corresponding denigration of "minor" parts of speech. A monstrous sentence, the "judgment" is a sentence all the same, or at least it is a collection of words that can masquerade

2. G. W. F. Hegel, *The Science of Logic*, trans. George di Giovanni (New York: Cambridge University Press, 2010), 558/565/567. Hegel's other examples of negative infinite judgments include "the spirit is not red [or] yellow" and "the understanding is not a table" (567).

3. Hegel, *The Science of Logic*, 567. Rather than coordinating a universal and a particular, a negative infinite judgment attacks the conceptual authority of the universal—its claim to order through inclusion, and its claim to offer some sort of negative determination via exclusion.

4. Hegel, *The Science of Logic*, 567.

5. Hegel, *The Science of Logic*, 567. Far from dismissing these nonsentential sentences as mere anomalies, Hegel accords them a crucial spot in his understanding of ethics and politics. Both in the *Logic* and when he returns to the topic in his *Encyclopedia Logic* and his *Philosophy of Right*, he cites crime, in particular the theft of property, as an example of the objective expression of a negative infinite judgment, because it is an act that violates not just someone's rights, but right as such.

as a sentence, if only for a short period of time. At other moments in Hegel's work, we encounter something closer to an abandonment of grammar. Perhaps the most famous example is found in chapter 1 of his *Science of Logic*, which opens with Section A, "Being," and begins: "*Being, pure being,*—without further determination."[6] In its first textual appearance, being appears in a sub- or protoformulation in which the very distinction between subject and predicate may not yet be operative. The dash in the middle of the two small sequences of words hardly simplifies matters. Among the marks used in formal writing, a dash is unique because it is never mandated by the rules of punctuation; electively inserted, it has an air of design about it and demands explication. At the same time, the ambiguity of the mark, which uncertainly heralds a decisive break, an aside, or a clarification or revision of what has just been stated, makes it difficult, if not impossible, to ascribe a dash an unequivocal role in a sentence. In practice, any given dash is thus often treated as if it were a different punctuation mark (e.g., a comma or semicolon) or simply ignored. At the opening of Hegel's *Logic*, there is no grammatical or logical statute to guide us as we seek to parse this "sentence"; no tidy substitution takes us "forward" across the dash to the prepositional phrase that follows, and no neat inversion takes us "back" to the words with which we began. Far from unusual, such rogue punctuation marks recur throughout Hegel's work, creating a kind of unscripted counterbeat to the rhythms of speculative logic—uniting and dividing, emphasizing and deemphasizing, and perhaps even suspending the very impulses that would normally give rise to propositions, however provisional, and their negations.

In Hegel, the overcoming of predicative statements by speculative thinking exposes linguistic forces that have no place in our canons of logic and grammar. That this sustained confrontation with novel discursive formations could be important for the study of literature has not gone unremarked. In *Marxism and Form*, Fredric Jameson declares: "I remain faithful to the notion that any concrete description of a literary or philosophical phenomenon—if it is to be really complete—has an ultimate obligation to come to terms with the shape of the individual sentences themselves, to give an account of their origin and formation."[7] In literary texts in particular, the hegemony of the subject-predicate

6. Hegel, *The Science of Logic*, 59 (Hegel's italics; punctuation corrected). For a superb study of the dash in Hegel, see Rebecca Comay and Frank Ruda, *The Dash—The Other Side of Absolute Knowing* (Cambridge, MA: MIT Press, 2018).

7. Fredric Jameson, *Marxism and Form: Twentieth-Century Dialectical Theories of Literature* (Princeton, NJ: Princeton University Press, 1971), xii.

form is routinely challenged by speculative dynamics. Whether or not our traditional conceptions of signification, representation, or expression can account for these tensions remains an open question.

Katrin Pahl has described the provocation of Hegel's speculative sentence as an insight into the poetics of thought: "Unlike the judgment, which is irreversible by law, the speculative proposition breaks with the linearity of *logos*. Like poetry, which forces us to turn at the end of the verse (*versus*), it has to be read backward and forward in a reading act that transforms discursive language into a multidimensional web arousing the reader to multiply connections while throwing her around in the rhythm of its beats."[8] If, as Pahl emphasizes, "the most vital question for Hegel the writer is . . . how to seduce the reader to read his propositions speculatively," then poetry, and perhaps literature in general, is the discourse in which the stability of the sentence form and the harmonious cooperation of grammar, logic, and representation cease to be givens.[9] Our task is therefore not simply to read "for" or "at the level of" the sentence, but to approach each and every verbal formulation as if it were constantly reevaluating its own claim to coordinate structure and content. For Hegel, the sentence names not a fixed compositional standard or model of expression, but a set of relationships that are forever in flux. Each time we encounter such a dynamic interplay of elements, we must learn to read all over again.

In Hegel, any proposition inexorably generates inferences that give rise to new propositions that conflict with it, thereby betraying its constitutive incompleteness and instability. Taken in isolation, no statement can be deemed true or false. As Theodor W. Adorno has put it, "every single sentence in Hegel's philosophy proves itself unsuitable for that philosophy."[10] For Hegel, truth is not an effect of the content of a given utterance, but of the ineluctable transformation of one utterance into another with which it can never completely accord. Under the scrutiny of the speculative reader, axioms, first principles, and foundational definitions lose their authority. An individual formulation never demonstrates itself to be entirely self-determining, establishes itself as

8. Katrin Pahl, "Speculative Rhythm," in *Hegel and Language*, ed. Jere O'Neill Surber (Albany, NY: SUNY Press, 2006), 243. Pahl continues: "Reading Hegel's prose resembles reading a poem aloud: one hesitates as to where to put the accent—is it in accordance with the meter, or with the syntax, or with the stress of the meaning? What if all three differ from one another? Where to articulate the beat? When to rest the foot?" (243).

9. Pahl, "Speculative Rhythm," 238.

10. Theodor W. Adorno, "Skoteinos, or How To Read Hegel," *Hegel: Three Studies*, trans. Shierry Weber Nicholsen (Cambridge, MA: MIT Press, 1993), 91.

the definitive iteration of a series, or has the last word. In fact, no individual formulation lays claim to doing much of anything.

Hegel's challenge to the alleged pithiness or weightiness of the solitary statement could scarcely be more direct. His Romantic contemporaries were equally concerned with the problem of how powerful a single sentence can be, but they approached the problem very differently. In considering the potential of individual formulations to realize the autonomy Hegel denies them, they had occasion to explore the powers of the aphorism.[11] Derived from the Greek *aphorismós*, "a pithy phrase containing a general truth," the aphorism and its cousins—maxims, sayings, adages, apothegms, and in Romanticism, the fragment—constitute a familiar if controversial topos of literary history. Even the writers who have become famous for their mastery of these short forms have been suspicious of them. Seeking to combine the self-evidence of an axiom with the authority of a dictum, aphorisms are threatening because they aspire to be independent of any conceptual or linguistic system that might understand or control them.[12] An aphorism is not a first principle and does not allow for clear lines of inference or deduction. Unlike an axiom, it does not present itself as a building block for anything larger. Unlike a dictum, it is not underwritten by or uttered in the name of any particular authority; its legitimacy comes not from the identity of its author or the situation in which it is articulated, but from the peculiar interplay of style and substance it effects, irrespective of context.

Above all, aphorisms do not ask for our assent or endorsement as much as they assume it. Reading one, we may find ourselves according it great significance before we have even begun to think about what it means. A sentence as miniature artwork, the aphorism holds our attention just long enough to win our applause, our near-reflexive affirmation of its profundity, and then releases us to contemplate another one. In the modern era, François de La

11. Although scholars sometimes refer to a Romantic "revival" of the aphoristic tradition, aphorisms are more of a constant presence than something that comes into or goes out of style. In the German tradition, Romantic-era authors such as Georg Christoph Lichtenberg, Friedrich Schlegel, and Friedrich von Hardenberg (Novalis) are considered to have been influential for a host of modernist writers, including Friedrich Nietzsche, Karl Kraus, and Franz Kafka. On these questions, see Ben Grant, *The Aphorism and Other Short Forms* (New York: Routledge, 2016); Richard T. Gray, *Constructive Destruction: Kafka's Aphorisms: Literary Tradition and Literary Transformation* (Tübingen: Niemeyer, 1987); and Joel Westerdale, *Nietzsche's Aphoristic Challenge* (Boston: Walter de Gruyter, 2013).

12. On aphorisms versus dicta, see Gary Saul Morson, "The Aphorism: Fragments from the Breakdown of Reason," *New Literary History* 34, no. 3 (Summer 2003): 409–29.

Rochefoucauld and René Pascal inaugurated the custom of publishing book-length collections of aphorisms in which each brief entry could be assessed in isolation. By the time of Samuel Johnson's 1755 *A Dictionary of the English Language*, "aphorism" had come to be defined as a "disconnected position."[13]

Not all aphorisms manifest themselves as novelties to be grouped together with their brethren. When one does appear as part of a larger argument, it can threaten to bring the discussion to a close even as it introduces a new premise that may push things in a different direction. Uncertainty about the scope of the claims aphorisms make muddies their logical or rhetorical ambitions. While some of the best-known classical aphorisms are ethical or ontological pronouncements of an ostensibly universal nature, they are not always general formulations of abstract truths that stand over and against facts of history or culture. For Francis Bacon, an aphorism was an instance of raw data, unsullied by any system of thought: "This delivering of knowledge in distinct and disjointed aphorisms doth leave the wit of man more free to turn and toss, and to make use of that which is so delivered to more several purposes and applications."[14] In Bacon's view, an aphorism was important not because it was the premise or conclusion of an argument, but because it contained information yet to be incorporated into the demonstration. It was not a gnomic insight, whether a product of intuition or lengthy rumination, but the fruit of empirical observation that could serve as the impetus for further reflection.

While the aphorism characteristically foregrounds the interdependence of its form and content, it stops short of affirming that they coexist harmoniously. There is often more than a hint that its artful crafting masks a deficit of substance; alternatively, one may suspect that the profundity behind the formulation is obscured by its rhetorical flair. The accomplished Viennese aphorist Karl Kraus offered the following aphorism about aphorisms: "An aphorism doesn't need to be true but rather should surpass [outstrip, outwit] the truth. It must get beyond it with one *Satz*."[15] Classically, a proposition can and must be judged to be either true or false. In declaring that an aphorism cannot be reduced to its logical status, Kraus plays on the ambiguity of the German *Satz*, which can mean "sentence" or "proposition" but also "leap" or "jump." His description of how an aphorism outstrips the truth becomes a call for a word to

13. Samuel Johnson, *A Dictionary of the English Language* (London: W. Strahan, 1755), 142.

14. Francis Bacon, *Maxims of Law*, cited in Stephen Gaukroger, *Francis Bacon and the Transformation of Early-Modern Philosophy* (New York: Cambridge University Press, 2001), 35.

15. Karl Kraus, *Aphorismen*, *Schriften*, vol. 8 (Frankfurt am Main: Suhrkamp, 1986), 117 (my translation).

outstrip itself—for *Satz* to mean more than *Satz*—the irony being that the word *Satz* cannot help but be polysemantic, although the sentences in which it appears may or may not be. Formulated as a proposition that illustrates precisely what it proposes, namely that it cannot be reduced to what it states, Kraus makes a case for why an aphorism cannot simply be treated as a representation of content, while suggesting that its significance will never be identical with its form, which it must always strive to outdo.

"Outwitting" the truth may sound sexy, but it is not clear where doing so will leave us. In introducing an aphorism into our argument, we change the rules of the game such that the only way to proceed further may be to follow the first aphorism with another. Rather than advancing smoothly from sentence to sentence, we may soon find ourselves springing from one gnomic observation to the next with no obvious way of accounting for where we are going or how we got there. In the process, the very notion of a "normal" sentence that can be coordinated with the sentences around it becomes increasingly chimerical.

The anxiety that aphorisms may pervert our systems of inquiry and reflection has had no small influence. Intellectual historians have characterized the rise of humanism in the fourteenth century as a backlash against the medieval *sententiae*, an attempt to squash the authority of autonomous maxims or proverbs by reasserting the importance of contextualizing individual claims within the work or corpus in which they appear, thus ensuring that the truth or falsity of any given proposition is anchored in a definite figure of authorship.[16] This may sound like a very broad claim, but one can readily think of cases in which such a competition has played out on a more local scale. Over time, the stock of maxims and adages rises and falls with different analytic trends as the standalone power of individual statements comes to be regarded as more or less of a threat to our models of argumentation and narration.

Aphorisms are often surrounded by an air of mystery. Lying on the side of inspiration rather than of logic or systematic proof, they are always under suspicion of being cleverer than they are substantive, ephemeral flashes of insight that fail to offer anything on which solid arguments, much less systems of thought, can be built. The contemporaries of Hegel who experimented with aphorisms were often viewed as provocateurs or sophists rather than consequential thinkers, the work of Friedrich Schlegel, one of the central figures of

16. As Charles Nauert writes, "from Petrarch onward, humanists insisted on reading each opinion in its context, abandoning the anthologies . . . and subsequent interpretations and going back to the full original text in search of the author's real meaning." Quoted in James A. Herrick, *The History and Theory of Rhetoric: An Introduction*, 5th ed. (New York: Routledge, 2012), 150.

early German Romanticism, being the archetypal example. Best known for his vertiginous pronouncements about irony, Schlegel offers a more systematic and comprehensive assessment of our ideas about language than is often supposed. Indeed, if Hegel railed against Schlegel and his circle for what he perceived to be the excesses of their methods, this may have been because some of their tactics were uncomfortably similar to his own. In his analyses of individual statements, Hegel demands that we go step by step and account for each assumption and inference we make in the course of characterizing the relationship between subject and predicate. Schlegel is no less exacting in the scrutiny he brings to bear on our grammatical and rhetorical schemas, albeit in a more idiosyncratic way. In discussions that appear at once whimsical and deadly earnest, he exaggerates the logic of particular ideas about thought and representation to the point that they threaten to become ridiculous or to collapse altogether.

In Hegel, the speculative analysis of a given statement inexorably gives rise to inferences that threaten to negate the original formulation, which is to say that any proposition is open to reversal or inversion; it can always be turned around. In a brief two-sentence fragment, Schlegel challenges this elemental discursive condition: "Whoever wants something infinite doesn't know what he wants. But this sentence can't be turned around [*umkehren*]."[17] If the first sentence sounds like an aphorism, it does not stand alone, for it is accompanied by a second one that could easily have been connected to it to make a single sentence but was not. This second sentence is less an inference to be drawn from the first sentence than a comment on it. It maintains that we cannot recast the premises and implications of the first sentence's various parts to produce a different—or opposite—claim. In this respect, the second sentence cautions us that we are at risk of not reading the first sentence properly, perhaps warning us that: "Whoever wants to make sense of this sentence doesn't know how to do what he wants."

At the same time, the second sentence sets in motion precisely the chain of inferences that Hegel leads us to believe is inevitable. Its first word, the adversative conjunction "but," suggests that it would be normal to anticipate that the first sentence could or should be reversed, whether because any pronouncement about knowing, wanting, and the infinite is bound to be somewhat fluid, or because, in line with Hegelian doctrine, any sentence is structurally open

17. Friedrich Schlegel, *Kritische Friedrich-Schlegel-Ausgabe*, vol. 2, ed. Hans Eichner (Munich: Ferdinand Schöningh, 1967), 153 (my translation). In German, the fragment reads: "Wer etwas Unendliches will, der weiß nicht was er will. Aber umkehren läßt sich dieser Satz nicht."

to being inverted. In marking the point at which the fragment ostensibly turns back on itself and comments on its first part, the word "but" is supposed to herald a turn away from the possibility of turning the first sentence around. In the process, however, the conjunction reminds us that the second sentence may also be at risk of being turned around, which would mean that the provocation of the fragment is that it invites us to reject its second claim and demonstrate that its first sentence can be reversed by turning the entire fragment around.

The first sentence of Schlegel's fragment foregrounds a distinction between wanting and knowing what we want that emerges when what we are seeking, or what we think we are seeking, is something infinite. In averring the impossibility of reversing the first sentence, the second sentence makes an indirect statement about the truth content of the converse of the first sentence, that is, the second sentence implies the falsity of: "Whoever doesn't know what he wants, wants something infinite." There is no reason, however, that the reversal or inversion of the first sentence must refer solely to the relationship between the statement and its converse. Perhaps turning the first sentence around generates its contrapositive: "Whoever knows what he wants doesn't want anything infinite." There is also the inverse to consider: "Whoever doesn't want anything infinite knows what he wants."

With each of these inversions—or perversions—of the fragment's first sentence, we have proceeded by flipping the syntax and transposing the words to produce a different result, reversing the conditions and consequences while preserving the explicit affirmations and negations. Other kinds of transformations are also possible. Rearranging the syntax of the sentence to produce a new claim is not self-evidently a more "authentic" or "organic" reversal than replacing "infinite" with "finite," or even inserting the word "not." We could just as well "turn things around" by rewriting the statement: "Whoever wants the finite doesn't know what he wants," or "Whoever wants the infinite knows what he wants." A priori, there is no reason to exclude these various formulations as less viable reversals of the original.

Schlegel's fragment reveals how cavalierly we use the terms "inversion" and "reversal." If his two-sentence text does not outright dismantle Hegel's basic tenet that any sentence can be turned around, it casts doubt on the putative self-evidence of the premise. In another fragment, Schlegel offers his own vision of what a truly independent sentence might be. He begins by casting aspersions on "the demonstrations of philosophy," which he deems to be "demonstrations in the sense of military jargon. The deductions are no better than political ones; even in the sciences, one first occupies a terrain and only proves his right to it after the fact."[18] Philosophical proofs never make good on their promise to effect an ineluctably logical march from premise to conclusion. Instead, an argument begins with the adoption of a position that is retrospectively understood to be the result of a series of steps emerging after the conclusion that they "produce." Possession is 10/10ths of the lawfulness of such an *ex post facto* law.

One might imagine that Schlegel would next contrast philosophy's flawed procedures with a form of proof in which demonstrations systematically unfold via inference and deduction, each step supported by solid data or sound logic. In fact, he calls into question the very need for proof with the somewhat improbable declaration: "The main point is that one knows something and that one says it. To want to prove or even explain it is in most cases wholly unnecessary."[19] This proclamation amounts to nothing less than a dismissal of much of what has passed for philosophical reasoning in the West. According to Schlegel, propositions articulated in anticipation of the demonstrations required to validate or refute them irremediably betray their own incompleteness. By asking to be proven, clarified, or exemplified, such statements acknowledge their reliance on future formulations; their concern with what needs to be spelled out in order for them to be understood detracts from their integrity, calling into question whether they really mean what they say. Far from autonomous, they are thoroughly dependent on sentences that have yet to be formulated.

Schlegel argues that proposing something is more difficult than proving it, not least since we can create all sorts of compelling proofs "for perverse and platitudinous propositions."[20] Proposals present original ideas that are products of genuine understanding, whereas proofs are the work of technocrats or sophists, who confirm the validity of others' claims—if not the validity of any and every claim—but never craft genial ideas of their own. At the conclusion of the fragment, Schlegel puts faces to this dichotomy by opposing one of the great conceptual innovators, G. W. Leibniz, with the quintessential mechanistic rationalist, Christian Wolff, who is famous for his deductive, almost

18. Schlegel, *Kritische Ausgabe*, vol. 2, 177 (my translation). In another fragment, Schlegel is even more explicit about the militaristic quality of philosophical demonstrations: "According to the way many philosophers think, a regiment of soldiers *en Parade* is a system." Friedrich Schlegel, *Philosophical Fragments*, trans. Peter Firchow (Minneapolis: University of Minnesota Press, 1991), 23.

19. Schlegel, *Kritische Ausgabe*, vol. 2, 177 (my translation).

20. Schlegel, *Kritische Ausgabe*, vol. 2, 177 (my translation).

mathematical models of demonstration: "Leibniz proposed and Wolff proved. Enough said."[21]

"The main point is that one knows something and that one says it." A sentence of the kind Schlegel envisions presents itself as self-evident in its veracity, betraying no need for any external support or confirmation. This may be a description of the aphoristic impulse in its purest form, although the question remains whether the opposition between those who create ideas and those who demonstrate the validity of what others have said is as stable as Schlegel implies. Far from following his own advice and rejecting any expectation that he defend or clarify what he is saying, he follows his statement about the unnecessariness of proofs by contrasting two famous thinkers to illustrate his point. Here the final remark of the fragment—"Enough said"—is decisive.[22] Schlegel argues that if a proposition is to stand on its own and genuinely say something rather than lay the groundwork for what will supposedly be said in the future, it cannot betray any anticipation of or dependence on any of the supplemental explanations or clarifications that will follow. In this sense, "enough said" is the implicit termination of all truly consequential statements. However, when it is explicitly articulated at the end of a fragment that maintains that "enough said" must be the message of all substantive pronouncements, this particular instance of "enough said" threatens to undermine the very argument it purports to conclude. Its appearance compromises the completeness of what has come before by suggesting that "enough said" has not already been said clearly enough. If "enough said" is the implicit full stop at the end of every autonomous sentence, it is the last parting remark this fragment should be offering. All of our propositions should say "enough said" without any of them actually having to be "enough said."

As a closing gesture that simultaneously says too much and calls into question whether one can ever say enough, "enough said" is a witticism. Since the seventeenth century, wit has been considered a key feature of aphorisms and other short forms. Typically described as a kind of cleverness distinguished by the ability to make unexpectedly illuminating connections, wit is more closely aligned with intuition than with conscious reflection—it is an "Aha!" moment rather than the culmination of a systematic chain of reasoning. As Schlegel describes it, wit's characteristic flash of insight, "a lightning bolt from the

21. Schlegel, *Kritische Ausgabe*, vol. 2, 177 (my translation).

22. In German, Schlegel's formulation reads: "Das ist genug gesagt." The expression will sound slightly odd to the contemporary German ear, for whom it will be less familiar than *Es ist genug gesagt worden* or *Es ist alles gesagt*.

unconscious world," can be disconcerting if not frightening.[23] It may be that we do not decide whether or not to make use of wit so much as we acquiesce to its designs, which are not within our control and may not be compatible with our goals at all.

A witticism is the consummate statement for which there is neither preface nor proof. It is a sentence that betrays no anxiety about whether it can explain what it means, a sentence that is entirely unconcerned with what is to follow. Taking this a step further, Schlegel proposes that a witticism may also be unconnected with whatever came before it, literally appearing out of nowhere, and yet somehow, serendipitously, contradicting what has just been said as inexorably as if the author were pursuing the speculative analysis of a sentence.[24] A witticism turns the claim that preceded it around despite the fact that there is no evidence that the previous claim was in any way responsible for the appearance of the witticism. As much as it gains its power from the way in which it interrupts what has come before it, a witticism always has the air of having emerged out of the blue. The result is Hegel's worst nightmare: "x is y" is countered by "x is not y," but it cannot be shown that the second statement "follows" from the first. An upending of inversion itself, wit is the reversal of a sentence that paradoxically threatens to have nothing to do with the original sentence. Far from simply undermining a given statement, a witticism jeopardizes our most basic assumptions about what it means for one sentence to come after another and how an argument is to be constructed by stringing a series of sentences together.

Schlegel invites us to move away from thinking about the aphorism as a type of sentence and instead consider the aphoristic impulse as a drive latent in any sentence—the desire for a sentence to be accepted as important without explanation, before it has been interpreted or understood. The quintessence of this impulse, a witticism does its work in a flash, immediately establishing itself as incisive and provocative irrespective of the reception it may receive. In this regard, it is similar to another kind of one-liner, the slogan. Whether it manifests itself in a battle cry, a political watchword, or a commercial catchphrase, a slogan seeks to create a loyal audience. Like an aphorism, it makes a case for its own power by calling attention to the unique relationship of form and content it claims to realize. In foregrounding the capacity of language to interpellate, a slogan boldly expands the dominion of linguistic performance,

23. Friedrich Schlegel, *Kritische Friedrich-Schlegel-Ausgabe*, vol. 12, ed. Jean-Jacques Anstett (Munich: Ferdinand Schöningh, 1964), 393 (my translation).

24. See Schlegel, *Kritische Friedrich-Schlegel-Ausgabe*, vol. 12, 393.

to the point of insinuating that it is impossible to speak or write without attempting to effect change.

While slogans appear to lie at the furthest remove from the recondite aphorisms of authors like Pascal or La Rochefoucauld, the two forms explore the power and limits of solitary sentences in similar ways. Both rely on brevity and wit to convey a sense of their own import, and both work to create a precarious balancing act between highlighting their own rhetorical flair and not permitting themselves to be dismissed as merely catchy or clever. Like the aphorism, the slogan does not invite a response or a rebuttal, but assumes our assent, if only insofar as we are willing to repeat it.

Etymologically the word "slogan" means "battle cry," suggesting a raw expression of passion or resolve. A direct and urgent utterance, it seems to share very little with a gnomic intervention that would tie us up in paradoxical reflections about our knowledge of the infinite. This putative straightforwardness notwithstanding, the slogan is more often than not an example of language in its most calculated form. Far from the unmediated imparting of an unadulterated emotion or idea, it is predicated on consideration and control, more like a carefully crafted maxim than a furious outburst. One may want to insist that slogans have a mercenary quality not shared by aphorisms, because they are overtly designed to encourage their audiences to do something: Attack! Vote! Buy! Nonetheless, slogans are not simply perlocutionary acts. As mottoes associated with a party or movement, they are nontrivial formulations of ideas, beliefs, or systems of thought, and once a cause or movement's identity has been tied to a slogan, the two will not easily be disentangled. In fact, support for any position, no matter how concrete or abstract, may require some reliance, whether implicit or explicit, on such exhortative utterances.

Having established the connection between slogans and aphorisms, we may wonder why we ever thought that there was a clear distinction between "highbrow" maxims and the self-promotional sayings of groups or causes. From philosophical treatises and bureaucratic debates to the mundane drudgery of the campaign trail, the fate of partisan discourse has rested on its capacity to exploit the provocations of the aphorism. Whether it be the graffiti that covered ancient Roman walls, the memorable adages of Niccolò Machiavelli or Carl von Clausewitz, or centuries of placards, billboards, posters, and now Internet memes, politics—as a theory and a practice—has always been an ecology of catchphrases, watchwords, and other one-liners that strive to impart rare wisdom with their pithy pronouncements while promoting, realizing, and sustaining various identities and programs. In perhaps no other forum is there such a strong sense that the shortest argument and the most identifiable position will prevail and that the brute repetition of a sentence is the best means of ensuring that its influence will be felt. In no other venue is it comparably difficult to decide whether an idea succeeds because of its substance or its packaging.

The temptation is to conclude that slogans constitute the seamy underside of public discourse. Heralding the devolution of ideas into bromides that can be uncritically embraced, they turn complex arguments into punchlines. Such prejudices, however, are far from universally held. Informed by both Hegelian and Romantic understandings of the sentence, Marxist thinkers reject the notion that slogans are mere simplifications. From Marx to Rosa Luxemburg, V. I. Lenin, Mao Zedong, and Fidel Castro, political ideas *are* slogans, that is, they are not simply statements of goals or beliefs, but polemical claims for the power of language to change the world. Nor should we imagine that we formulate our concepts first and only later craft catchy mottos for them as a kind of afterthought. To the contrary, it may only be possible to think through a problem insofar as we can devise battle cries for our positions along the way.

Today, the association of slogans with commercial advertising is so strong that they have come to be regarded as the language of consumer capitalism, evidence of the way in which commodity fetishism shapes the signifying realm and helps to sustain the existing relations of power. For Marxist revolutionaries, in contrast, slogans have a self-abnegating quality that bespeaks their potential for subversion. In trumpeting our own battle cries, we disparage the emptiness of our opponents' calls to arms, even as we are painfully aware of how tenuous the very act of drawing this distinction may appear. Whatever convictions we have about the superiority of our cause, the slogans we use to champion it are bound to have as much an aura of the contrived or the mercenary as those of our enemies. If slogans make genuinely partisan argument possible and affirm the transformative power of language, they also raise suspicions about their own identity, suggesting that they are important precisely because, unlike the catchphrases of the other side, they are not "just" slogans.[25] In this way, slogans are at once the most powerful and the emptiest of utterances, the most self-confident and most self-sabotaging of exhortations.

25. In the 2016 mayoral race in Portland, Oregon, campaign posters for the ultimate winner boasted: *Ted Wheeler for Mayor—No Slogans, Just Solutions*. While our inevitable response will be that *No Slogans, Just Solutions* is itself a slogan, it is arguably not just a slogan, but a slogan that reveals an essential truth about all slogans, namely that they must resist being deemed "mere" slogans. Alternatively, *No Slogans, Just Solutions* may be predicated on a misunderstanding insofar as the claim of any slogan is precisely that what a slogan says and does *is* the solution. In this respect, Wheeler's slogan would be an anti-slogan, a slogan that seeks to contravene the claim to practical wisdom that makes slogans what they are.

While this has seldom been identified as a major theme of his work, Marx spilled a considerable amount of ink exploring the political catchphrases of his day. Mindful of Hegel's challenge to the density or pithiness of the solitary formulation, he repeatedly called attention to the potential disjunction between high-blown oratory and the uncertainty and haplessness characteristic of the empirical agency it was advertising. Alone, verbal audacity proves neither symptomatic of nor productive for practical wisdom. If anything, the appeal to various forms of rhetorical force threatens to become an obstacle to political change, as some of the slogans that prove most effective turn out to represent causes with little or no future.

Slogans that do not meet with Marx's approval are disparaged as "phrases." In German, "die Phrase" can be equivalent to the English "phrase," but it also designates a tired or trite saying, a "catchphrase." Marx condemns "mere phrases," "banal phrases," and above all "empty phrases," labels he uses so often that the charge itself starts to seem empty. "Phrases" are the ghosts of words and ideas, the antithesis of true knowledge and genuine verbal praxis.[26] For this reason, they are potentially powerful interventions, giving voice to something that may have had no voice or creating something that did not previously exist. Ideologically charged one-liners, their mode is necessity rather than actuality; they tell us what must or should happen, irrespective of the prospects that it will take place. At the very moment when we feel most confident in dismissing them as tools of mystification and deception, phrases have a way of revealing themselves as essential to shifting the line between the possible and the impossible, and hence as vital to social or political change. An instructive example is "Liberty, Equality, Fraternity," the French Revolutionary slogan that acquired quasi-official status in 1848. Marx may be quick to dismiss the bourgeois concepts that inform it, particularly as deployed in the mid-nineteenth century, but he has to acknowledge that the catchy trio of terms has demonstrated staying-power, leading him to the more general conclusion that there is no easy way to distinguish between revolutionary and reactionary slogans, between the *bons mots* of stasis and those of change.

As often as Marx condemns "phrase-mongering" and "phraseology," he cannot dispense with it entirely, and at various points, he intervenes creatively in the discourse, penning slogans of his own. One thinks immediately of the *Communist Manifesto*—"Proletarians of all countries, unite!"—although his most lasting contribution from this period is arguably: "The revolution is

26. See Karl Marx, "The Eighteenth Brumaire of Louis Bonaparte," *Marx/Engels Collected Works*, vol. 11 (New York: International Publishers, 1975), esp. 193ff.

dead!—Long live the revolution!"[27] This memorable pair of sentences is a reworking of the proclamation that posited the transfer of sovereignty in the French monarchy: "The King is dead, long live the King!" While it may be difficult for us to get past the sense of cliché that surrounds the formulation, we should ask ourselves why this phrasal template has been earnestly invoked in so many political struggles around the globe over the past 150 years.

The slogan appears at the end of the first section of a series of articles Marx wrote in 1850 that were published together posthumously as *The Class Struggles in France*. These pieces constitute a key moment in the development of his theory of revolution. It is here that he describes the working class replacing the bourgeoisie as the vanguard of revolution and first uses the phrase "dictatorship of the proletariat"; these articles also represent his first detailed attempt to spell out the inherent limitations of nonproletarian movements in effecting radical change.[28] Although the centrality of sloganeering to these reflections is not widely recognized, the argument of the first essay is structured around an effort to reject the popular understanding of one catchphrase and replace it with another. Marx opens by insisting that although the banner "Defeat of the revolution!" heads "every more important part of the annals of the revolution from 1848 to 1849," the revolution was by no means defeated, or rather, what appeared to be setbacks allowed for a genuinely revolutionary party to emerge.[29] In Hegelian fashion, "defeat has created all the conditions under which France can seize the *initiative* of the European revolution"; and Marx concludes with: "And we exclaim: The revolution is dead!—Long live the revolution!"[30] Rhetorically speaking, this slogan constitutes a precise intervention into a dialectic of victory and defeat that is aligned—although by no means precisely—with an uncertain relationship between life and death. Given the complexities, we must ask whether this battle cry is as passionate as we may suppose, and whether we actually know what it is designed to do.

The pronouncement that served as the model for Marx's slogan expressed continuity as a coordination of particulars—"one monarch is dead, and a new one stands ready"—in order to prove a general point, namely that the system of

27. Karl Marx and Friedrich Engels, "Manifesto of the Communist Party," *Marx/Engels Collected Works*, vol. 6, 519 (translation modified); Karl Marx, *The Class Struggles in France*, *Marx/Engels Collected Works*, vol. 10, 70.

28. Marx, *The Class Struggles in France,* 127.

29. Marx, *The Class Struggles in France*, 47. With a few decades of hindsight, Engels will dryly note that he and Marx were overly optimistic about the prospects for revolution in Europe.

30. Marx, *The Class Struggles in France,* 70.

royal succession is not dependent on any given ruler because there will always be a successor waiting in the wings. The balancing act the declaration aims to effect is anything but trivial. In fifteenth-century France, it initially specified singular individuals ("King Charles is dead, Long live King Henry!"); it was not until more than half a century later that "The King is dead, long live the King!" became standard, perhaps betraying a concern that the move from the particular transfer of sovereignty to a general claim about the resiliency of the monarchy was not as easy as it appeared.[31] The comma at the center of the proclamation separates the indicative mood from the formulaic subjunctive and symbolically marks the uneasy moment at which there is no king. In France, the inheritance of the throne had to be ratified by the princes, meaning that in some cases years might pass between the burial of one sovereign and the ascension of the next. As much as the punctuation mark bespeaks a need to bridge the divide between the death of one king and the moment when his replacement takes power, there is also a need to keep the two apart—the "old" king had better be dead, or we may find ourselves contending with two monarchs. Tasked with nothing less than bridging the divide between life and death while keeping them rigorously separate, the two halves of the announcement want to swap roles, the first striving to become a wish ("Let the King be dead!"), and the second aspiring to be an indicative assertion ("We have a new King!").

Marx's rewriting of the pronouncement alters the relationship between its two halves. While "The revolution is dead!" refers to a particular event, that is, the revolution of 1848, "Long live the revolution!" does not seek to empower a ready-to-hand substitute but is rather the "declaration of the permanence of the revolution" for the whole of Europe.[32] Although Marx offers a detailed description of how the various elements of society win different kinds of power in their struggles with one another and with existing institutions, he has little to say about the power of such a battle cry. The second sentence—"Long live the revolution!"—gains its force by following the first and turning it around, as if there were a dialectical reversal taking place as life emerges from death. Perhaps most striking is Marx's confidence that the phrasal template will be adaptable enough that we can substitute one term for another—even when the terms in question are "king" and "revolution"—without creating any problems for the form. Given his concern about the potential evils of phraseology, the

31. Ralph E. Giesey, *Cérémonial et puissance souveraine: France, xve–xviiie siècles,* Cahier des Annales 41 (Paris: Éditions de l'EHESS, 1987), 123.

32. Marx, *The Class Struggles in France,* 127.

subtext of the proclamation may in fact be: "The original terms of the slogan are dead!—Long live the slogan!" What is dead one moment and risen from the ashes the next is less the monarchy or the revolution than the slogan itself.

While the slogan "Long live the revolution!" did not originate with Marx, it was not born as an expression of passionate radicalism, either. Plenty of slogans of the form "Vive X!" were in circulation in France around 1790 ("Vive la nation!"; "Vive la constitution!"; "Vive la république!"), but there is little evidence that "la révolution" figured in any of them. The phrase seems not to have been shouted by the Jacobins themselves so much as it was attributed to them by their opponents.[33] When "Vive la révolution!" appeared on posters denouncing Charles X and the nobility during the 1830 revolution, it had been appropriated from the verbal toolkit of the right rather than the left.[34] One of the most famous nineteenth-century European catchphrases was thus not originally a call to arms, but a watchword that from the outset was belated in its enunciation and distorted in its meaning, a fact not lost on contemporary observers of the events in France, who commented that cries of "Long live X!" often signified "Long live Y!"

We may begin to suspect that Marx's invocation of "Long live the revolution!" is somewhat tongue-in-cheek. In his writings about the events of 1848 and their aftermath, he repeatedly cites examples of "Long live X!" and periodically punctuates his argument with his own versions of the exclamation. He never, however, presents the formulation as worthy of emulation, much less as the model for a catchphrase that will stand the test of time. To the contrary, this seemingly straightforward affirmation of someone or something's future generally appears in passages in which the tone is bitterly sarcastic and in which Marx seems determined to debunk the slogan's ostensible power. He often writes "Long live X!" when he is making fun of someone's commitment to X.

33. One of the earliest associations of "Long live the revolution!" with the Jacobins occurs in a 1797 text by the conservative Gérard de Lally-Tollendal, who describes the "monsters" who cried out "Vive la révolution!" See Gérard de Lally-Tollendal, *Défense des femmes, des enfans et des vieillards émigrés, pour faite suite à l'ouvrage* (Paris: Poignée, 1797), 20. Relating the events surrounding Napoleon's ascension, Alexis de Tocqueville writes that "everything is done to the cry of 'Long live the republic!' . . . [and] 'Long live the republic!' meant: 'Long live the revolution! No Royalist reaction!'" Alexis de Tocqueville, *The Old Regime and the Revolution,* vol. 2: *Notes on the French Revolution and Napoleon*, trans. Alan S. Kahan (Chicago: University of Chicago Press, 2001), 240. I am grateful to Dan Edelstein, Mary Ashburn Miller, and James Swenson for helping me trace the genealogy of this slogan.

34. See Pamela M. Pilbeam, *The 1830 Revolution in France* (New York: Palgrave Macmillan, 1991), 42.

Alternatively, he uses the line as a way of indicating that X has been outlawed or relegated to the scrapheap of history, underscoring the futility of the slogan, which will not bring any ideals back to life by its repetition. In other cases, he makes it clear that the chant of "Long live X!" was made at gunpoint, so that it was "uttered mechanically, coldly, and with a bad conscience," the automaticity of the slogan's recitation rendering its "intent" suspect.[35] In a colorful passage, Marx even scoffs at the way in which the self-proclaimed Napoleon III attempted to emulate his namesake and bolster his troops' morale by offering them champagne and sausages. The hapless "pseudo-Napoleon," as Marx terms him, failed to realize that the soldiers crying out "Long live Napoleon! Long live the sausage!" were mocking their ruler, since the French word for "sausage" was slang for "buffoon."[36] Taking stock of Marx's use of the form "Long live X!" one begins to wonder whether he is directing his scorn more at those who believe in the possibility of X (e.g., freedom or democracy) or at those who think that bellowing slogans will change the world.

Given how systematically Marx expresses his skepticism about expressions of support taking the form "Long live X!" we might ask whether "The revolution is dead!—Long live the revolution!" is designed to attack the very hegemony of the proclamation's venerable form. This would make it no less a call to arms, although it might indicate that any revolution worthy of the name must contend with established lineages of verbal authority. Classically, the ultimate power of the sovereign was the ability to wage war or to exercise capital punishment. From this perspective, "The King is dead, long live the King!" speaks in the name of a more fundamental proclamation, "Long live the power to sentence people to death!" To unsettle the discourse of monarchy, then, we must challenge the centrality of the sovereign's death sentence as the sentence of sentences that grounds the power of language in the right to kill.

Marx was by no means the first to reach this insight. More than a decade before the events of 1848, Georg Büchner explored the means of resisting sovereign proclamations in a drama about the Revolutionary Terror. In the final scene of *Danton's Death*, a distraught Lucile, the wife of one of Danton's deputies, watches her husband mount the scaffold to be executed. She cries out, "Long live the King!"—whereupon the stage directions explain: "She is surrounded by the watch and led off," and the play concludes.[37] The most

35. Marx, *The Class Struggles in France,* 105.

36. Marx, *The Class Struggles in France,* 143.

37. Georg Büchner, *Complete Works and Letters*, trans. Henry J. Schmidt (New York: Continuum, 1991), 123.

common interpretation of this outburst is that Lucile has resolved in her despair to perish with her husband. In the revolutionary context, her exclamation of "Long live the King!" is an act of suicide.

Lucile's outburst turns the ultimate affirmation of immortality—the royal line will never end—into a death sentence for herself and the monarchy. Whereas Marx's "Long live the revolution!" attacks the language of sovereignty by preserving the form but altering the content, Lucile does the same thing, and arguably more, by retaining the monarchical formulation itself. Her exclamation serves as a reminder that if "The King is dead, long live the King!" was a situational celebration of one ruler following another, it was not strong enough to keep the monarchy on its feet and may have been a proleptic death sentence all along.

In his *Meridian Address*, Paul Celan discusses the conclusion of Büchner's play and the cry "Long live the King!" as an attack on the monarchy. He deems Lucile's final exclamation a counter-act or "counterword"—more than mere parody, it is an instance in which language betrays language.[38] Celan is particularly struck by the fact that this "act of freedom" breaks the genealogical chain of sovereign power through the very verbal performance designed to give shape to the historicity of sovereignty.[39] In *Danton's Death*, the force of this proclamation gone rogue is manifest in the terrible irony that while the verbal ceremonies of royal succession did not prevent Louis XVI from being guillotined, the slogan "Long live the King!" did keep killing anyone brave enough to utter it well after the last king was dead and buried.

It is by no means clear why the language of sovereignty should be vulnerable to attack not just by a single sentence, but by a single sentence of its own devising. In his 1949 essay "Literature and the Right to Death," Maurice Blanchot cites the Terror and the Marquis de Sade as models in declaring writing to be a revolutionary act: "Any writer who is not induced by the very fact of writing to think, 'I am the revolution, only freedom allows me to write,' is not really writing."[40] Much has been written about this claim, although less attention has been paid to the fact that Blanchot's argument relies on the introduction of yet another string of sovereign pronouncements and counterpronouncements. A rewriting of Louis the XIV's "I am the state," "I am the revolution" has

38. Paul Celan, *The Meridian*, trans. Pierre Joris (Stanford, CA: Stanford University Press, 2011), 3.

39. Celan, *The Meridian*, 3.

40. Maurice Blanchot, "Literature and the Right to Death," *The Work of Fire*, trans. Charlotte Mandell (Stanford, CA: Stanford University Press, 1995), 321.

long been attributed to Napoleon Bonaparte, who supposedly made the declaration during his rise to power.[41] The quotation is likely apocryphal, which underscores that for Blanchot absolute creativity produces not utterances of unparalleled originality, but citations of well-established battle cries that may never have been uttered in the heat of battle at all. To write is to write as a revolutionary, as Sade or an engineer of the Terror, but this means inserting oneself into a complex chain of repetition and parody in which the contest for power takes place as a struggle between rival slogans of uncertain or even spurious provenance.

In referencing Napoleon's "I am the revolution," Blanchot does not include the second sentence that purportedly preceded the first, "The revolution is over."[42] Together, Napoleon's two lines offer a proleptic rejoinder to Marx's "The revolution is dead!—Long live the revolution," which was certainly in dialogue with the emperor's—possibly fictitious—boast. Although he does not invoke the second half of the suspect citation, Blanchot does take Napoleon at his word in a way that few others have done when he argues that speaking necessarily puts an end both to oneself and to the subject of one's remarks. Lucile's "Long live the King!" is a death sentence, a sentence that betrays the dark truth that the subtext of every sentence uttered by a monarch in the name of sovereignty is "Long live death!" Blanchot generalizes this point in arguing that *every* sentence is the death sentence of both its subject matter and its speaker. We are familiar with the notion that a sign functions in the absence of its referent, but Blanchot takes this negative aspect of signification to the extreme, maintaining that language actively destroys the existential composition of that about which it speaks. In his example, to say "this woman" is to announce her mortality and presage her ultimate demise, since the utterance that takes her as its object of reference reveals that she can "be detached from herself, removed from her existence and her presence, and suddenly plunged into a nothingness [i.e., language] in which there is no existence or presence."[43]

Going a step further, Blanchot adds that it is only because this woman is capable of dying that he can refer to her at all and thereby perform this "deferred assassination, which is what [his] language is."[44] In these terms, mortality is

41. See David P. Jordan, *Napoleon and the Revolution* (New York: Palgrave Macmillan, 2012), 71.

42. Jordan, *Napoleon,* 71.

43. Blanchot, "Literature and the Right to Death," 323.

44. Blanchot, "Literature," 323. This leads Blanchot to one of his most provocative claims about literature: "When I first begin, I do not speak in order to say something; rather, a nothing

the precondition of signification, applying not just to the person about whom one speaks but to the speaker as well: "When I speak, I deny the existence of what I am saying, but I also deny the existence of the person who is saying it"; one speaks "out of his power to remove himself from himself, to be other than his being."[45] If every sentence is a murder-suicide, Blanchot's intervention into the chain of political slogans transforms "I am the revolution" into "I kill both myself and the revolution."[46]

Far from challenging the verbal praxis of classical sovereignty, Blanchot intensifies the logic according to which "I sentence you to death" comes to be the defining utterance of power. In this regard, his argument remains quite conventional. At least since Kant, philosophers have proposed that the human being can only confirm its status as a creature of reason subordinate to the rule of universals by rising above the limits of its biological existence, which means by risking or even sacrificing its own life.[47] In Victor Hugo's *Les Misérables*, the insurgents of June 1832 who decline to leave their positions on the barricades despite near-certain doom cry out "Long live death!"[48] This is not

---

demands to speak, nothing speaks, nothing finds its being in speech, and the being of speech is nothing. This formulation explains why literature's ideal has been the following: to say nothing, to speak in order to say nothing" (324). Blanchot's model of language accords near-absolute privilege to names and naming. At a key juncture, he cites an early text of Hegel: "Adam's first act, which made him master of the animals, was to give them names, that is, he annihilated them in their existence (as existing creatures)" (cited in Blanchot, "Literature," 324). Blanchot adds: "Hegel means that from that moment on, the cat ceased to be a uniquely real cat and became an idea as well" (324).

45. Blanchot, "Literature," 324.

46. In his *Arcades Project*, Walter Benjamin cites a statement by Charles Baudelaire that in the context of Blanchot's reflections assumes an ambiguity of diabolical dimensions: "I am no dupe, and I have never been a dupe! I say, 'Long live the revolution!' as I would say, 'Long live destruction! Long live expiation! Long live punishment! Long live death!'" Walter Benjamin, *The Arcades Project*, trans. Howard Eiland and Kevin McLaughlin (Cambridge, MA: Harvard University Press, 1999), 245.

47. As Jacques Derrida describes this tradition: "The dignity of man, his sovereignty, the sign that he accedes to universal right and rises above animality is that he rises above biological life, puts his life in play in the law, risks his life and thus affirms his sovereignty as subject or consciousness. . . . The very idea of law implies that something is worth more than life and that therefore life must not be sacred as such; it must be liable to be sacrificed for there to be law." Jacques Derrida, *The Death Penalty*, vol. 1, trans. Peggy Kamuf (Chicago: University of Chicago Press, 2014), 116.

48. Victor Hugo, *Les Misérables* (New York: Simon & Schuster, 2005), 471. References to the battle cries of fascist Spain and Italy—"Viva la muerte!" and "Viva la morte!"—frequently

a dark parody of "Long live the revolution!" but an expression of the way in which slogans maintain their authority by confirming the paradoxical power of language to give life to its own power to kill. What emerges from Blanchot's ostensible attack on the classical discourse of sovereignty is a heightened form of the classical discourse of sovereignty. He preserves rather than challenges the deadly core of this ideology of sentential might.

Having opened Pandora's box, Blanchot cannot stop invoking slogans for which he should have no need. "Revolutionary action," he writes, "explodes with the same force and the same clarity as the writer who has only to set down a few words side by side in order to change the world."[49] But which words? Having proposed that revolutionary action is not a means to an end but an act that is itself the end, he adds that for this event, "the only tolerable slogan [*la seule parole supportable*] is Freedom or Death."[50] Beyond the problem of how this new battle cry will coexist with the implicit "I am the revolution," what role is the slogan to play at the moment when "freedom aspires to be realized in the *immediate* form of *everything* is possible, [when] everything can be done"?[51] One presumes that this "passage from nothing to everything, the affirmation of the absolute as event and of every event as absolute," will not need to externalize its program in a catchy instrumental formulation.[52] Surely any slogan that comes on the scene at such a juncture is bound to disappoint, appearing either too early or too late—indeed, one wonders whether the very fact that a slogan *could* manifest itself at such a moment suggests that the coincidence of possibility and actuality for which the free revolutionary aims is anything but perfect. Moreover, the particular slogan in question—"Freedom or death!"—is at odds with the rest of Blanchot's argument, which offers an

---

name "Vive la mort!" as the model, deeming it a Jacobin slogan, but as with "Vive la révolution," evidence suggests that this was a line attributed to the French revolutionaries rather than one used by them. In the earliest reference I have been able to find to the exclamation, the conservative Rétif de La Bretonne reported that Parisian crowds shouted "Long live death!" during the September massacres of 1792. Nicolas-Edme Rétif de La Bretonne, *Les nuits de Paris, ou Le spectateur nocturne,* vol. 16 (London: np, 1788–94), 376. Writing a few years later, Chateaubriand famously made a similar claim. See François-René de Chateaubriand, *Génie du christianisme* (Paris: Éditions de La Pléiade, 1978), 915. On the construction of a genealogy of this and other nineteenth-century slogans, see Jean-Claude Milner, *La puissance du détail: phrases célèbres et fragments en philosophie* (Paris: Grasset, 2014).

49. Blanchot, "Literature and the Right to Death," 319.

50. Blanchot, "Literature," 319.

51. Blanchot, "Literature," 318.

52. Blanchot, "Literature," 319.

account of freedom *through* death. The theme of his essay is not "Give me liberty or give me death!" but "I am capable of principled free action precisely because I can have a relationship with the fact of my own finitude!" The assertion of freedom occurs as the negation of the reality of particular lives. It is, as Blanchot writes, the "freedom of the decapitated head"; the flesh-and-blood individual dies so that the idea will live on.[53]

A truly revolutionary overturning of the language of classical sovereignty must fashion slogans that do not predicate the possibility of the future on the implicit or explicit announcement of the ambition, if not the power, to kill. While Blanchot's account of language as a medium of existential annihilation suggests that this is impossible, Marx may be less pessimistic. As we have seen, his reflections on efforts to appropriate monarchial slogans for postmonarchial causes culminate in the ambiguous closing line: "The revolution is dead!—Long live the revolution!" Two years later, he revisits the issue in *The Eighteenth Brumaire*, where he maintains that previous revolutionaries have mobilized the battle cries (*Schlachtparole*) of earlier political movements, borrowing from these discourses to glorify their struggles as well as to deceive themselves about their own agendas. His examples include the embrace of Old Testament motifs and adages by Cromwell and his allies and the adoption of Imperial Roman mythopoetics by the revolutionaries who deposed the French monarchy. In both cases, the languages of the past were appropriated on a short-term basis. In due course, the revolutionaries cast off the older phraseology and fashioned new vocabularies of their own. In contrast, 1848—the infamous "farce"—sees not another attempt to use historical models as a springboard from which to engage with "the spirit of revolution," but the resurrection of an old language with no indication that a new one will emerge to take its place.[54] Eschewing the violence and sacrifice that changing the world requires, the would-be radicals of 1848 parody prior reappropriations of the past, obscuring the very distinction between phrase and content. Once we begin playing around with other people's slogans, we may discover that we are stuck reciting them without any ability to recode them for our own purposes.

Marx calls on the radicals of the nineteenth century to reject older political jargon and fashion a discourse no longer shaped by the dynamics of citation: "The social revolution of the nineteenth century cannot draw its poetry [*Poesie*] from the past but only from the future. . . . Earlier revolutions required

53. Blanchot, "Literature," 320. On the ideological questions raised by Blanchot's essay, see Derrida, *The Death Penalty*, 111–20.

54. Marx, "The Eighteenth Brumaire of Louis Bonaparte," 105.

recollections of past world history in order to anesthetize themselves to their own content. In order to arrive at its own content, the revolution of the nineteenth century must let the dead bury their dead. There the catchphrase [*Phrase*] went beyond the content—here the content goes beyond the catchphrase [*Phrase*]."[55] One might surmise that the difference between *The Class Struggles in France* and *The Eighteenth Brumaire* is that in the latter text Marx has stopped trying to dabble in catchy phrases, however ironically, and begun systematically characterizing the historicity of contemporary political jargon in order to lay the groundwork for a new political language and perhaps even to realize a clean break with slogans. A closer examination of this passage reveals that he has by no means abandoned catchphrases or watchwords. The disparagement of slogans is eminently catchy, complete with a slick chiasmus and a memorable New Testament quotation about letting the dead bury their dead, a line flashy enough that a number of Marx's contemporaries, including Mikhail Bakunin, adopted it as their own. Marx is not "joking" here, yet as with "The revolution is dead!—Long live the revolution!" it is hard to reconcile the content of his remarks with the form in which they emerge, a problem that is particularly vexing given that the inevitable disjunction between form and content is the subject of the passage. If in Marx's text the content goes beyond the catchphrase, this may be because the catchphrase goes beyond the content, as well.

As *The Eighteenth Brumaire* continues, Marx proposes that nineteenth-century revolutionaries must be relentlessly self-critical, their "poetry" a discourse of indefatigable introspection and self-determination. In this Enlightenment language of self-reflection, self-awareness is to be the guarantor of sound judgment. The role of slogans in such a campaign is far from obvious. Rallying cries are exhortative and directive rather than self-doubting, raising the question of what a self-critical slogan might look like. In a passage in which the rhetorical momentum of the sentence mimes the event Marx is characterizing, as if neither content nor catchphrase could get the upper hand, he writes:

> Proletarian revolutions like those of the nineteenth century criticize themselves constantly, interrupt themselves continually in their own course, come back to the apparently accomplished in order to begin it afresh, deride with unmerciful thoroughness the inadequacies, weaknesses, and paltrinesses of their first attempts, seem to throw down their adversary only in order that he may draw new strength from the earth and rise again, more gigantic, before them, recoil

55. Marx, "The Eighteenth Brumaire of Louis Bonaparte," 106.

ever and anon from the indefinite prodigiousness of their own aims, until a situation has been created which makes all turning back impossible, and the conditions themselves cry out:

Hic Rhodus, hic salta!
Here is the rose, here dance![56]

In Ciceronian fashion, the long sentence prior to the quotation zig-zags back and forth, gaining speed as it proceeds to its preordained conclusion, but taking time along the way to parallel the trials of the revolutionaries with Hercules' battle with the giant Antaeus, who was refreshed by his mother Gaia each time the hero knocked him down. Given the effort at rhetorical buildup, the punchline becomes almost comical, taking us from the most systematic of reflections to something far more inscrutable. Remarkably, Marx has nothing to say about the slogan with which he punctuates this virtuoso sentence. Having presented us with a Latin citation and its German "translation," he simply begins a new paragraph and starts making some relatively mundane observations about the events of 1848.

When self-critical proletarian poetics effects real change, it speaks not in German but in Latin.[57] In Schlegel, we encountered a two-sentence fragment in which the second member of the pair commented on the impossibility of inverting the first. With our various versions of "X is dead! Long live X!" we have seen examples of asymmetrical inversions that call into question the meaning of their terms and the relationships between them, particularly with regards to the link between life and death. Here, however, we have a single sentence presented in two different languages, as if to suggest that the best slogans occur in a tongue we may not understand. Far from direct and immediate in substance and consequence, the revolutionary battle cry is an exhortation that must, like the Bible, be translated.

In fact, the relationship between Marx's Latin and his German is more confusing than any of this would suggest. The citation comes from Erasmus's Latin translation of one of Aesop's fables, written in Greek, that tells the story of a braggart who claimed to have excelled in the long jump at Rhodes and was challenged to "put up or shut up," that is, to demonstrate his abilities on

56. Marx, "The Eighteenth Brumaire of Louis Bonaparte," 106–7.

57. This same Latin quotation appears at the end of chapter 5 of the first volume of *Capital*, where it is also cited without comment, as if its significance were self-evident.

the spot.[58] The formulation as Erasmus writes it is: "Hic Rhodus, hic saltus" ("Here [is your] Rhodes, here [is your] jump").[59] Marx's version of the verb is different. He ends the line with "salta," the singular imperative of the verb *saltare*, which can mean "to dance" or "to jump." A Latin student would translate Marx's line as: "Here is Rhodes, jump/dance here!"

In offering "the rose" (*die Rose*) for "Rhodus," Marx indicates that he is citing—or rather, nearly citing—Hegel's near-citation of Erasmus in the Preface to the *Philosophy of Right*. In contrast to Marx, who quotes the line in Latin and then in German, Hegel presents the original Greek along with a Latin version, but no German one. A few sentences later, it becomes clear that Hegel is not completely satisfied with either form of the statement when he observes: "With a little alteration, the saying just quoted would read: '*Here* is the rose, *here* dance.'"[60] Unlike Marx, Hegel gives some indication as to why he offers the citation in the first place, declaring that the task of philosophy is "to comprehend *what is*," and adding: "It is just as foolish to imagine that any philosophy can transcend its contemporary world as that an individual can overleap his own time or leap over Rhodes."[61] The remark about leaping over an entire island has led some scholars to suggest that Hegel may not have been familiar with the fable from which he took the line, or at least he did not fully understand it.

As it turns out, the Greek that Hegel presents as the "original" quotation is actually a hybrid of the two existing Greek versions of Aesop's fable, the one translated by Erasmus together with a second in which the relevant line reads: "Look—Rhodes, and leap off from (it)!" In creating his own Greek version of Aesop and then "complementing" it with Erasmus's Latin translation of one of the two standard versions, Hegel juxtaposes two lines from two foreign languages as if the one were a translation of the other, when in fact it is not. By the time Hegel arrives at his rewriting of the Latin in German as "Here is the rose, here dance," it is virtually impossible to determine what motivates his individual "emendations." He may be relying on etymology, that is, he may think, as some scholars of the period did, that the name Rhodes came from the Greek word for rose, *rhodon*, or he may simply be fashioning a pun based

58. Aesop, *Aesop's Fables*, trans. Laura Gibbs (Oxford: Oxford University Press, 2002), 106.

59. Desiderius Erasmus, *Adages: IIvii1 to IIIiii100, Collected Works of Erasmus*, vol. 34, trans. R. A. B. Mynors (Toronto: University of Toronto Press, 1992), 455.

60. G. W. F. Hegel, *Elements of the Philosophy of Right*, ed. Allen W. Wood (New York: Cambridge University Press, 1991), 22.

61. Hegel, *Philosophy of Right*, 21–22.

on the first syllable of Rhodus.[62] Hegel's proposed shift from *saltus* (the noun "jump") to *salta* (the imperative "Dance!") raises similar questions.[63] Suffice it to say that no two accounts of this passage in the *Philosophy of Right* or of Marx's quasi-citation of it agree on what is wordplay, what is well-founded scholarly reflection, and what is outright mistake.[64]

What occurs in *The Eighteenth Brumaire* when Marx reads Hegel by countering Hegel's slogan about philosophy's inability to transcend its time and place with a slogan of his own, which is of course also Hegel's? Having called on the revolutionaries of the nineteenth century to go beyond the traditional play of living and dead languages, Marx punctuates his account of the linguistic mobilization of the proletariat by coming close to quoting Hegel's near-quotation, or misquotation, an exercise in misprision that spans three languages, living and dead. Although Hegel and Marx both claim to craft a discourse of the here and now, their use of such citations confounds the relationship between the putative proximity and contemporaneity of German and the then and there of the Greek and Latin. If Hegel "quotes" Aesop, or some fabular hybrid of Aesop, in order to emphasize the importance of philosophy not attempting to exceed its own time, Marx's mobilization of Aesop, Erasmus, and Hegel reveals Hegel's citational practice to be a challenge to the possibility of ever knowing if the language one is speaking is one of the past, present, or future.

Hic Rhodus, hic salta! is the battle cry of proletarian revolutionaries, the moment at which, contra Hegel, they exceed their own time and place. In trumpeting it, the speaker is at least as daring as Aesop's athlete, springing from one language to another without necessarily being able to return to the old one or land safely in the new one, much less coordinate the old with the new. Indeed, having jumped, we can no longer be sure that what we were jumping from was in fact our own language. In this respect, *Hic Rhodus, hic salta!* is what Marx

62. For a review of nineteenth-century speculations about the etymology of this place name, see F. G. Tomlins, *A Universal History of the Nations of Antiquity* (Halifax: W. Milner, 1844), 625.

63. See Hegel, *Philosophy of Right*, 391 n.26. Some of Hegel's immediate predecessors also quoted the Erasmus line as "hic Rhodus, hic salta," possibly because they wanted a more directive version of the formulation, possibly because they were working with the other version of Aesop's text. In such cases, it is not always clear whether *salta* was intended to be read as "Jump!" or "Dance!"

64. Many scholars have weighed in on these passages and inveighed against the "errors" of others' explanations of the interlinguistic complexities. For help with these discussions, I am grateful for the assistance of my colleagues Walter G. Englert and Nigel Nicholson.

in various texts terms a *salto mortale*.[65] Such a linguistic act becomes truly revolutionary by freeing itself of any claim to be "of" a particular language, old or new. It is not simply that such a slogan pits its message against the messages of other slogans; it pits itself against its own capacity to be paradigmatic. Grammatically or stylistically, any sentence is in principle a model for other sentences, but Marx envisions a revolutionary battle cry as an irreducibly partisan intervention that does not serve as a prototype for any other utterance, even another slogan. Ruthlessly a-systemic, this sentence (or *Satz*, recalling Kraus's account of the aphorism) is always a leap (*Satz*), a speculative gesture that risks ignominy or oblivion without any guarantee of being rewarded for its daringness.

Marx characterizes the articulation of pure practical speech as something that takes place when the self-reflective agency of the proletarian revolution reaches the point at which turning in on itself any further becomes impossible, a point beyond the language of inversions and reversals that is Hegel's discourse of speculative sentences. The slogan that emerges at this juncture cannot, as Schlegel's fragment puts it, be turned around. Contrary to what Hegel would have us believe, it is not a product of preexisting claims and will not produce inferences that contravene or contrapose it, despite the fact that its appearance, like the lightning bolt of a witticism, makes all the difference in the world.[66] As the intrusion of a foreign language into a familiar tongue, a slogan of the kind for which Marx calls flirts with inscrutability, and to the extent that it appears to be an enigmatic outburst that is simply incomprehensible,

65. In an early text on Hegel's *Philosophy of Right*, Marx observes that Germany lags behind other European nations in political emancipation because in Germany, theory runs ahead of material exigency. Accordingly, he suggests that Germany must, through a *salto mortale*, surmount the fact that it does not yet experience the same barriers as other European nations, that is, Germany must leap over the absence of what needs to be there to be leaped over. See Karl Marx, "Contribution to the Critique of Hegel's *Philosophy of Law*," *Marx/Engels Collected Works*, vol. 3, 183. Years later, this *salto mortale* will reappear in *A Contribution to the Critique of Political Economy* and *Capital* to describe the "leap" of value from the body of the commodity to gold, the first step of C–M–C circulation.

66. Marx's commitment to the curious dance motif from Hegel's *Philosophy of Right* hints that there may be an odd kind of celebration at this point of no re-turn, a fact that will not be lost on Nietzsche or Bataille, among others. As urgent as the stakes may be, the language of the revolution is potentially open to a kind of revelry, if not to genuinely Dionysian excess. In any case, we can be forgiven for being a little suspicious about whether a complex joke is afoot and for being more than a little unsure who is its butt. On dancing in Marx, see David Riff, "Was Marx a Dancer?," *e-flux journal* 67 (November 2015), http://www.e-flux.com/journal/67/607156/was-marx-a-dancer/.

whether by the discourse that produced it or by the discourse that receives it, it is always at risk of being ignored or dismissed.

While Marx's inheritors accord slogans a central role in their thinking, they may not always appreciate the nuances of his theory of the revolutionary battle cry.[67] Lenin offers an intriguing contribution to the discussion in the form of a 1905 essay in which he proposes that what a slogan says is less important than that its message be unequivocal. While every individual political situation warrants a rigorous analysis guided by relevant theoretical and historical considerations, it is imperative that once our assessment of the situation is complete, "the concrete questions of our political conduct [have] absolutely clear answers—*which do not permit of a double interpretation*."[68] The product of our deliberations, the slogan, must be devoid of any nuance or innuendo that might complicate its message. In the end, Lenin argues, we should be able to boil our battle cry down to a simple "yes" or "no." A slogan is charged with saying everything, yet it must do so in such a minimal fashion that it says next

67. In "The Mass Strike," an essay written in the wake of the failed 1905 Russian revolution, Rosa Luxemburg treats slogans as the expressions of an ethos that helps to maximize a movement's potential. In revolutionary action, she writes, the most important task of the group that assumes the provisional leadership role is "to give the slogan [*Parole*]—the direction—to the struggle; to establish the *tactics* of the political struggle such that in every phase and at every moment the entire sum of the available power of the proletariat . . . will find expression in the fighting posture of the party." Rosa Luxemburg, *The Essential Rosa Luxemburg: Reform or Revolution & The Mass Strike*, ed. Helen Scott (Chicago: Haymarket Books, 2008), 149 (translation modified). Although Luxemburg is generally thought to emphasize the spontaneity of mass phenomena as opposed to a top-down organization of revolutionary praxis, here she seems to say that slogans create organization precisely because they are the kernel—even the form—of an intrinsically spontaneous dynamic.

In *History and Class Consciousness*, György Lukács treats this passage as a lynchpin of Luxemburg's thought, glossing it as follows: "Knowledge becomes action, theory becomes slogan [*Parole*], the masses act in accordance with the slogans and join the ranks of the organized vanguard more consciously, more steadfastly, and in greater numbers." György Lukács, *History and Class Consciousness: Studies in Marxist Dialectics*, trans. Rodney Livingstone (Cambridge, MA: MIT Press, 1972), 42 (translation modified). So taken is Lukács with Luxemburg's account of slogans that he neither acknowledges the complexity of the relationships he is describing between knowledge and theory or action and slogans nor elucidates the consequences of his remarks. His main point seems to be that slogans fall on both sides of the theoretical/practical divide, perhaps even rendering the distinction obsolete, and in any case, they are essential to the formation of radical consciousness.

68. V. I. Lenin, "Argue about Tactics, but Give Clear Slogans!" *Collected Works*, vol. 9 (Moscow: Progress Publishers, 1977), 262.

to nothing. Like a logician attempting to develop a formal system whose propositions will never be vague or ambiguous, Lenin calls for a language beyond subject-predicate constructions in which a one-syllable adverbial intervention becomes a decisive signifying act precisely because it stands alone, outside any larger syntactic or semantic dynamic.

Lenin never stopped revising his theory of slogans. In an essay from late 1917, "On Slogans," he acknowledges that political battle cries function more smoothly in theory than in practice. He opens by echoing his 1905 remarks about the rational nature of sloganeering, maintaining that the correct and meaningful slogan must be "deduced from the totality of specific features of a definite political situation."[69] In fact, a particular moment's status as decisive for the revolutionary struggle can only be identified thanks to the way in which slogans give shape to the temporality of praxis. The problem, Lenin observes, is that "too often it has happened that when history has taken a sharp turn, even progressive parties have for some time been unable to adapt themselves to the new situation and have repeated slogans which had formerly been correct but had now lost all meaning—lost it as 'suddenly' as the sharp turn in history was 'sudden.'"[70] If slogans shape the development of the struggle, they have a short half-life, and we have to work constantly to fashion new "class and party categories" if we are to have any hope of seeing our exhortative utterances remain current.[71] While this observation is in no way intended to disparage the role slogans play in revolutionary praxis, it underscores the need to develop new ones in order to keep pace with the volatility of circumstances.

Lenin's main example is the eminently familiar "All Power to the Soviets!" While it may be difficult to think of a more successful twentieth-century political catchphrase, Lenin points out that it did not do what it was designed to do, that is, it did not actively facilitate, or even passively witness, the transfer of power to the Soviets. To the contrary, he says, history moved too quickly. From February 27 to July 4, 1917, "All Power to the Soviets!" made sense as a rallying cry because for this exact period of time it was conceivable that power might be seized peacefully. During these months, the slogan was an essential feature of transpiring events. In contrast, Lenin argues, chanting "All Power to the Soviets!" after July 4 was "quixotic or mocking," because the Soviets

69. V. I. Lenin, "On Slogans," *Revolution at the Gates: Selected Writings of Lenin from 1917*, ed. Slavoj Žižek (London: Verso, 2002), 62.

70. Lenin, "On Slogans," 62.

71. Lenin, "On Slogans," 68.

had come to be dominated by Menshevik and Socialist-Revolutionary forces.[72] Now it was the proletariat, including the peasantry, who had to lead the revolution, and they had to do so by turning their backs on the counterrevolutionary elements within the Soviets. "All Power to the Soviets!" was not just a motto whose sell-by date had passed, but an exhortation that would have been actively harmful had it continued to be used. For this reason, Lenin maintains, it was best forgotten.

Lenin appears confident that when the changes that have taken place since July 4, 1917, are recognized, a new slogan calling for the overthrow of counterrevolutionary elements will emerge and play an important role in what unfolds. Nonetheless, his point is that slogans, whatever their creative or agentive powers, are always on the brink of expiration. Like the lightning flash of Schlegel's witticisms, slogans are sentences that do their work and then take their leave. They are simultaneously the most memorable and the most forgettable examples of language. "All Power to the Soviets!" clearly failed to meet this near-impossible standard. Its function as a token of identity proved independent of its success or failure as a political tactic at a specific period in time, and it has survived to this day, a living ghost of the Russian Revolution, cited by many who have no idea what the Soviets were or why relying or not relying on them at a particular moment would have been controversial.

Almost as if to excuse this curious afterlife, the entry on "All Power to the Soviets!" in the third edition of the *Great Soviet Encyclopedia* (1969–78) explains that the slogan initially had a specific meaning, just as Lenin describes, but was then "suspended" at the Sixth Congress of the Russian Social Democratic Labor Party at the beginning of August 1917, since it had outlived the situation.[73] The *Encyclopedia* goes on to say that the slogan was "reissued" with a new meaning several months later. With the bolshevization of the Soviets complete, "All Power to the Soviets!" became a call to use these organs to establish a dictatorship of the proletariat, a goal that was triumphantly realized in the October Revolution. In effect, the Brezhnev-era *Encyclopedia* "supplements" Lenin's account of the slogan by telling a different story in which "All Power to the Soviets!" was not a one-time verbal phenomenon whose vibrancy was tied to a specific dynamic of political change, but an empty form that could be deployed for a while and then put in mothballs until the appropriate circumstances arose for it to be revived.

72. Lenin, "On Slogans," 64.

73. "All Power to the Soviets," *Great Soviet Encyclopedia*, 3rd edition, ed. A. M. Prokhorov, vol. 1 (New York: Macmillan, 1973), 24–25.

At this point, we are far from Marx's *salto mortale*, a deadly leap that we cannot risk taking more than once. While Lenin maintains that we can deduce the proper slogan for each individual situation from each individual situation, here two different situations appear to require the "same" slogan, even though it will not be the same in both cases at all. If such an utterance is designed to make history, it must itself paradoxically have no history. Lenin insists that we can distinguish between genuine slogans that encapsulate "the totality of specific features of a definite political situation" and idle talk or "phrasemongering," for example, casual boasting about one's revolutionary ambitions.[74] On the basis of his key example, however, we may wonder how stable an opposition this can be, since the competing accounts of "All Power to the Soviets!" suggest it is both genuine and phrasemongering.

In *The Eighteenth Brumaire*, Marx stresses the need for the content to go beyond the catchphrase. Lenin struggles with the fact that a catchphrase has an uncanny way of outliving its usefulness, as if the rhetorical form had more stamina that the substance of the utterance, however revolutionary the message. Is this simply to say that the catchphrase *is* the content? György Lukács seems to have recognized this as a problem inherent in Lenin's theory. In *History and Class Consciousness*, he acknowledges the need to ignore the mottoes of the party if they fail to accord with the empirical realities of the moment, but he insists that "when [slogans] are seen from a true revolutionary point of view," the "final goal" of proletarian struggle is "present dialectically in every slogan from the day."[75] With some effort, the clever dialectician will discern the kernel of truth in even the most outdated slogan. With this claim, Lukács comes close to emptying the slogan of its autonomy as a transformative verbal act that remakes political language in the course of reshaping the political landscape. In contrast to Marx's *salto mortale*, in which there is always the possibility that the message will be unreadable, Lukács envisions a discourse of hyperlegible sentences that all say exactly the same thing.

Lukács describes political rallying cries that may appear to be out of step with empirical circumstances but will confirm their essential meaningfulness when analyzed properly—their content should be durable. Lenin's slogans are designed for particular situations but tend to survive well past their expiration dates—their form is almost too durable. From the perspective of Marx's argument in *The Eighteenth Brumaire*, we might conclude that neither Lukács nor Lenin is willing to accept the possibility that the truly political discourse may

74. Lenin, "On Slogans," 66.

75. Lukács, *History and Class Consciousness*, 328.

be one we can never entirely control. As with *Hic Rhodus, hic salta*! the emergence of a transformative slogan marks the point at which we no longer know for sure what we are saying or whether anyone listening will be able to make it out. Our claim to a language of our own is exposed as chimerical even as our need to speak, and to speak with absolute authority, intensifies.

While Schlegel led us to consider whether there was an aphoristic potential in every sentence, the audacious impulse to claim that it can do everything on its own, Marx and his inheritors suggest that every sentence has the potential to become a slogan, an utterance seeking to foreground the power of language to effect social change. This insight has never been lost on the poets. Reflecting on the interplay of the Idealist and Romantic traditions as Marx had before him, Walter Benjamin characterizes slogans not as the battle cries of the mob but as the "language of artists."[76] One of the artists he had in mind was undoubtedly his friend Bertolt Brecht. Benjamin notes that Marx was "a teacher of satire" and that "it is with Marx that Brecht has gone to school."[77] Whatever the style of pedagogy, the subject was definitely the slogan. Brecht arguably never wrote a text without at least one prominent catchphrase, and many of his plays are expositions of mottoes introduced at the start.

This is certainly the case in the play *Man is Man* [*Mann ist Mann*], first performed in 1926, in which the guiding slogan is already offered in the work's title. Set in British colonial India, the drama focuses on three soldiers who need someone to impersonate the fourth member of their unit, who has gone missing due to drunken misadventure. Seizing on the first available substitute, they enlist the aid of a packer by the name of Galy Gay, and little by little, he is transformed from a mild-mannered civilian into a cavalier destroyer of cities. Gay learns the bearing and conduct of a soldier by imitating the relevant gestures, so that as the audience watches him acquire a military identity, they witness not only the metamorphosis of his character but the construction of Brechtian acting itself, with its uniquely self-conscious performance of the microscopic aspects of human behavior.

Depending on one's taste, Brecht's plays may seem overly formulaic, but in this text, the power of formulas and formalization is precisely what is at issue. Everything in this drama turns around what is proposed, posited, or hypothesized by its title: *Man is Man*. From the opening scene, these three words set

76. Walter Benjamin, *One-Way Street*, in *Selected Writings,* Vol. 1: *1913–1926*, ed. Marcus Bullock and Michael W. Jennings (Cambridge, MA: Harvard University Press, 1996), 460.

77. Walter Benjamin, *Understanding Brecht*, trans. Anna Bostock (New York: Verso, 2003), 1984.

in motion a series of assertions of identity and difference that at once drive and interrupt the action. Whether one thing can stand in for another is constantly up for debate, but in such a way that we are never sure if what we should be afraid of is something for which there is a ready substitute or something for which there is not.

The play's original title was *Man = Man*. Brecht gradually, perhaps begrudgingly, settled on *Man is Man*, although he occasionally regressed and reinstated the equals sign. In fact, long after he had allowed the verb "to be" into the title, he continued to highlight the play's arithmetic parameters. In the 1931 production he directed in Berlin, simple equations were projected on screens above the stage to characterize the action of each scene, so that when one of the four soldiers goes missing, we see $4 - 1 = 3$; when they enlist Galy Gay to stand in for their comrade, we see $3 + 1 = 4$; and in the fateful scene in which the protagonist first answers to his new name in the roll call, we see $1 = 1$.[78] The question of whether a sentence is implicitly an equation, or vice versa, haunts the play. Most immediately, it appears to be impossible to decide whether "man = man" is equal or equivalent to "man is man."[79] If the sentence can be reduced to a mathematical expression, then the putative content of "man" is perpetually at risk of becoming a minimal articulation of self-sameness, that is, MAN becomes a mere variable, just one more A, B, or C. This danger is directly thematized as the soldiers work to turn the protagonist Galy Gay into Jeraiah Jip, which would be tantamount to demonstrating that GG = JJ.

With so many different kinds of formalization at work, it is far from clear whether the title of the play is in any sense self-identical. The theme of the drama is that one man can become another, or as one might say in English—and this is how the title is sometimes translated—"A man's a man," that is, "one man is as good as another." Once we begin to introduce indefinite articles and determiners such as "one" or "another," we are no longer speaking about a strict statement of equivalence, not $1 = 1$ but $3 =$ some other number. Still, a number's a number, right? One of the inspirations for Brecht's title was a late eighteenth-century Robert Burns song, an expression of Scottish egalitarianism called "A Man's a Man for A' That." "For all that" compromises the balance of the equation even further insofar as "man is man" is no longer an expression of self-identity, but a statement about one of man's attributes, as in "man is

78. For details about the early performances of the play, see Brigid Doherty, "Test and Gestus in Brecht and Benjamin," *MLN* 115, no. 3 (April 2000): 453.

79. In line with Schlegel's reflections on propositions, we could also ask whether it is possible to turn these statements around.

good" or "man is mortal." In this vein, "man is man" serves at various points in the play as an acknowledgment that man is by nature lascivious, greedy, or violent, as in "men will be men." Part of the provocation of the title, then, is that even the simplest verbal assertion of equivalence, the perfect substitution of a word by itself, does not hold up, meaning that the putative self-identity of any term is in jeopardy.

From this perspective, we can begin to discern an irreducible element of negativity at work in the play. Galy Gay is introduced as "a man who cannot say no," but it turns out that the play does not share this problem.[80] The assertion "man is man" is constantly countered by invocations of idiomatic phrases that appear to offer overt contradictions, including "Einmal ist keinmal" (literally "once is never") and "Einer ist keiner" (literally "one is none" or "one person is no one").[81] At a crucial juncture, we are told that "the human being is nothing whatsoever," which is presented as a gesture against anthropocentric thinking, although in this context one might be suspicious of the "whatsoever," as if the very need to intensify the "nothing" already betrayed that it was at least a little more or less than nothing, i.e., that not even nothing is perfectly equal to itself.[82]

Once the integrity of "man is man" is challenged, other kinds of equivalences emerge to displace the central, putatively human identity posited by the play's title. The key to effecting the transition of the packer Galy Gay into the soldier Jeraiah Jip lies in convincing Galy to sell a patently artificial elephant. The elephant is fake, the transaction is fake, the buyer is fake, and the seller is certainly fake—but as we are reminded, "Elephant is elephant, especially when it's sold."[83] In this falsest of false transactions, a mere pantomime of commerce underwrites assertions of equivalence between anything and everything. Such a scene is precisely what Adorno had in mind when he defended Brecht's plays against the charge that they were too abstract—yes, Adorno allows, abstraction *is* a formal principle in Brecht, but this is because the foundational field of capitalist society is now exchange, which is a dynamic of abstraction in which difference is predicated on identity and not the other way around.[84]

80. Bertolt Brecht, *Gesammelte Werke* I, *Stücke 1918–1932* (Frankfurt am Main: Suhrkamp, 1967), 334. All translations from this text are my own.

81. Brecht, *Stücke*, 314, 360.

82. Brecht, *Stücke*, 340.

83. Brecht, *Stücke*, 343.

84. See Theodor W. Adorno, "Commitment," *Notes to Literature*, vol. 2, trans. Shierry Weber Nicholsen (New York: Columbia University Press, 1992), 82.

The iterability of the title is explicitly at issue in the play's interlude when we are told "Herr Bertolt Brecht maintains [*behauptet*]: Man is man. / And that is something that anyone can maintain."[85] Turning on itself, the play presents its foundational assertion of identity less as a proposition whose truth one can aver or deny than as a chip to be wagered at a casino table. If the skeptical view of slogans is that they are ideas that have been reduced to tokens deployed for instrumental purposes, here the drama appears to sloganize its own defining slogan. Schlegel argued that "the main point is that one knows something and that one says it." Taking this to the extreme, Brecht's play asserts that anyone can assert that "man is man," although doing so may jeopardize the speaker's ambitions to be a "man." With the slogans of sovereign power, we were dealing with beheadings, *Enthauptungen*—in particular with the fact that anyone's head can be chopped off, including a monarch's. Here we move from *Enthauptung* to *Behauptung*, an assertion that anyone can make—literally anyone can "be the head"—although the statement itself gains no authority from this fact. The implication is not that one becomes a human being by averring that "man is man." Indeed, the play scrupulously does not equate "man is man" with the arguably equivalent statement "a human being is a human being." Moreover, nobody in the drama can successfully assert that "man is man," that is, nobody can speak with, to, or about this slogan in such a way as to demonstrate its integrity, at least not for long, or not without nearly losing their head. In a play marked by injuries, from lost chunks of hair to self-castration, "man is man" lingers as a kind of primordial wound in the language. We can all assert that "man is man," but despite our best efforts, the slogan threatens to become generic, a variable statement, if you will, of no greater or lesser distinction than A = A or B = B.

The Marxist theory of political catchphrases suggests that the foundational verbal paradigm is not the subject-predicate schema of classical logic and grammar, but the slogan. Part battle cry and part motto, such an utterance foregrounds the interpellative powers of language as it seeks to create and sustain partisan identities and to effect change. With "man is man," Brecht takes a putatively straightforward grammatical construction and reveals that it has the power to reduce any sentence to an assertion of equivalences between empty variables. On the one hand, Brecht thereby invites us to approach each and

85. Brecht, *Stücke*, 336. One of Benjamin's most famous statements about Brecht's epic theater is that it tries to make gesture citable. See his "What is Epic Theater?," *Selected Writings*, Vol. 4: *1938–1940*, ed. Howard Eiland and Michael W. Jennings (Cambridge, MA: Harvard University Press, 2003), 305.

every clause with an eye to its potential, latent or manifest, to become a slogan. On the other hand, he reminds us that every slogan emerges as a kind of discursive injury, altering our usual understanding of how we do things with words without necessarily offering any hope that its impact on our customary verbal practices will easily be repaired, regardless of how many equals signs we muster. Having braved Marx's deadly leap, we are much the worse for wear.

The guiding formulation of Brecht's play may be read as a commentary on another slogan that pits itself against both the language of sovereignty ("The king is dead!") and the language of radicalism ("The revolution is dead!"). Today, Nietzsche's infamous "God is dead!" has become a rallying cry for a host of countercultural impulses. The versatility of the catchphrase is perhaps unsurprising given that it was already a slogan when it first appeared. In *The Gay Science*, it is the "madman" who declares that we have killed God, that he is dead, and that he remains dead.[86] In *Zarathustra*, we learn: "But when Zarathustra was alone he spoke thus to his heart: 'Could it be possible! This old saint in his woods has not yet heard the news that *God is dead*!'"[87] In both cases, the infamous utterance, one of the most consequential ontotheological assertions conceivable, manifests itself as a claim whose source is either markedly unreliable or permanently absent and whose truth or falsity has little bearing on its significance. Like a rumor that irrepressibly gathers steam, "God is dead" gains force with each repetition, becoming more powerful the further removed it is from the site of its original articulation, assuming there ever was one. In Marx's terms, Nietzsche's sentence is a political utterance because no entity—human or divine—can control it or claim it as its own. In Brecht's terms, it is a slogan because it inflicts an indelible wound on the language. In the wake of "God is dead," any act of predication is at risk of appearing comparatively insignificant, as if language's declaration of the demise of the divine were equally an announcement of its own status as irremediably fallen.

Benjamin may have had Brecht in mind when he declared slogans to be the "language of artists," and he may have been thinking of himself when he added that this is a language that criticism must also speak.[88] The writings of Adorno, himself a careful reader of Benjamin, Brecht, and Nietzsche, offer another example of a critical discourse that explores the power of slogans and their re-

86. Friedrich Nietzsche, *The Gay Science*, trans. Josefine Nauckhoff (New York: Cambridge University Press, 2008), 119–20.

87. Friedrich Nietzsche, *Thus Spoke Zarathustra*, trans. Adrian Del Caro (New York: Cambridge University Press, 2007), 5.

88. Walter Benjamin, *One-Way Street*, 460.

lationship to the aphoristic potential of all sentences.[89] Perhaps nowhere in Adorno's work are these issues more at the forefront than in *Minima Moralia*, which like many of Benjamin's writings is an experiment with shorter forms. Subtitled *Reflections on a Damaged Life*, it comprises 153 texts ranging from one to several pages in length. Much has been said about the book's polyvalent style and its resistance to traditional genre classification. Prose poetry or humorous anecdote at one moment, it can become intense personal rumination or didactic ethical pronouncement the next.

No interpretation of *Minima Moralia* can get far without asking what these 153 "reflections" are. In the dedication, which ostensibly serves as an account of the book's methodology, Adorno terms them "aphorisms." The stylistic inspiration is Nietzsche, who used the same term for his collections of paragraph-length texts and boasted of his ambition "to say in ten sentences what other people say in a book."[90] Adorno is explicit that he is trying to call

89. It would be intriguing to explore the work of Ludwig Wittgenstein as a philosophy elaborated through slogans. In this regard, one thinks immediately of the numbered sections of the *Tractatus* and its famous opening line, "The world is all that is the case." Ludwig Wittgenstein, *Tractatus Logico-Philosophicus*, trans. D. F. Pears and B. F. McGuinness (New York: Routledge, 2001), 5. The *Philosophical Investigations*, however, is no less rife with adages, and Wittgenstein's arguments often proceed by reflecting on the ways in which their most gnomic or lapidary formulations prove to be difficult to integrate into the larger trajectory of the discussion.

90. Friedrich Nietzsche, *The Anti-Christ, Ecce Homo, Twilight of the Idols and Other Writings*, trans. Judith Norman (New York: Cambridge University Press, 2005), 223. Gerhard Richter has argued that Benjamin, Adorno, Ernst Bloch, and Siegfried Kracauer all produced versions of "thought-images" (*Denkbilder*), an example of which would be the reflections of *Minima Moralia*. Richter writes: "This *Denkbild*, as this group of friends conceived of it, is a brief aphoristic prose text typically ranging in length between a few sentences and a couple of pages that both illuminates and explodes the conventional distinctions among literature, philosophy, journalistic intervention, and cultural critique." Gerhard Richter, *Thought-Images: Frankfurt School Writers' Reflections from Damaged Life* (Stanford, CA: Stanford University Press, 2007), 7. Adorno's description of Benjamin's *Denkbilder* is quite similar to his account of the aphorisms that make up *Minima Moralia*. He argues that in Benjamin's short pieces, what would normally be regarded as merely subjective or contingent phenomena prove to be what is most consequential, if not outright laying claim to objective status. At the same time, one has to question to what degree Adorno's reflections "arrest thought in an image composed of words," not least given his sustained polemic with Benjamin about the role of mediation when it comes to capturing the particularities of sociocultural experience (Richter, *Thought-Images*, 13). The *Denkbild* as Richter describes it may not even do justice to all of the sections of *One-Way Street*, a number of which are numbered lists of theses. Seeking to cast doubt on the generalizability of the *Denkbild* as a model for the writings of this intellectual cohort, Andreas Huyssen stresses that Benjamin himself called the sections of *One-Way Street* "aphorisms" and that these pieces

attention to Hegel's neglect of the partial and the incomplete by producing short texts that accord significance to singular phenomena and fleeting experiences rather than shoring up the authority of universals. Based on what Hegel says, Adorno proposes, his philosophy allows for no privileging of the general over the particular and opposes any simple acceptance of the primacy of the whole; but when it comes to what Hegel does, his thought betrays exactly these prejudices. If there is going to be a true tarrying with the negative, someone else will have to do it—hence the aphorism. "Dialectical theory," Adorno writes, "abhorring anything isolated, cannot admit aphorisms as such. In the most lenient instance they might, to use a term from the *Preface* to the *Phenomenology of Spirit*, be tolerated as 'conversation.'"[91]

The relationships between the individual sentences in Adorno's reflections vary widely. Sometimes statements seem to follow one another as smoothly as in the soundest of logical proofs. At other moments, the connections between them seem off, if not outright illusory, and the various propositions begin to drift apart, threatening to devolve into lists of statements. As if to show us—or warn us—what the entire book might have looked like, a few sections offer lists of one-sentence witticisms of enviable cleverness: "Every work of art is an uncommitted crime"; "It is Proust's courtesy to spare the reader the embarrassment of believing himself cleverer than the author."[92] In other places, Adorno considers what happens when such an adage becomes part of a larger prose sequence. "There is no right life in the wrong one," one of the book's most oft-cited maxims, is the last sentence of an "aphorism" several pages in length that contains a number of other sentences that could also stand alone as isolated nuggets of wisdom.[93] It is no simple matter to decide whether or not the final line is a sound conclusion growing out of what preceded it, or if one could never have anticipated it before one read it, at which point one simply has to accept its authority as the gist of the passage by a leap of faith. In sum, some of Adorno's "recollections" read like mini-essays, with few if any sentences that appear worthy of being pondered in isolation; others are expository texts punctuated by sayings or maxims that may or may not be easily coordinated

differ greatly from the ones he published in a collection under the title *Denkbilder*. Andreas Huyssen, *Miniature Metropolis* (Cambridge, MA: Harvard University Press, 2015), 119.

91. Theodor W. Adorno, *Minima Moralia: Reflections on a Damaged Life*, trans. E. F. N. Jephcott (New York: Verso, 2005), 8 (translation modified).

92. Adorno, *Minima Moralia*, 111, 49.

93. Adorno, *Minima Moralia,* 39 (translation modified).

with the sentences around them; and still others are strings of individual aphorisms, set apart from one another on the page.

These differences notwithstanding, each section of *Minima Moralia* begins not with a statement or a question, but with a brief collection of italicized words—a phrase or proto-clause—followed by a period and a dash.[94] Some of these opening collections of words are riffs on well-known titles of works of literature or philosophy ("*The Health unto Death*"; "*This side of the pleasure principle*"; "*Unmeasure for unmeasure*"), while others invoke idiomatic sayings ("*Fish in water*"; "*Baby with the bathwater*") or offer rejoinders to sayings that have appeared in previous aphorisms ("*Tough baby*").[95] Some are specimens gathered from the quotidian verbal landscape ("*English spoken*"; "*No exchanges*") or distortions thereof ("*Do not knock*"), while others have a maxim-like quality with comic undertones ("*Savages are not better human beings*"; "*Ego is id*").[96] In referencing a range of cultural, historical, and linguistic facts of varying degrees of obscurity, these introductory blurbs function like mini-tests, even shibboleths, allowing the reader to confirm her status as "in-the-know" if she gets the joke.

These italicized "bits" of text are *salti mortali*, evidence of the sloganistic potential of all language. Grouped together, they have the appearance of verbal detritus. They are fragments of what could or might once have been fully-fledged formulations—ideas for arguments, articles, even whole books. We might think of them as efforts to write the shortest aphorism possible. Alternatively, we might imagine cutting *Minima Moralia* into pieces and pasting some of the blurbs together to make a Futurist or Dada poem.

The opening of each section of *Minima Moralia* is also, however, a warning. Taken together, the period and dash (".—") that separate the italicized text from the rest of the reflection become curiously ambiguous. The dash threatens to undo the finality of the period, but it may also extend the punctuation mark's authority, widening the gap between the "introduction" and the aphorism proper. Alternatively, the dash may invert the presumed hierarchy between the introductory snippets and what follows, as if the "main" part of each text were simply a gloss on or footnote to the shorter section that preceded it.

94. Gerhard Richter suggests that in *Minima Moralia* Adorno is continuing Benjamin's efforts to recreate the baroque emblem and that "the short, epigrammatic titles that head the *Denkbilder* . . . of Adorno's *Minima Moralia* . . . reenact this function of the baroque emblem's *inscription*" (*Thought-Images*, 11).

95. Adorno, *Minima Moralia*, 58, 60, 103, 23, 43, 45.

96. Adorno, *Minima Moralia,* 47, 42 (translation modified), 40, 52 (translation modified), 63.

As in Hegel, Adorno's dashes threaten to become unbridgeable divides that the would-be parser of his text's sentences cannot hope to traverse unless she is willing to risk a *salto mortale*. The key point is that for Adorno such punctuated "gaps" in the text are only the most obvious examples of disjunctions that can lurk anywhere and everywhere. This is explained in the final aphorism of the book's opening section, "*Gaps.—*", in which Adorno inveighs against the notion that a writer must "show explicitly all the steps that have led him to his conclusion, so enabling every reader to follow the process through and, where possible—in the academic industry—to duplicate it."[97] In one fell swoop, the basic contract of intelligibility and communicability that usually obtains between author and reader is deemed not simply inessential, but misguided. "Texts which anxiously undertake to record every step without omission," Adorno declares, "inevitably succumb to banality, and to a monotony related not only to the tension induced in the reader, but to their own substance."[98] We must not aspire to pen "mere statements [*einfache Aussagen*]," self-effacing language that docilely evaporates in the course of giving the reader access to a set of facts.[99] Instead, our sentences must retain an element of independence from their subject matter; they must over- or under-shoot their putative referents; they must betray an element of the virtual that will never be "fulfilled," as Adorno puts it, by any instance of factuality or actuality.[100] What we need to write, in other words, are sentences that are slogans before they are propositions, sentences that become verbal provocations before they are instances of predication. Unlike a mere statement, a slogan never operates under the illusion that it can be understood by reconstructing the steps that led to its articulation; and it certainly never imagines that its success will be a factor of the ease with which it can be digested by others.

Lukács proposes that one should be able to find the truth of the proletarian struggle in any slogan, no matter how out of step with circumstances it appears to be. In *Minima Moralia*, Adorno broadens this argument, but not in order to prove that each and every element of culture reveals the all-pervasive evils of the capitalist system. His suggestion is rather that insofar as every word, phrase, or clause is informed by its potential, latent or manifest, to become a catchphrase or a buzzword, we must approach even the most staid proposition as a "dead" slogan and realize that a sentence cannot be fully understood

97. Adorno, *Minima Moralia,* 80.
98. Adorno, *Minima Moralia,* 80.
99. Adorno, *Minima Moralia,* 127.
100. Adorno, *Minima Moralia,* 127.

until we have discerned its primal battle cry, its core conviction about its own capacity to change the world. In this respect, every sentence is partisan because it has an inherent tendency—call it aphoristic or sloganistic—to assert its independence from any and every other linguistic formation. At the same time, every rallying cry is its own worst enemy, inevitably prompting the question of whether it offers a reduced or debased version of an idea or argument. The more powerful the slogan, the more doubts it will raise about its mode of expression, the more scrutiny it will bring to bear on itself, and the harder it will become to distinguish from the Hegelian speculative sentence to which it should be diametrically opposed. Like Kraus's *Satz*, a formulation driven by the ambition to overstep its own coordination of form and content, a slogan can have the last word about everything except itself and its kind. The more forcefully any given slogan tells us what is to be done, the more it guarantees that we will never be done with it.

CHAPTER 2

The Poetic Line

Did you ever read one of her Poems backward, because the plunge from the front overturned you? I sometimes (often have, many times) have - a Something overtakes the Mind -

EMILY DICKINSON, fragment

The requirements of the rules of punctuation and those of the subjective need for logic and expression are not compatible.

T. W. ADORNO, "Punctuation Marks"

Even a brief foray into the literary universe will turn up innumerable variations on the sentence. Ornate or austere, improbably long or arrestingly brief, experimental verbal formations can be as troubling when they follow the rules as when they flaunt convention. In some cases, the innovations are essentially stylistic—instances of compositional creativity that do not fundamentally alter the paradigm. In others, more radical transformations force us to reevaluate our ideas about what sentences are, how they shape our experience of language, and what they can and cannot do.

Poetry tests the authority of the sentence in unique ways. By foregrounding rhythms and other cyclical or repetitive patterns that are less obvious in—although by no means absent from—prose, it highlights organizational parameters that coexist alongside or may even be at odds with syntactic ones. In this chapter, we will explore challenges to the sentence form that emerge in the work of two of the most distinctive voices in the nineteenth-century American literary canon, Walt Whitman and Emily Dickinson. Situated on the cusp of modernism, both continue the transformations of aesthetics that began in Romanticism even as they anticipate the avant-garde movements that will emerge at the turn of the twentieth century. While the maximalist syntax of Whitman's sprawling sentences would never be mistaken for Dickinson's short ballad stanzas, both find possibilities in verse for unsettling the hierarchies inherent to traditional grammatical structures, if not the hegemony of the subject-predicate construct itself. Freeing phrases from the clauses to which they are ordinarily thought to be subordinate, pitting diction against syntax, and testing the distinction between poetry and prose, their poems offer a glimpse of what it would mean for us to read a literary text without the expectation that it is exclusively—or even principally—governed by the sentence form.

Traditionally, poetry's most obvious affront to the authority of the sentence is versification, which separates groups of words, phrases, or clauses from one another by line breaks whose frequency and placement is dictated not by grammatical rules or extratextual factors (e.g., how many words fit across the piece of paper, screen, or clay tablet), but by considerations internal to the poem. A line may end after a certain number of iambs or because the typographic layout of the text has been designed to create the shape of a violin. Lineation is one of the easiest features of a poem to recognize, but it is hard to specify precisely what role it plays in shaping the meaning of a text, whether in individual cases or in general terms. As the poet and critic James Longenbach writes, "While line is central to our experience of poetry, it is notoriously difficult to talk about—much more difficult than meter, rhyme, or syntax, even though our experience of all of these poetic elements is bound up with our experience of line."[1]

As objective a feature of a poem as the line break may be, observations about how it works tend to be extremely subjective. The end of a line of verse is often treated as a kind of pause. The momentary arrest, however fleeting, becomes part of the rhythm of the phrases or clauses and is often marked by punctuation. Of course, if the end of a line of verse is a break in its own right, then closing it with a comma or dash is arguably redundant. The punctuation mark papers over the line break, recoding it as a phenomenon that could take place in any prose sentence and thus bringing the verse structure back into

1. James Longenbach, *The Art of the Poetic Line* (Minneapolis: Graywolf Press, 2007), xi. The poet Denise Levertov characterizes lineation as a form of punctuation: "The line-break is a form of punctuation additional to the punctuation that forms part of the logic of completed thoughts. Line-breaks together with intelligent use of indentation and other devices of scoring represent a peculiarly poetic, alogical, parallel (not competitive) punctuation." Denise Levertov, "On the Function of the Line," *New and Selected Essays* (New York: New Directions, 1992), 79. Levertov's emphasis on the "alogical" quality of the line break would appear to overtly contradict her notion that this second punctuation is "parallel" but "not competitive" with the standard one. Either standard punctuation does help clarify relationships between elements of sentences that respect logical parameters and hence does conflict with her second punctuation, or else standard punctuation is also "alogical," in which case there are good reasons to suppose that it might "compete" with lineation.

the standard grammatical fold. In this regard, it has been argued that the term "line break" is misleading, particularly if "break" is taken to imply something unanticipated, since it overstates the degree to which the conclusion of one line and the beginning of the next are imperfectly connected or coordinated.[2] In regular meter or prosody, the end of a line is eminently predictable thanks to patterns of stress and intonation. In irregular verse, there can be abrupt pauses, but they are just as likely to appear internal to lines as at their close.

In lieu of the term "break," one can speak of one line "turning" into the next; in the traditional plane geometry of poetics, it is precisely the "turns" of poetry that are said to distinguish it from *prosa oratio*, "straightforward or direct speech."[3] Virgil famously played on the sense of *versus* as a "furrow" to characterize units of verse text as narrow trenches plowed in a field. This figure arguably raises as many questions as it answers, since it ambiguously presents poetic lines as similar, precisely bounded iterations of one another; as irreducibly linked elements; or as independent units that exist in parallel and yet never actually meet, their only point of contact being the grammatical structures that straddle them. Sometimes the "turns" of verse are treated as if they were figures for the inherently self-reflexive nature of poetic language, the way in which poetry takes its own mode of expression into account, but the implications this holds for the understanding of the relationship between the verse form and a text's content are rarely spelled out.

In formal poems, versification may not appear to pose much of a challenge to the authority of sentence grammar. Lines end tidily at the close of phrases and clauses, frequently with standard punctuation, and as often as not the resulting rhythms work in tandem with the syntactic divisions. In free verse, the potential for a divergence or even outright clash between line and sentence is more pronounced. Once line lengths are no longer determined by a regularized syllable count, meter, or a translineal rhythm or rhyme scheme, the end of one line and the beginning of the next call out to be ascribed particular significance.[4] The lines stop where the poet wanted them to stop, and it is up to the

2. Longenbach prefers the term "line ending" (*The Art of the Poetic Line*, xii).

3. The word "verse" comes from the Latin *versus*, the past participle of *vertere*, which means "turned toward or against."

4. Joshua Clover argues that as free verse becomes more prevalent, "the line, excepting prose poetry (that official exception, verse's loyal opposition), persists as poetry's distinctive formal feature but abandons its historical task as a quantitative instrument measuring similar and repeating units. At this point, the longstanding drama between sentence and line, period and carriage return, point and counterpoint, ascends as a dominant formal fact of poetics." Joshua Clover, "Value and Temporality in Poetics," *Representations* 126, no. 1 (Spring 2014): 19–20.

reader to explain why. In this regard, free verse may be less formal poetry gone astray than prose with a series of extragrammatical interruptions that demand clarification.[5]

Lineation or typographic experimentation in general, however radical, has lost much of its capacity to shock. Our constant engagement with texts on computer screens, phones, and tablets has accustomed us to every imaginable configuration of words "on the page," and we will be familiar with the possibility that any given eccentricity of layout may be less evidence of creativity on the part of the author than the sign of a flawed e-mail client or an overly aggressive word-processing program. Marjorie Perloff has suggested that "the response to lineation must itself be historicized,"[6] maintaining that we cannot assume that an eighteenth- or nineteenth-century reader's reaction to a particular example of versification would be comparable to its reception by someone who has grown up with Twitter and Snapchat. As persuasive an argument as this may be, we should be cautious about assuming that there was a magical moment in the past when lineation was precisely codified and processed accordingly by readers. Its significance has always varied widely from author to author if not from text to text.

The most explicit clash between syntax and versification is enjambment, which sees a sentence continue from one line to the next with no clear pause or juncture to mark the transition or break.[7] This forces the reader to

5. Derek Attridge describes free verse as "the introduction into the continuous flow of prose language, which has breaks determined entirely by syntax and sense, of another kind of break, shown on the page by the start of a new line, and often indicated in a reading of the poem by a slight pause." Derek Attridge, *Poetic Rhythm: An Introduction* (Cambridge: Cambridge University Press, 1995), 5. For an attempt to systematically coordinate metrical analysis with other types of interpretation and ultimately to "read meter and grammar as intersecting codes," see Donald Wesling, *The Scissors of Meter: Grammetrics and Reading* (Ann Arbor: University of Michigan Press, 1996), 56. Wesling's project is guided by his sense that "modern theories of poetic meter . . . are unable to relate their formalizing gestures to any adequate exegesis" (vii).

6. Marjorie Perloff, "After Free Verse: The New Non-Linear Poetries," *Poetry On & Off the Page: Essays for Emergent Occasions* (Tuscaloosa: University of Alabama Press, 2004), 145. Perloff continues: "In a contemporary context of one-liners on the television screen and the computer monitor, as well as lineated ads, greeting-cards, and catalog entries, the reader/viewer has become quite accustomed to reading 'in lines.' Indeed, surfing the Internet is largely a scanning process in which the line is rapidly replacing the paragraph as the unit to be accessed" (145).

7. It has been suggested that the possibility of enjambment—a line ends but the sentence or clause does not pause or stop—is the only feature that truly distinguishes poetry from prose. As Giorgio Agamben writes: "Awareness of the importance of the opposition between metrical segmentation and semantic segmentation has led some scholars to state the thesis (which I

recognize that any conclusions she draws about the structure and meaning of given phrases or clauses must be regarded as provisional until she has actually arrived at a terminal punctuation mark. In revealing the putative linearity of the reading experience to be a complex dynamic of pro- and retrospection, enjambment underscores something that we know in theory but forget in practice, namely that processing a sentence is less a matter of proceeding sequentially through a string of words than of deciphering the hierarchical relationships that compose each part of a syntactic tree.[8] In this regard, to speak of enjambment as inherently destabilizing is a simplification. The very fact that we register a sentence as "running over" into the next line may be evidence that we are implicitly relying on syntax to hold things together, irrespective of how the words are laid out. Far from defying the structural authority of the sentence, enjambment reveals the sentence's elasticity, the fact that it can still function no matter how many lines or even stanzas it spans.

Versification creates units that may not have a clear relationship with the grammar of the sentence in which they appear, but the possibility that they are units of sense in some other regard cannot be discounted. The result is a degree of uncertainty about when—if ever—we can regard our scan of a particular line of verse as "final," yet no matter how often we remind ourselves of the need for caution, the impulse to coordinate the lineation and the sentence grammar, and typically to subordinate the one to the other, is all but irrepressible.

In creating false expectations about how a given phrase or clause will end, enjambment is often characterized as a form of playful trickery, although the dexterous author hardly needs line breaks to effect such feints. In this vein, Joshua Clover has argued that the tensions between lines and sentences that emerge in poetry bring into relief the dialectical relationship between prospection and retrospection that is in play in any text, verse or otherwise. Insofar as there will always be conflicts between the linear and hierarchical dimensions of a sentence, the assumptions one makes about its overarching structure and the role and relative priority of its various parts must necessarily remain

share) according to which the possibility of enjambment constitutes the only criterion for distinguishing poetry from prose." Giorgio Agamben, *The End of the Poem: Studies in Poetics*, trans. Daniel Heller-Roazen (Stanford, CA: Stanford University Press, 1999), 109.

8. One could argue that the English language is unusually accommodating of a belief in the linearity of sentences given the degree to which word order is standardized. Other languages, e.g., classical Latin, are much more flexible.

provisional until the arrival of the terminal punctuation mark—the *point de capiton* or "quilting point," to use the term Clover takes from Lacan.[9]

Clover emphasizes that as we read, we are constantly recalibrating our sense of the relations that obtain between the various grammatical elements. While his argument challenges the tendency to privilege linearity over hierarchy in our conception of sentences, it still betrays a bias in favor of sequence insofar as he maintains that it is the end of the sentence that brings things to a close by offering a stable perspective from which to take stock of the whole. The features of the grammar that prove decisive for the entire structure can be anywhere or everywhere in the sentence; instead of one quilting point, there may be many.

Persuasive or not, the idea that a sentence does not truly take shape until it ends forms the basis for one of the most venerable stylistic forms, the so-called "periodic" sentence. Thought to have achieved its apotheosis in the work of Cicero, this is a carefully balanced structure in which the syntax is organized such that it is not until the final clause, phrase, or word that the core grammatical and semantic logics reveal themselves. The Ciceronian sentence is often opposed to the nonperiodic, "cumulative," or "loose" sentence, which is "more relaxed and conversational in its effect—the component members are continuous, but so loosely joined that the sentence would have been syntactically complete if a period had been inserted at one or more places before the actual close."[10] Considered as a product of style rather than as a result of the way in which the reader processes it, the periodic sentence does not, as Clover

9. Clover writes: "The contingency of meaning itself, the continuous activity of reinterpretation, the simultaneous motion by which each step forward must throw the mind backward as well—as Lacan shows, this is a characteristic of grammar in general. Always there, humming in the background" ("Value and Temporality," 20). Lacan's summary pronouncement on this topic comes in his third seminar: "The sentence only exists as completed and its sense comes to it retroactively." Jacques Lacan, *The Seminar of Jacques Lacan (Book III): The Psychoses 1955–56*, trans. Russell Grigg (New York: W. W. Norton, 1993), 262–63. Explaining this idea, Clover writes: "While one is still within the regime of syntax, any outcome to the sentence remains possible, and thus the significance of the sentence's beginning is unknowable until one departs the regime of syntax for that of sentence by arriving at the period, the *point de capiton,* at which point one can now arrange the preceding signification into meaning. Syntax gives onto grammar only then. Reading is retcon" ("Value and Temporality," 19).

10. M. H. Abrams and Geoffrey Galt Harpham, *A Glossary of Literary Terms*, 10th ed. (Boston: Wadsworth Cengage Learning, 2009), 385. Seneca is usually invoked as the classical stylistic alternative to Cicero. See George Williamson, *The Senecan Amble: A Study in Prose Form from Bacon to Collier* (Chicago: University of Chicago Press, 1951).

would have it, facilitate dialectical thinking, but is considered exceptionally stable or even static—a sort of contrivance—whereas it is the loose or cumulative sentence, in which the final phrase or clause is not nearly as decisive, that is viewed as a representation of a dynamic mind at work. This basic question of what the spontaneity of thought looks like on the page plagues all discussions of sentence style, as one person's depiction of the volatility of consciousness is another person's stable emblem or trope.

Regardless of the assumptions we make about when and how the overarching structure of a sentence reveals itself, breaking one into lines denaturalizes the primacy of sequence and the forward trajectory of language. Whatever sense of motion seems to be organizing our experience of given phrases or clauses, versification forces us to recognize that this momentum is constitutively open to interruption, if not reversal, and in this space of provisionality and uncertainty, we are forced to articulate new ways of understanding what it means to read a sentence.[11] One author who makes a strong case for the urgency of this task is Walt Whitman. In terms of formal innovation, Whitman scores well by almost any measure. Credited as the "father" of free verse, he became famous for poems that lacked rhyme, standard meter, or regularized line lengths.[12] Notoriously ambitious, he loudly declared his intention to produce nothing less than an aesthetic discourse capable of sustaining American democracy, and his stylistic experiments and ideological positions were to have an enormous influence on avant-garde artistic movements in the Americas and Europe well into the twentieth century. So numerous are the provocations of his texts that it is difficult to pin down the force of individual gestures, and there is such broad scholarly agreement about his oeuvre's importance that one is apt to find oneself simply repeating familiar accolades.

11. Michal Ginsburg and Lorri Nandrea argue that prose, no less than poetry, has disruptive turns that break the forward trajectory of language: "True, poetry highlights 'turns' in the form of line breaks, as well as rhyme and meter, whose effect depends on what came before (turning back), in contrast to prose whose sense depends on what lies ahead (the end of a sentence; the next event in the plot of a novel). But various forms of 'linking forward' occur in verse (cf. enjambment), and pauses in which one rests and reflects back regularly occur in prose (paragraph and chapter breaks, as well as the final rupture of forward movement that constitutes the end)." Michal Ginsburg and Lorri Nandrea, "The Prose of the World," in *The Novel*, vol. II, ed. Franco Moretti (Princeton, NJ: Princeton University Press, 2006), 245.

12. Definitions of free verse are legion. Charles O. Hartman has characterized "the prosody of free verse" as "rhythmic organization by other than numerical modes." Charles O. Hartman, *Free Verse: An Essay on Prosody* (Princeton, NJ: Princeton University Press, 1980), 24–25.

The first edition of *Leaves of Grass* opens with a ten-page text, now referred to as the Preface, which is—nominally—in prose; it is followed by twelve untitled verse texts that span some 85 pages. In subsequent editions, the Preface disappears, although sections of it return as parts of the various poems, which acquire titles of their own and multiply until they number almost three hundred. Thanks to the survival of Whitman's voluminous notebooks, coupled with the multiple printed editions of his *magnum opus*, scholars have been able to reconstruct his writing process in detail. One of its distinctive features is the way in which he constantly rearranged pieces of text, treating individual lines like building blocks to be organized into countless different configurations.[13] In some cases, he separated manuscript pages into single-line strips and reordered them as he saw fit—the phrase "cut and paste" recurs in the commentaries.[14] Inasmuch as each line's position vis-à-vis the others is the result of extensive deliberation and field testing, we may be tempted to conclude that—at least in the final extant version of each poem—everything is exactly where it should be. We might equally well infer, however, that the fact that the individual lines of text can be treated in a modular fashion reveals that the placement of any one of them retains an irreducible trace of contingency, since it could have landed somewhere else without serious consequences. In these terms, each section of Whitman's poems has the potential to switch places with any other, even as we must hold open the possibility that any given arrangement is the result of an exactingly precise design, that is, that he did—finally—get it right.

Insofar as Whitman's text exists in a state of quasi-flux, it is hard to take anything about it for granted. As Ed Folsom explains, "Early reviewers of *Leaves*

13. As Ed Folsom describes it: "Whitman formed entire lines as they would eventually appear in print, but then he treated each line like a separate entry, a unity available to him for endless reordering, as if his lines of poetry were portable and interchangeable, could be shuffled and almost randomly scattered to create different but remarkably similar poems." Ed Folsom, "Database as Genre: The Epic Transformation of Archives," *PMLA* 122, no. 5 (2007): 1574–1575. Folsom and Kenneth M. Price add that "this habit of composition may well have derived from Whitman's experience as a typesetter, where lines of text were separate, moveable units assembled into galleys." Ed Folsom and Kenneth M. Price, *Re-Scripting Walt Whitman: An Introduction to His Life and Work* (Malden, MA: Blackwell, 2005), 32.

14. Matt Miller characterizes this practice in explicitly Deleuzian terms as the deterritorialization of different images and statements: "a visualization of language as made up of multiple, interdependent, plant-like entities that are put together in an irregular, centerless and asymmetrical structure." Matt Miller, *Collage of Myself: Walt Whitman and the Making of "Leaves of Grass"* (Lincoln: University of Nebraska Press, 2010), 101.

of Grass weren't sure what genre Whitman was writing in, and certainly Ralph Waldo Emerson wasn't when he wrote his famous letter in 1855 greeting Whitman 'at the beginning of a great career' but never once mentioning poetry as the thing that made him rub his eyes 'to see if this sunbeam were no illusion.'"[15] Jacques Rancière has argued that Whitman's goal was not to mix genres, but rather to produce a new kind of discourse that was neither poetry nor prose.[16] I want to propose that uncertainties about the generic classification of Whitman's texts arise because of the shock to which he submits both the traditional sentence and the traditional line of verse. In this respect, his writing invites us to consider whether one—largely unacknowledged—function of conventional genre categories has been to give us tacit instructions about how to read the sentences in a given work, especially when it comes to according them autonomy with respect to one another or treating them as integrally interconnected.

To get a sense of what is at stake, we can examine a passage from the Preface of the 1855 edition of *Leaves of Grass*:

> To him [the bard] enter the essences of the real things and past and present events—of the enormous diversity of temperature and agriculture and mines—the tribes of red aborigines—the weather-beaten vessels entering new ports or making landings on rocky coasts—the first settlements north or south—the rapid stature and muscle—the haughty defiance of '76, and the war and peace and formation of the constitution . . . . the union always surrounded by blatherers and always calm and impregnable—the perpetual coming of

15. Folsom, "Database as Genre," 1572. Folsom argues that Whitman "experimented throughout his life with mixing poetry and prose sometimes on the same page, testing the boundaries of genre and performing typographical experiments that forced readers to engage the printed page in ways they were not accustomed to, by slipping across the bounds of genre" (1571–1572). The nominally "poetic" part of the first edition, adds Folsom, "with its cascading lines, mixed diction, and endless catalogs of the commonplace, itself reads more like some cross between journalism, oratory, and the Bible" (1572). Whitman's own notebooks betray uncertainty about what *Leaves of Grass* would be: "Novel?—Work of some sort ^Play? . . . A *spiritual novel*?" (cited in Folsom, "Database as Genre," 1572).

16. Rancière argues that in his quest to transcend the poetry/prose divide, Whitman offers one of the first versions of the "modernist axiom" that "there is a mode of presenting common things that subtracts them both from the logic of the economic and social order and from the artificiality of poetic exception"; the resulting text is "neither the account book that maintains things in their commodity value, nor the poetic speech that separates its chosen subjects and rhythms from commonplace occupations." Jacques Rancière, *Aisthesis: Scenes from the Aesthetic Regime of Art*, trans. Zakir Paul (New York: Verso, 2013), 72.

> immigrants—the wharf hem'd cities and superior marine—the unsurveyed interior—the loghouses and clearings and wild animals and hunters and trappers . . . . the free commerce—the fisheries and whaling and gold-digging—the endless gestation of new states—the convening of Congress every December, the members duly coming up from all climates and the uttermost parts . . . . the noble character of the young mechanics and of all free American workmen and workwomen . . . . the general ardor and friendliness and enterprise—the perfect equality of the female with the male . . . . the large amativeness—the fluid movement of the population—the factories and mercantile life and labor-saving machinery—the Yankee swap—the New York firemen and the target excursion—the southern plantation life—the character of the northeast and of the northwest and southwest—slavery and the tremulous spreading of hands to protect it, and the stern opposition to it which shall never cease till it ceases or the speaking of tongues and the moving of lips cease.[17]

It strains credulity to treat this grouping of words as a single sentence. The formation portends unboundedness, giving no indication that it will ever stop or ever need to stop. Its content seems fated to proliferate endlessly; and yet it does come to a close, and it does so—coyly or ironically—on the third repetition of the word "cease," which in the final instance is specifically the halting of the movement of speaking lips. In this way, the opening capital letter and the last single dot (period or full stop) do appear to frame a sort of unit, whatever we may decide to call it, although it is by no means clear whether this unit is primarily syntactic, rhythmic, or semantic in character, or something of an entirely different order.

With its multidimensional content, Whitman's "sentence" ranges over space and time, introducing various narratives and subnarratives less than it briefly alights on them and then moves on as it links past, present, and future in a tone that is part eschatological and part fairy tale, part encyclopedia entry and part journalism. The developmental trajectory is not teleological, which is to say that the individual sections do not gain their ultimate significance from the contribution they make toward reaching the end; nor do they individually acquire a retrospective significance when we finally arrive at the full stop. No part of the whole gives any indication that it regards itself as "just" a part. In this regard, Angus Fletcher has argued that one of Whitman's great

17. Walt Whitman, *Leaves of Grass* (1855 edition), The Walt Whitman Archive, ed. Ed Folsom and Kenneth M. Price, http://whitmanarchive.org/published/LG/1855/whole.html (ellipses in original).

innovations was to craft a language of phrases, an alternative to the traditional syntactic hierarchies of superordinate and subordinate clauses that normally organize the discursive realm. In *Leaves of Grass*, Fletcher writes, "no phrase is ever *grammatically* superior to any other phrase."[18] The result is that in a sentence such as the one just cited, the individual parts do not pile up as if they were lumped together indiscriminately, but exist harmoniously in parallel—true parataxis.

Present participles are crucial to many of the phrasal gestures that make up Whitman's lengthy constructions. Several scholars have suggested that the prominent use of this verb form prevents his exceedingly long sentences from turning into lists by creating a kind of perennial present or "a syntax of continual restarting."[19] The result, writes Wai Chee Dimock, is that in Whitman's syntax "the fact of prior occurrence is in no way a determining condition for what follows," "as if the significance of each [element] were exhausted by its appearance, so that each departs as it arrives, leaving behind no residue, no constraints on the syntax, nothing to make it less open or less ready for more parallel additions."[20] Previously, we considered how verse may foreground the dialectical nature of the sentence, highlighting the prospection and retrospection required to grasp the unfolding relationships between the different elements of a grammatical unit. In Whitman's "syntax of continual restarting," we find the extreme alternative in which any given moment in a sentence is informed neither by what came before it nor by what will follow. No phrase reveals the truth of one of its predecessors, whether by fleshing out what had been implicit or negating it; no phrase lays the groundwork for what is to come.

In subsequent editions of *Leaves of Grass*, material from the "prose" Preface is set into verse, making it more orderly, as if putting the sentences into a lineated form had the effect of suspending the reader's expectation that the parts should work together to articulate predicative statements, the rhythm helping to make up for the glaring paucity of finite verbs. Here, pieces of the section from the 1855 edition cited above return in the 1856 "Poem of Many in One":

18. Angus Fletcher, "The Whitman Phrase," in *Walt Whitman*, ed. Harold Bloom (New York: Chelsea House Publishers, 2006), 219.

19. Ed Folsom, "Walt Whitman's Invention of a Democratic Poetry," in *The Cambridge History of American Poetry*, ed. Alfred Bendixen and Stephen Burt (New York: Cambridge University Press, 2015), 334.

20. Wai Chee Dimock, *Residues of Justice* (Berkeley: University of California Press, 1998), 116.

The picturesque looseness of their carriage, their
 deathless attachment to freedom, their fierce-
 ness when wronged,
The fluency of their speech, their delight in
 music, their curiosity, good-temper, open-
 handedness,
The prevailing ardor and enterprise, the large
 amativeness,
The perfect equality of the female with the male,
 the fluid movement of the population,
The superior marine, free commerce, fisheries,
 whaling, gold-digging,[21]

Prefaced by a seven-word exclamation—"Race of races, and bards to corroborate!"—the sentence in which these lines appear is already over five hundred words long by the time they make their entrance.[22] This gargantuan construction begins with an indirectly referenced subject—"Of them, standing among them, one lifts to the / light his west-bred face"—and then unfolds in

21. Whitman, *Leaves of Grass* (1856 edition), Whitman Archive, http://whitmanarchive.org/published/LG/1856/whole.html. These lines appear basically unchanged in the 1891–1892 version, where as part of a poem called "By Blue Ontario's Shore," they are still imbedded in an immensely long sentence, although it has undergone some minor changes.

There have been many attempts to characterize Whitman's verse style. The King James Bible is frequently invoked as one of his principal models. Sometimes he is said to be mimicking the cadence of oratory, sometimes the patterns of regular speech. Although the lines and stanzas of his poems vary in length, grammatical and rhetorical patterns as well as repetitions of sounds do network the different parts of the poems, as would be the case in more conventional verse. Nonetheless, if one can identify distinct syntactic, metrical, and semantic rhythms, it is unusual for any one of them to predominate. These factors in mind, Derek Attridge locates Whitman's prosody in a "border area" between meter and language rhythm, "where regularity remains only half-realized, and a shadowy metrical set prevents sense and syntax from wholly determining the rhythmical character of the line, but does not itself govern the movement of the verse." Derek Attridge, *The Rhythms of English Poetry* (New York: Longman, 1982), 322. The potential complexity of Attridge's claim becomes clear when we consider just how tenuous—or potentially obscure—the very distinction between meter and language rhythm may be. Charles O. Hartman characterizes Whitman's texts as metrical verse that has been fragmented (*Free Verse: An Essay on Prosody*, 121–23).

22. Whitman, *Leaves of Grass* (1856 edition), Whitman Archive, http://whitmanarchive.org/published/LG/1856/whole.html.

clusters of similarly structured phrases that describe the features of a country permeated by the spirit of this "one" who lifts his face to the light, the bard.[23]

In the course of this lengthy sentence, various forms of repetition loosely link different strings of phrases, as in the section above, in which each line begins with the same definite article. At other points, the same present participle or exclamation is repeated at the beginning of several consecutive lines. Considered together, Whitman's phrases are not crypto-clauses. They do not feel fragmentary or intimate that they are ellipsed sections of something larger, not least because their grammar is in many respects quite conventional, with standard word order, use of modifiers, etcetera. If anything, one wonders whether the term "phrase" captures what is happening here, insofar as it implies that these parts of the poem are subsentential elements. Each small group of words seems more akin to a label affixed to a section of an annotated painting or photograph, a node in a composite picture helping to make up a graphic array of information not beholden to any syntactic tree.

One might argue that there is nothing especially disruptive going on in these verbal constructions beyond their length, since such a "sentence" is really just a kind of list, the role of the participles in creating a perennial present notwithstanding. Rejecting this conclusion, Gilles Deleuze maintains that each monstrous formation of *Leaves of Grass* does something extraordinary in setting loose an asyntactic force:

> It is as if the syntax that composes the sentence, which makes it a totality capable of referring back to itself, tends to disappear by setting free an infinite *asyntactic* sentence, which prolongs itself or sprouts dashes in order to create spatiotemporal intervals. . . . It is an almost mad sentence, with its changes in direction, its bifurcations, its ruptures and leaps, its prolongations, its sproutings, its parentheses.[24]

23. Whitman, *Leaves of Grass* (1856 edition), Whitman Archive, http://whitmanarchive.org/published/LG/1856/whole.html.

24. Gilles Deleuze, *Essays Critical and Clinical*, trans. Daniel W. Smith and Michael A. Greco (Minneapolis: University of Minnesota Press, 1997), 57–58. Eric Wilson invokes Deleuze and Guattari in characterizing Whitman's poetry as Lucretian: "Inflecting Lucretius' atomism through his desire for motion, Whitman in his first version of 'Song of Myself' uproots the radicle symbols of Platonism and pantheism—plant, leaf, tree, parts controlled by an orderly whole—and replaces them with Deleuze and Guattari's rhizomes: unstable gatherings of free parts moving in an unfettered whole." Eric Wilson, *Romantic Turbulence: Chaos, Ecology, and American Space* (New York: St. Martin's Press, 2000), 119.

In the a-sentential sentence Deleuze finds in Whitman, there is no longer a tension between the linearity of the words following one another and the pyramid-like hierarchy of grammar that organizes their relationships into phrases and clauses. Instead, the structure is multidimensional, any given moment connecting with any other. What we typically refer to as the beginning and the end of the sentence lose their authority, since the dynamics of the language can no longer be characterized in terms of prospective or retrospective vectors that allow clear figures of development or inversion to emerge. In Deleuze's terms, this would be a rhizomatic discourse in which there is no shortage of movement, but the patterns of motion never assume a fixed form that would serve as a firm ground of sense. Equally disruptive, there is no longer an implicit or explicit subject—"the poetic voice"—by reference to which everything gains its significance. Whitman's sentences supersede any figure of intention that would claim them for its own. Like Frankenstein's monster, these sprawling constructions are as much the creator of their creator as they are his creation.

Deleuze is hardly the only reader of Whitman to think along such lines. It has been proposed that the fluid language of *Leaves of Grass* disrupts established social and political paradigms and points the way toward progressive reconceptualizations of, among other things, ethnicity and gender.[25] At the same time, it seems difficult to give up on the romanticized figure of the poet who ambiguously resides either inside Whitman's text, as the lyric self, or outside it, in the form of the empirical author and his aesthetic project. This is partly due to the fact that Whitman was far from shy about detailing his ambitious plans for his work, making it difficult not to evaluate it by his lofty standards. Perhaps best known is his grand declaration that he was writing the verse that his countrymen needed. "Has not the time arrived," he asked, "when, (if it must be plain said, for democratic America's sake, if for no other) there must imperatively come a readjustment of the whole theory and nature of Poetry?"[26]

Despite the degree to which Whitman claimed to be embracing Wordsworth's proverbial "language of real men," some of his modernist readers were skeptical that his writing was intrinsically democratic, arguing that

25. For an influential account of the transformative potential of *Leaves of Grass*, see Michael Moon, *Disseminating Whitman: Revision and Corporeality in* Leaves of Grass (Cambridge, MA: Harvard University Press, 1991).

26. Walt Whitman, "A Backward Glance O'er Travelled Roads," *Complete Poetry and Collected Prose*, ed. Justin Kaplan (New York: Library of America, 1982), 662.

its difficulty necessarily limited the scope of its reception.[27] More recently, scholars have taken a different approach to the political potential of Whitman's work, asking whether there is something intrinsically egalitarian about the phrasal dynamics of the sentences themselves. If the different lines are, improbably, all on an equal footing with one another, is this "democratic" in the sense in which all the members of a polity enjoy the same rights, and perhaps more importantly, does the very existence of such a nonhierarchical language have the potential to foster and sustain the political spirit of a nation, as Whitman himself suggests? Angus Fletcher insists that Whitman's unique phrasal gestures constitute "a new grammar of status relations," although he is vague about the implications of this claim, writing that to Whitman's mind, "the only way for a Jacksonian democracy and its refusal of subordination to thrive, in symbolic terms, would be to get rid of the clauses of sentences as much as possible."[28] The qualification "in symbolic terms" raises the question of what the relationship is between a discursive democracy such as *Leaves of Grass* and a "nonsymbolic" one. Fletcher also has little to say about the fact that Whitman never fully abandoned clauses. As we will consider below, some of his best-known lines are grammatically unremarkable.

Wai Chee Dimock argues that insofar as the main force structuring Whitman's writing is equivalence, his language offers "a democratic hospitality to the world, a refusal to tolerate exclusions, a refusal, indeed, to register distinctions, an openness as impartial as it is impersonal."[29] In her view, the very fact that so many different figures and topics could appear serially in the lengthy sentence we have just been considering is evidence of a kind of semantic leveling that parallels the paratactic grammar. Extending a common critique of the narcissism of Whitman's writing, Dimock notes that this openness results

27. If Whitman is routinely celebrated for having tried to write the poetry of American democracy, scholars have largely discussed this in terms of his rejection of meter, rhyme, and conventional diction and his embrace of a so-called plain style, despite the fact that, as Patrick Redding points out, Whitman himself never puts these four features together or systematically explains how they would constitute a "democratic poetics." Patrick Redding, "Whitman Unbound: Democracy and Poetic Form, 1912–1931," *New Literary History* 41, no. 3 (2010): 671. Some modernist critics found Whitman much too egotistical, essentially writing for himself, as it were. In this regard, they contrasted him with Edgar Allan Poe, who on their view sought to produce texts with universal appeal (Redding, 681).

28. Fletcher, "The Whitman Phrase," 213, 219.

29. Wai Chee Dimock, "Whitman, Syntax, and Political Theory," in *Breaking Bounds: Whitman and American Cultural Studies*, ed. Betsy Erkkila and Jay Grossman (New York: Oxford University Press, 1996), 71. See also Dimock, *Residues of Justice,* 116.

in an idealized subject who confronts the world as a group of ideas and objects that are all of equal interest to it, which is to say that they may all equally be of no interest.[30] When anything can enter the text and enjoy the same standing as everything else, no element is more or less important than any other, and complete openness to the world shades into complete indifference to it. With an egocentric bard as its controlling instance, the poem presents a democracy of "me" with no real value placed on a collective "we." Whitman's radically egalitarian sentences would thus betray an implicit hierarchy after all, with the poet, biased against nothing, reigning sovereign over everything.

The notion that everything in *Leaves of Grass* is subordinate to a domineering figure of subjectivity appears to be substantiated by countless passages, but is perhaps nowhere so directly confirmed as in a few short lines, now among Whitman's best known, that in the original version of the book were part of the first untitled poem, which in later editions was called "Poem of Walt Whitman, An American," "Walt Whitman," and finally "Song of Myself." These lines read: "Do I contradict myself? / Very well, then, I contradict myself; / I am large—I contain multitudes."[31] Starkly contrasting with the sprawling syntactic monstrosities we have been examining thus far, these short, even conversational statements have become Whitmanian aphorisms. They certainly seem to support the notion that his discourse is grounded in a figure of subjectivity "always open to new experience, but always unencumbered by that experience."[32]

Puzzlingly enough, the defining expression of the poetic voice's posture toward literally everything appears to manifest itself in sentences that are structurally unremarkable. It is similarly puzzling how enthusiastically these claims have been embraced by Whitman's readers as an account of his poetics. As experimental as he is taken to be, scholars have regarded these statements and others like them as grounds for treating large sections of *Leaves of Grass* as if they were straightforwardly autobiographical, in effect endorsing a very traditional model of the text as an expression of an individual—its feelings, memories, and ambitions. This line of interpretation is not so much the result of conventional critical impulses as it is a side-effect of the move to parallel

30. See Dimock, *Residues of Justice*, 115, 118.

31. Whitman, *Leaves of Grass*, Whitman Archive, http://whitmanarchive.org/published/LG/1867/whole.html. Whitman is typically thought to be responding to Emerson's famous "Suppose you should contradict yourself; what then?" Ralph Waldo Emerson, *The Annotated Emerson*, ed. David Mikics (Cambridge, MA: Harvard University Press, 2012), 168. It is in this context that Emerson offers his well-known adage, "A foolish consistency is the hobgoblin of little minds" (168).

32. Dimock, "Whitman, Syntax, and Political Theory," 75.

the paratactic grammar of the sprawling sentences with a semantic leveling in which no particular thing represented in the poem is subordinate to any other. Having decided to treat form and content as if they mirror one another, assuming that they remain distinguishable at all, an analysis of Whitman's book, however attentive to the complex dynamics of individual sentences, is fated to confirm the overarching unity and cohesiveness of the representational features of the text, which are then readily figured as the product of a subject's interior ruminations.

One might counter that Whitman was trying to write the "perfect" sentence in which structure and substance are one and the same insofar as all the parts coexist in a nonhierarchical field. The question remains, however, whether the result of such an endeavor must be a celebration of the power of a poetic self. A priori, there is no reason that the tolerance of or open indifference to its subject matter that shapes the representational posture of *Leaves of Grass* should not extend to the manifestations of selfhood in it as well. A hint as to how we might proceed can be found in the first version of the canonical lines about a capacious subjectivity: "Do I contradict myself? / Very well then . . . . I contradict myself; / I am large . . . . I contain multitudes."[33] Here we encounter one of the most distinctive—and notorious—features of the 1855 edition of *Leaves of Grass*, the ellipses. Ranging from three to as many as nine dots in length, they abound in both the Preface and the verse sections.[34] Strikingly, this feature of the text disappears completely in the following edition, never to return in any of the book's subsequent versions.

Formally, an ellipsis represents a relationship between presence and absence. It indicates that something has been left out, customarily with the implicit suggestion that the omitted material is inessential. Something is missing, but it need not be missed. The ellipsis has a well-established rhetorical pedigree, most commonly in its capacity as an uncertain trailing off at the end of a sentence that may be playful, ironic, or ominous. Recalling our earlier question about what kind of sentence, if any, can illustrate the dynamic spontaneity of a mind at work, Whitman's readers have generally characterized this explosion

33. Whitman, *Leaves of Grass* (1855 edition), Whitman Archive, http://whitmanarchive.org/published/LG/1855/whole.html.

34. Anne Toner explains that the use of three dots was not an established convention in the nineteenth century. As late as 1927, the *Chicago Manual of Style* specified four dots for omitted material in English sentences, three dots for omitted material in quotations from Romance languages. See Anne Toner, *Ellipsis in English Literature: Signs of Omission* (New York: Cambridge University Press, 2015), 153.

of difficult-to-explain punctuation as a sign of the inchoate quality of the thought processes being represented. The strings of dots are read as simulations of "a mind groping for the next word, image, or idea, not really knowing what is coming next, joying in its own improvisations."[35] Rather than marking something that has been removed, the ellipses become place- or time-holders that put something back in. Opinions differ as to whether this is tantamount to saying that the ellipses hold the disparate pieces of the sprawling sentences together, or if they foreground the essentially fragmentary quality of the language, whose parts can never truly be coordinated.

It has been suggested that the ellipsis-ridden 1855 text of *Leaves of Grass* is the oral version of the poem that is redacted into a more conventional written document in later editions. One could equally well argue, however, that the ellipses strewn throughout the book's first version ironize the very idea of lyric poetry as an instance of the "spoken voice" for the simple reason that it would be impossible to vocalize their distinctiveness, as if one could pause differently for seven as opposed to eight dots in a spoken presentation.[36] Far from using eccentric punctuation to represent the vagaries of spontaneous speech, Whitman may be slyly making fun of J. S. Mill's famous notion of the lyric as "an utterance overheard" by cautioning us that our imagined eavesdropping is fated to be only partially successful, since whole chunks of text may prove inaudible to even the most careful listener. Instead of celebrating subjectivity, individual or universal, Whitman's poem would underscore the incompleteness of any account of its language as the discourse—ruminations, reflections, or self-affirmations—of a self. From this perspective, the ellipses are no longer a representation of the mind of the bard searching for his next word, but instances of language that decline to belong to anyone, including the poet. Anti-clauses, they are verbal structures free of any compulsion to facilitate predication, reference, or signification. They may be an expression of linguistic egalitarianism, but only insofar as they reveal the truth that a genuinely democratic language is one with nothing to say and no need to pretend otherwise. Alternatively, we could understand them to be a graphic confirmation of the poetic self's indifference to everything, with each set of dots steadfastly unconcerned with saying anything in particular.

35. Eric Wilson, "Whitman's Rhizomes," *Arizona Quarterly: A Journal of American Literature, Culture, and Theory* 55, no. 3 (Autumn 1999): 11.

36. Rancière suggests that Whitman's ellipses are an effort to displace and even transcend the speech/writing dichotomy itself by abolishing the "separation between the signs of speech and graphic images" (*Aisthesis*, 73).

The ellipses are absent from every other edition of *Leaves of Grass*, as if having flirted with them as a way of radicalizing the sentence form, Whitman opted to retain the curious mix of sprawling syntactic dynamics and short, almost laconic assertions while avoiding any further reliance on ambiguous strings of dots.[37] Just how transformative his experiments with the sentence are remains an open question. In Deleuze's view, Whitman's more extreme constructions disrupt the status of predication as the controlling representational principle and explode our assumptions about the bounded nature of a sentence, the basic idea that it must start somewhere and finish somewhere else. There seems, however, to be a countervailing tendency in Whitman's writing to subordinate its verbal excesses to the figure of an all-controlling self who stands sovereign over every piece of the puzzle and in some cases, as in the lines just under consideration, expresses its authority with simple

37. While the ellipses vanish, Whitman's experimentation with punctuation does not end. This becomes clear when we compare the different versions of the canonical lines just cited (*Leaves of Grass*, Whitman Archive, https://whitmanarchive.org/published/LG/index.html):

1855

Do I contradict myself?
Very well then . . . . I contradict myself;
I am large . . . . I contain multitudes.

1860

Do I contradict myself?
Very well, then, I contradict myself,
I am large—I contain multitudes.

1891–92

Do I contradict myself?
Very well then I contradict myself,
(I am large, I contain multitudes.)

By altering the punctuation while leaving the words untouched, Whitman changes the relationships among the elements of the sentences. In the second line, the force of "then" and the connection it articulates between what precedes and follows it modulate slightly in each version. In the final line, it may be hard to characterize the difference between the function of the ellipsis and the dash, but the introduction of parentheses in the last version has the odd effect of turning arguably the most canonical statement in the book into a supplementary explanation or aside.

first-person statements. In this respect, Whitman reveals just how deeply our ideas about sentences are grounded in an understanding of subjectivity. If, as Nietzsche would have it, our paradigm of individual agency is structured by subject-predicate schemas—if we believe that there is a doer behind the deed because grammar tells us so—Whitman shows us that the converse is equally true and that we cannot conceive of the sentence as a formation that could exist in the absence of an expressive self. Less clear is whether this self is intrinsically democratic in nature.

Whitman's constant revisions of his magnum opus make it difficult to say whether he left us with multiple versions of a poem, with several distinct poems, or with one giant work that manifests itself as manifold iterations. The question of whether there is a "final" or "definitive" version of any of the poems of his contemporary Emily Dickinson is an even thornier issue.[38] While Whitman constantly rearranged the pieces of his texts and meticulously oversaw every detail of their typesetting, sometimes stopping the presses during a print run to correct mistakes, Dickinson left us handwritten documents on all varieties of paper that resist tidy formalization on the printed page. As R. W. Franklin proposes at the beginning of his facsimile edition of her manuscripts, her works "resist translation into the conventions of print. Formal features like her unusual punctuation and capitalization, line and stanza divisions, and display of alternate readings are a source of continuing critical concern."[39]

Dickinson's punctuation alone represents a major challenge, since in some cases the marks on the page appear to be more akin to musical notation than to commas, dashes, and periods, and even her most assiduous devotees are occasionally accused of not being able to keep the graphic subtleties straight, particularly with regards to the idiosyncrasies of her handwriting. With so many different features of her oeuvre identified as unique, she can at times seem to be writing in a semi-private language that borders on the unreadable.

38. To compare and contrast these two poets, whether on the basis of their styles, genders, or commercial ambitions, is a standard topos of literary history. For a classic account of the duo, see Sandra Gilbert, "The American Sexual Poetics of Walt Whitman and Emily Dickinson," *Reconstructing American Literary History*, ed. Sacvan Bercovitch (Cambridge, MA: Harvard University Press, 1986), 123–54.

39. *The Manuscript Books of Emily Dickinson*, vol. 1, ed. R. W. Franklin (Cambridge, MA: Harvard University Press, 1981), ix. High-resolution images of Dickinson's manuscripts are available online at the *Emily Dickinson Archive* (EDA), http://www.edickinson.org/.

With these concerns in mind, some Dickinson scholars have made a concerted effort to privilege the holographic over the typographic. Traditionally, transcriptions of her handwritten documents followed the metrical and stanzaic cues; it is in this form that most of us first read her texts and most editions still present them. The problem is that there are frequently additional breaks in the metrical lines on her manuscript pages. To call them all "runovers," as if she had simply run out of room on the right-hand side of the page and finished a given metrical line in the space directly below it, would be an oversimplification. There are numerous instances in which the "breaks" acquire semantic significance in the context of the individual passages, often becoming visual or verbal puns or overtly commenting on the tensions between the arrangement of the words and the laws of grammar. Acknowledging these facts, some scholars nevertheless resist the conclusion that the poems should be laid out to show the manuscript lineation. Meter and rhythm, they maintain, are so important in Dickinson's writing that one cannot risk subordinating them to a "visual" lineation. Nor is typesetting the poems "as she wrote them" necessarily a guarantee of graphic fidelity. Doing so is apt to produce a thin column of verse on a largely blank page, whereas she sometimes made her script larger such that only a few words would span the width of a sheet of paper. Ultimately, one may have to resign oneself to the fact that any given rendition of a Dickinson text is a sort of approximation.

Of course, even to speak of exploring Dickinson's "poems" is to overlook the fact that any given text's generic identity may be very much in doubt. "Editors and scholars," writes Cristanne Miller, who is both, "do not agree as to what constitutes a 'poem,' a version of a poem, metered prose, a letter-poem, or even whether to call Dickinson's work 'poems' (some prefer 'manuscript writing')."[40] This is hardly a new idea. More than half a century ago, the poet Jack Spicer suggested that Dickinson's verse texts and her correspondence could not be systematically distinguished as poetry versus prose, a point that seems incontrovertible when one considers that she often uses the same meters and rhythms for both. Reviewing Thomas Johnson's variorum edition of Dickinson in 1956, Spicer writes: "The reason for the difficulty of drawing a line between the poetry and prose in Emily Dickinson's letters may be that she did not wish such a line to be drawn. If large portions of her correspondence are considered not as mere letters—and, indeed, they seldom communicate information, or have much to do with the person to whom they were

40. Cristanne Miller, "Introduction," *Emily Dickinson's Poems: As She Preserved Them*, ed. Cristanne Miller (Cambridge, MA: Harvard University Press, 2016), 11.

written—but as experiments in a heightened prose combined with poetry, a new approach to both her letters and her poetry opens up."[41]

Despite these complexities, Dickinson appears at first glance to be a more traditional writer than Whitman. She uses ballad forms that were already quaint in her day; her syntax does not sprawl in impossibly protracted sequences; and while he pens long lines of verse of varying lengths, she writes extremely short ones with more uniform syllable counts. At second glance, the results prove to be anything but simple. Dickinson's work is less programmatic than Whitman's, and there is no centralizing voice to unite the different thematic strands, which means that in any given text the relationship between tone and content can be quite obscure. Thanks to her frequent reliance on common meter, we can hum many of her poems to the tunes of nursery rhymes we have known most of our lives, adding an air of lightness, even whimsy, to the verses that can clash with the weightiness of the subject matter.[42]

In spite of the degree to which the theme or argument of individual texts remains obscure, Dickinson has always been an eminently quotable writer, and many of her sentences stand on their own as wise adages or wry quips.[43] The reader's experience of these constructions as sentences is, however, tempered

41. Jack Spicer, *The House That Jack Built: The Collected Lectures of Jack Spicer*, ed. Peter Gizzi (Middletown, CT: Wesleyan University Press, 1998), 234. More recently, Virginia Jackson has argued that considerable violence has been done to Dickinson's writings by tearing them from their singular contexts, printing them in metrically defined stanzas, and reading them as instances of "lyric." See Virginia Jackson, *Dickinson's Misery: A Theory of Lyric Reading* (Princeton, NJ: Princeton University Press, 2005).

42. The regularity or irregularity of Dickinson's verse forms is a more complex matter than one might anticipate. Cristanne Miller emphasizes the continuity across the texts, observing that "the great majority of [Dickinson's] poems are written in iambic or catalectic meter or in a popular beat-based rhythm, typically combining the rising rhythms of iambs and anapests. Almost all her poems rhyme, albeit often irregularly or slant. Similarly, Dickinson's verse typically maintains a metrical base, even among its irregularities of rhythm, rhyme, line length and stanzaic structure. Alternatives generally maintain a poem's meter" (Miller, "Introduction," 8). John Shoptaw counters that while "Dickinson is mostly thought of as a poet of hymnodic quatrains and there's no doubting she was partial to hymn meters," it is also the case that she frequently invented a meter for a poem and used it only once. John Shoptaw, "Listening to Dickinson," *Representations* 86, no. 1 (Spring 2004): 39.

43. Forest Pyle has shown that the first lines of many of Dickinson's poems constitute striking verbal events, in the wake of which the rest of the text can feel like something of a disappointment. As he explains: "the values or positions established by these aphoristic beginnings are often reversed or annulled or overturned or even abandoned in the course of the poem, and their currency as adage is likewise undone or ironized. And yet never entirely . . ." Forest Pyle,

by the way in which her versification splits them up across several short lines or in some cases across multiple stanzas, foregrounding the status of each individual phrase or clause as a part of a larger syntactic pattern, almost as if the poems were diagramming their own grammatical structures. This effect is intensified by the rhythms, which highlight the prevalence of enjambment by bringing many lines to a decisive "conclusion" even as syntactically they end midphrase or midclause.

Coupled with the staccato rhythms and frequent use of dashes, the tension between sentence grammar and versification, particularly when it is further complicated by the manuscript lineation, can create the impression that we are being confronted with the pieces of a puzzle, ostensibly arranged in their proper places but by no means fitting snuggly together. As with Whitman, we may find ourselves reading Dickinson's texts less "for" the sentence—that is, with the expectation that a given group of words will coalesce into standalone statements, questions, or commands—and more for the phrase. The effect is not necessarily displeasing. Along with the familiar meters, the notion that we are being given a schematic presentation of the various pieces of a work can contribute to our sense that the material is accessible, its obscurities notwithstanding.

In addition to calling attention to their own status as verbal constructions, Dickinson's poems are often explicit about the challenges, if not threats, presented by writing, not to mention the dangers involved in reading what one has written. The tone of such reflections is almost invariably ambiguous, as in this example:

> I read my sentence - steadily -
> Reviewed it with my eyes,
> To see that I made no mistake
> In it's extremest clause -
> The Date, and manner, of the shame -
> And then the Pious Form
> That "God have mercy" on the Soul
> The Jury voted Him -
> I made my soul familiar - with her extremity -
> That at the last, it should not be a novel Agony -
> But she, and Death acquainted -

Art's Undoing: In the Wake of a Radical Aestheticism (New York: Fordham University Press, 2013), 109.

Meet tranquilly, as friends -
Salute, and pass, without a Hint -
And there, the Matter Ends -[44]

This poem turns around the dual meaning of the word "sentence" as "an organized set of words" and "the assignment of an official punishment." The imagery and logic of the text are flexible enough to accommodate what appear to be two very different interpretations. Either the poet is literally writing about reading a death sentence and metaphorically writing about the way in which she relates to her sentences as if they were death sentences, or the other way around. If initially it is ambiguous whether the sentence in question is specifically for the first-person speaker or written by her for another, the latter lines appear to stress the personal nature and consequences of the existential verdict.

Dickinson's poem may be playful or somber, lighthearted or consequential.[45] There is undeniably something funny about the fact that we all despise our own writing, and there is undeniably something terrifying about the prospect of reading one's own death writ. The difficulty of deciding between the two interpretations is heightened by the ending, which seems to describe the condemned soul, now figured as independent of the poem's speaker, as untouched by a personified Death. Indeed, in a curiously contradictory fashion the soul and death "Salute, and pass, without a hint."

This poem about reading a "sentence" carefully in order to be sure that it says what one thinks it should challenges the reader to repeat the act of reading characterized in it. That this is a potentially impossible trial is augmented by an ambiguity in the text's second word. Until we reach the first word of the second line, "Reviewed," we do not know whether the verb "read" in the first line is in the present or past tense. Our inability to read the poem's sentences carefully enough to be certain that we are reading the word "sentence" correctly is thereby heightened by our inability to read the word "read" with any

44. Emily Dickinson, *The Poems of Emily Dickinson*, ed. R. W. Franklin (Cambridge, MA: Harvard University Press, 1998), #432. Subsequent references to this edition will be cited as "Fr" along with the number Franklin assigns to the text. In contrast to most earlier editors, Franklin presents the horizontal lines in Dickinson's texts as hyphen-length marks rather than em or en dashes, but I will continue to refer to them as "dashes," since the term is iconic in the secondary literature. For a facsimile of the manuscript page, see Franklin, *The Manuscript Books of Emily Dickinson*, vol. 1, 324.

45. On the comic in Dickinson, see Suzanne Juhasz, Cristanne Miller, and Martha Nell Smith, *Comic Power in Emily Dickinson* (Austin: University of Texas Press, 1993).

confidence, at least on first pass, that is, we can only read "read" with assurance once we are rereading it, although we do not know this the first time we encounter it. The word "read," moreover, may not be the same word the second time around, which is precisely the concern that the first-person speaker has about the sentence she is trying to read. No less than the poet, we will run into trouble in attempting to decide when our reading of the text at hand has really gotten going and when it is complete.

The text questions the authority of its own "sentences," legal or otherwise, by foregrounding the possibility that there may be mistakes to be found in the composition it is describing. If we follow the poet's lead and go in search of her writing's "extremest clause" in lines 5–8, we find only phrases, and when the extreme does make an explicit return in an actual clause ("I made my soul familiar - / With her extremity"), the verse form suddenly changes. Based on the rhythm and rhyme scheme up to this point, we would expect the text to read: "I made my soul familiar - / With her extremity - / That at the last, it should not be / A novel Agony -". In fact, if we follow the metrical lineation as constructed by Franklin, these four lines become two ("I made my soul familiar - with her extremity - / That at the last, it should not be a novel Agony -"). On the manuscript page, they appear as three lines, although not in a way that would fit the pre-established rhyme scheme, so the second line ends with "not" rather than "be": "I made my soul familiar - with her extremity - / That at the last, it should not / be a novel Agony -". Every time this poem about a sentence tries to zero in on its own sentences, it fails to finalize a particular set of relationships between its parts and the patterns that organize them. Dickinson's text is always in its "extremest clause," or better, every clause is perpetually *in extremis*, as if it can do no more or less than announce that it is a death sentence for language itself. The way in which the poem closes ("And there, the Matter Ends -") only confirms this predicament. The syntax and rhythm demand that we read the last word as a verb, and there is something decidedly tidy about the poem finishing on the act of ending. The problem is that Dickinson almost never capitalizes a verb, meaning that we cannot neatly bring our reading of the final word to an end without at least speculating on whether "Matter Ends" is some sort of substantive. If it certainly matters that the end of someone sentenced to death will be nothing more or less than matter, "Matter-Ends" also matter precisely because they are not simply the end of anything.

Dickinson's poem plays with the word "sentence" while challenging our ability to read its words and sentences, and its ultimate irony may be that because we have read it, we are no longer in a position to decide what is confusing about it. Other Dickinson texts are no less strident in challenging the authority of both sentential syntax and versification by pitting the referential and signifying powers of the word and the sentence against one another. In the early 1860s, Dickinson began writing lists of variant terms on the page below the main body of her texts, a practice she would continue with increasing frequency for the rest of her career. For one or more words in a poem, she would provide "alternatives"—some scholars prefer to call them "additional" words. While we might anticipate that this would offer insight into the process by which a specific noun or adjective was selected from among the many options on offer in the language, Dickinson tended to list possibilities without indicating that one in particular was being privileged over the others. With some texts, she did produce so-called "clean" copies in which choices appear to have been made, but there is no consensus among her readers about which version, if any, should be regarded as "definitive" or "final"—be it the first, the last, or the one she shared with a particular friend or relative.

For some scholars, these lists of alternative words, each of which can seemingly function equally well in the same place in a given line of verse, are evidence that Dickinson strove to refine her diction as exactingly as possible.[46] Contesting this conclusion, Sharon Cameron has argued that what is represented by the variants is "the representation of not choosing," since "in the poems the choice of particular words implied by the lyric frame to be imperative is rather shown to be impossible."[47] While the grammar and verse structure necessitate the selection of a word for a particular slot in the syntax and the line, the string of "additional" terms never yields up one "winner." In this respect, Dickinson's writing, no less than Whitman's, challenges our customary notion of a "finished" text, suggesting that the persistence of manifold possibilities is not proof that a piece is still in draft form, but an indication that what distinguishes these poems is their openness to alternative possibilities.[48]

46. Scott Donaldson maintains that "the multitude of variants standing on [Dickinson's] work-sheets make it clear that she never chose words casually." Scott Donaldson, "Minding Emily Dickinson's Business," *New England Quarterly* 41, no. 4 (December 1968): 574.

47. Sharon Cameron, *Choosing Not Choosing: Dickinson's Fascicles* (Chicago: University of Chicago Press, 1992), 23. Other scholars who follow Cameron in this line of interpretation to some degree include Jerome J. McGann, *Black Riders: The Visible Language of Modernism* (Princeton, NJ: Princeton University Press, 1993), Martha Nell Smith, *Rowing in Eden: Rereading Emily Dickinson* (Austin: University of Texas Press, 1992), and Marta L. Werner, *Emily Dickinson's Open Folios: Scenes of Reading, Surfaces of Writing* (Ann Arbor: University of Michigan Press, 1996).

48. Cameron draws just such a comparison between the two poets: "As Whitman does not choose—as the thematic principle of *Song of Myself* is one of inclusion, and the principle of

In contrast to Whitman's gargantuan sentences, where the presence or absence of a given noun or adjective might go unnoticed, Dickinson's short rhythmic lines ensure that every word stands out, heightening the potential provocation of her variants. In the following poem, the relationships between the text's syntactic and lexical features are foregrounded through a reflection on one of the foundational works of the Western tradition, the Bible. From line to line, the subject-predicate model imposes itself and vanishes, predominating at one point, completely absenting itself the next. Presented in Franklin's edition to show the metrical lineation, it reads:

The Bible is an antique Volume -
Written by faded Men
At the suggestion of Holy Spectres -
Subjects - Bethlehem -
Eden - the ancient Homestead -
Satan - the Brigadier -
Judas - the Great Defaulter -
David - the Troubadour -
Sin - a distinguished Precipice
Others must resist -
Boys that "believe" are very lonesome -
Other Boys are "lost" -
Had but the Tale a warbling Teller -
All the Boys would come -
Orpheus' Sermon captivated -
It did not condemn - (Fr. 1577 C)

The list-like quality of the resulting verses is even more graphic when one considers the manuscript lineation:

The Bible is an
antique Volume -
Written by faded
Men

successive editions is one of textual variation—so the identity of Whitman's texts, much like that of Dickinson's, must be understood in terms of those textual variants. Variants and variation are strategies for redefining the boundaries of a Whitmanian as well as of a Dickinsonian text" (*Choosing Not Choosing*, 61).

At the suggestion
of Holy Spectres -
Subjects - Bethlehem -
Eden - the ancient
Homestead -
Satan - the Brigadier -
Judas - the Great
Defaulter -
David - the Troubadour -
Sin - a distinguished
Precipice
Others must resist -
Boys that "believe"
are very lonesome -
Other Boys are "lost" -
Had but the Tale
a warbling Teller -
All the Boys would
come -
Orpheus' Sermon
captivated -
It did not
condemn -[49]

Typical of Dickinson's treatment of religious themes, the tone of this piece is complex. Despite the overt playfulness, humor, and even sarcasm in the staged clash between Holy Scripture and classical poetry, there is more than a note of respect for both discourses.[50] A poem about choosing words for a poem,

49. This version of the poem (ca. 1882) is based on a signed pencil copy sent by Dickinson to her nephew Ned. For a facsimile of the manuscript page, see http://www.edickinson.org/editions/1/image_sets/236701.

50. The jejune tone of the first part of the poem is ostensibly clarified by the fact that the earliest draft of Dickinson's text had a title that does not appear in later versions: "Diagnosis of the Bible, by a Boy -". In its latter lines, however, the text shifts gears and begins to comment on the "boy" and others like him who might develop relationships with the Bible, balancing the juvenile and the adult. The question, then, is whether the "mature" voice ever entirely frees itself of the immaturity with which the text opens. In this regard, the earlier versions of the first lines were arguably even cheekier: "The Bible is an *untold* Volume - / Written by *unknown* Men / At the suggestion of *hallowed* Spectres -" (Fr. 1577 A). On the complexities of Dickinson's

the text systematically calls attention to the precariousness of its own diction. The near absence of verbs in the first two-thirds of the verses coupled with the string of unexpected combinations of adjectives and nouns invites the reader to rearrange the different elements to produce the "correct" or at least the "anticipated" formulations. "Antique Volume" would customarily be "Ancient [from metrical line 5] Volume," and one is tempted to rewrite "faded Men" as "distinguished [from metrical line 9] Men." In a similar vein, "Spectres" stands out as a poor substitute for the expected *Ghost*, as does "homestead" for the more customary *Homeland*. By opening with such odd turns of phrase, the poem forces us to think from the start about the status of the individual adjectives—and by extension all the words in the text—as choices.[51]

Heightened by the unexpected pairings of nouns and adjectives, the list-like quality of the main section of the poem contrasts starkly with the sentences at the end, as if at its close the text were reasserting the authority of the subject-predicate schema. In the meantime, the poet apparently loses confidence in her ability to choose her words. Having introduced an alternative to biblical poetry in the form of Ancient Greek mythopoetics and Orpheus, the poem becomes markedly skeptical toward its own language: "Boys that 'believe' are very lonesome - / Other Boys are 'lost' -". Recourse to scare quotes is not unusual for Dickinson, but here one worries that they are characteristic of the writing of faded men more than that of captivating poets.[52] Qualifying "believe" and "lost" in this way suggests that producing a poem is less an issue of choosing exactly the right word than of settling for euphemisms. The text deploys "believe" and "lost" without confirming its ability to capture their full range of meanings, or perhaps more importantly, without confirming its ability to come up with something better with which to replace them. If glosses are offered for Eden ("ancient Homestead") or Judas ("the Great Defaulter"), no synonyms are suggested for this final verb and adjective. This poem about choosing words thus closes with a glaring challenge to its own ability to make such choices.

---

engagement with Christianity, see Linda Freedman, *Emily Dickinson and the Religious Imagination* (New York: Cambridge University Press, 2011).

51. Parallel to this odd exercise in mispairing adjectives and nouns is the poem's reading of the Bible in metrical lines 4–9, which does not, as would be customary, involve quoting, summarizing, or decoding the text. Instead, individual figures (Eden, Satan, Judas) are selected and given epithets as if they were characters in genre fiction.

52. In many of Dickinson's poems, the density of qualifications effected by scare quotes and italics can be intimidating: "And after *that* [*Death]*- there's Heaven - / The *Good* Man's - '*Dividend*' - / And *Bad* Men - 'go to Jail' - / I guess -" (Fr. 249). See also Fr. 179.

As it turns out, the poem's last lines do not have the last word regarding its diction. While the second and third versions of the text present a "warbling Teller" in metrical line 13 ("Had but the Tale a warbling Teller -"), the first version reads "thrilling Teller," and "thrilling" is supplemented by a fourteen-word variant list:

typic
hearty
bonnie
breathless
spacious
tropic
warbling
warbling
ardent
friendly
magic
pungent
winning
mellow (Fr. 1577 A)

Following Cameron, we might try to treat all the words in this variant list as equally plausible options that could be inserted, one by one, into the slot in the syntax right before "Teller." This could mean reading the line of which each is potentially a part as if all fourteen were there simultaneously, thereby shattering the verse form; imagining the co-presence of many different versions of the line; or viewing the variant list as an independent vector of the text, an autonomous tangent that complements or counters the verse and sentence structure of the poem with a string of words that is not subordinate either to the patterns of lineation and meter or to a subject-predicate paradigm.

Pursuing the implications of Cameron's argument that Dickinson chooses not to choose, Marjorie Perloff has argued that "an examination of the variant word lists that begin to appear on the fringes of Dickinson's poems . . . suggests that [she] did not believe that words were in themselves irreplaceable."[53] Far from evidence of the extreme care she took in selecting her words, Dickinson's habit of listing variants would instead reveal that for her poetic precision is not

53. Marjorie Perloff, "Emily Dickinson and the Theory Canon," http://writing.upenn.edu/epc/authors/perloff/articles/dickinson.html.

a factor of diction but of structure or rhythm. As intriguing as this idea may be, it is easy to show that with this particular list of terms, Dickinson chose her "non-choices" very carefully. Semantically, etymologically, and phonically, the fourteen words resonate with one another and with other terms in the poem.[54] The list is also notable for what it does not include. As a substitute for "thrilling," Dickinson might have offered the most obvious synonym for "warbling," "trilling," thereby preserving both the semantics of the sentence and the insistence of Ts and Ls: *Had but the Tale a trilling Teller*. Instead, "trilling" haunts this line of verse and the variant list as a term that did not quite make the cut. Like tropic, trill is etymologically related to the verb "to turn," and turning is one of the defining predicates of Orpheus. Rapidly alternating between two notes and two sounds, the poem is an Orphic trilling/warbling of language.

We should not assume that these additional terms irremediably compromise the grammar of the sentence they supplement. If the variant list constitutes a nonsentential axis of the poem, its members are all adjectives with the capacity to modify the noun "Teller" if, and only if, they are placed in front of it. Of course, when every word in a poem about Orpheus and the Bible comes under suspicion of being the tip of a variant list iceberg, even these hallowed figures may be reduced to the status of *a* poet and *a* book. This points to a difficulty inherent in the very notion of perfecting one's diction. If a word is to manifest itself as exactly the right one, it must seem essential and irreplaceable, as if it could not have yielded its spot to any alternative without deleterious consequences for the entire composition. The problem is that such a word must also appear to be the product of a genuine choice—the "right" choice—and hence there must be some sense in which another word could hypothetically have been selected in its stead. Only insofar as there is evidence of the possibility for error can the success of each word choice come into full relief.

With typically understated irony, Dickinson shows us what this intersection of necessity and contingency involves by including "warbling" not once but

54. *Typic* suggests this text is preoccupied with typological exegesis, which is not infrequently a topic in Dickinson's writing. *Warbling* comes from the Old High German *werbel*, "something which revolves," meaning that it is a synonym for the term in the variant list that directly precedes it: *tropic* (from the Greek *trópos*, "a turn"). As this list of words starts to turn back on itself instead of marching along from one item to the next, it invites us to look to the figure who famously turned around just a little too soon, the Orpheus of metrical line 15 of the poem. Like Odysseus, the legendary poet got the better of those other great singers, the Sirens, but unlike Odysseus (Homer's "trope master"), Orpheus couldn't always rein in his tropic impulses when necessary. Presented as a warbler, Orpheus both celebrates poetry and warns of its dangers.

twice in her variant list for "thrilling." This may simply be an indication of the importance of this particular word, which after all was the term that appeared in the later drafts of the poem, unaccompanied by variants. Alternatively, it may be symptomatic of the utter indifference of each term to the others in the variant list, as if Dickinson, perhaps echoing Whitman's interminable ellipses, could just as well have written one word fourteen times over with no real consequence. Pushing this logic a step further, one might ask whether the second instance of "warbling" in the list is a variant on the first. Like Orpheus, who must not turn around as he leads Eurydice out of the Underworld, we must decide as we proceed through the list whether the manifestation of a second "warbling" forces us to turn back to the previous one in order to see if it was in fact identical to the new word with which we are now confronted.

With startling succinctness, "warbling / warbling" distills the potentially paralyzing feature of enjambment down to its essence. Instead of scanning backward and forward in order to evaluate the dialectical relationships between the parts of a sentence, we find ourselves stuck between two "lines" of a list, between "warbling" and "warbling," with no sense of whether we are progressing or regressing as we flit from one word to the other while it gradually dawns on us that now it is we who are warbling or wavering.

Perhaps it is not surprising that we have become embroiled in such a list, given that the heart of the poem it supplements is also a list, a six-line string of names and epithets, the last line of which is reintegrated into a standard sentence form by becoming the object of the subject-verb construction in metrical line 10 ("others must resist sin"). With grammar and predication put aside, the substantives—David the Troubadour, Satan the Brigadier, even implicitly God the Father—appear at least temporarily to be set free of the expectation that they should be parts of a sentential structure; their status as signifiers is significant enough.[55] At the same time, "warbling," a participial adjective, "is derived from a verb, not a noun, which is why it can be used to describe the verbal activity of the entire poem. Like the other term in the variant list that begins with *w*, "winning," the preeminence of "warbling" does not hint at a discourse in which proper nouns enjoy an authority independent of their status as parts of sentences. Predication remains the dominant form of signification, although in

55. In this parody of the Adamic scene of naming, Dickinson's curious list foregrounds the paradigmatic status of the figures it names with the definite article—*the* Homestead, *the* Brigadier—while implying that they may nonetheless be mere examples of larger categories, i.e., Eden is one homestead among others, Satan is the book's token brigadier, David its token troubadour, and so on.

the form of participles, as in Whitman's poems, rather than as finite verbs that could become the roots of independent clauses.

In "The Bible is an antique Volume," the integrity of the sentence is challenged by momentarily liberating words from the demand that they occupy a place within a syntagm. In other Dickinson texts, we encounter more overt forms of grammatical confusion, precarious juxtapositions of phrases and clauses that give rise to myriad ambiguities when we attempt to read them together as the parts of complete sentences. In some cases, the very assumption that a sentence ever can or should be "complete" seems to be the central concern.[56] In the following piece, Dickinson's uncharacteristic reliance on polysyllabic, non-Anglo-Saxon words introduces an air of abstraction that contrasts with the structural simplicity of the individual phrases. Against this backdrop, coordinating the different lines with one another proves to be a daunting task:

A nearness to Tremendousness -
An Agony procures -
Affliction ranges Boundlessness -
Vicinity to Laws

Contentment's quiet Suburb -
Affliction cannot stay
In Acres - It's Location
Is Illocality - (Fr. 824)

Cristanne Miller proposes that "the poem claims, in simple paraphrase, that agony brings us close to or procures boundlessness."[57] The term "simple" seems out of place here, for on any reading, this text is obscure. There is no obvious connection between its implied "speaker" and its content, and no particular experience or phenomenon is introduced to illustrate its claims. Miller's effort to articulate the gist of the two stanzas looks even more daring when we realize how difficult it is to decide whether the poem's phrases and clauses can be connected with each other to produce statements that will complement, or at least not outright contradict, one another. In contrast to Whitman, where the proliferation of parallel elements does not lead to grammatical incoherence,

56. For a version of "unfinished" Dickinson, see David Porter, *Dickinson: The Modern Idiom* (Cambridge, MA: Harvard University Press, 1981), 134–35.

57. Cristanne Miller, *Emily Dickinson: A Poet's Grammar* (Cambridge, MA: Harvard University Press, 1987), 42.

here we are severely challenged in our attempts to identify the subject and object of verbs, to determine where individual "sentences" begin and end, and to decide what is and is not an appositive. Rarely is the paradox inherent to the hermeneutic circle so glaringly in evidence: to understand the parts we have to have an account of the whole, but to have an account of the whole, we must understand the relationships between the parts.

Miller's summary that "agony brings us close to or procures boundlessness" is sound if one understands the poem to say: "Agony effects transcendence; affliction roams without restraint. Affliction cannot stay in a particular location; its location is illocality." What this gloss does not account for are the fourth line of the first stanza and the first line of the second one: "Vicinity to Laws // Contentment's quiet Suburb -".[58] Taken individually, these two noun phrases can certainly be grouped with or pitted against other elements in the poem. "Contentment" stands in opposition to "Agony" and "Affliction"; "Vicinity" lines up with "Suburb" and contrasts with "Illocality," but confusingly, it also recalls the "nearness" in "A nearness to Tremendousness." In any case, identifying these various semantic relationships does not help us coordinate "Vicinity to Laws" and "Contentment's quiet Suburb" with the other six lines. If one posits that the stanzas delimit "sentences," then "Vicinity to Laws" may modify "Boundlessness" for the simple reason that it follows the word, although the dash between them—not to mention their divergent meanings—potentially speaks against this. Ignoring the stanza divide, one can treat "Contentment's quiet Suburb" as an appositive for "Vicinity to Laws," which may seem plausible semantically, but now the two phrases are syntactically unrelated to what precedes or follows them in an extremely short poem. If one decouples the two outlier lines and tries to integrate them individually into larger clauses, multiple possibilities emerge for constructing sentences that include them, yet many of the resulting statements overtly conflict with what appears to be the poem's main claim about the transcendent effects of agony.[59]

"Vicinity to Laws" and "Contentment's quiet Suburb" are so difficult to incorporate into clauses in a way that would allow for a consistent interpretation of the poem that one is tempted to read them as a sort of aside, a

58. For some reflections on these lines of "A Nearness to Tremendousness," see Sharon Leiter, *Critical Companion to Emily Dickinson: A Literary Reference to Her Life and Work* (New York: Infobase Publishing, 2007), 39–40.

59. Dorothy Huff Oberhaus argues that these eight lines constitute two distinct texts that have to be disentangled from one another. See Dorothy Huff Oberhaus, *Emily Dickinson's Fascicles: Method and Meaning* (University Park: Pennsylvania State University Press, 1995), 98–108.

conclusion whose peculiarity is heightened by the fact that the two phrases are separated by a stanza break. Perhaps because these vexing lines are at the center of the text and yet somehow not a part of it, more than one critic has observed that "the poem seems to be *about* nearness, how words and phrases assume meaning by their contiguity to other words."[60] From this perspective, this short piece exposes our reliance on rarely articulated but absolutely fundamental ideas about what the proximity of one word, phrase, or clause to another "means," especially when we try to reconcile the hierarchy of sentence grammar with the linear unfolding of the terms of a text, and in this case a text divided into lines.

The poem stages this problem of nearness from the outset, the first line proving to be the object rather than the subject of the verb "procures" in the second line, although on a first scan one might assume that the initial noun phrase was the subject of the sentence and conclude that the poem's inaugural claim was that a nearness to tremendousness is agonizing rather than the other way around. As with the first instance of the word "read" in Dickinson's death-sentence poem, we finish evaluating the grammar of the first line only once we are well past it. Indeed, the process may not be complete until we have reached the second stanza and seen that "Affliction" appears twice as the subject of a sentence, retrospectively confirming that its synonym "Agony" is a subject, as well. Nevertheless, the noun phrase that is the first line of the first stanza never entirely loses some claim to being a subject rather than a direct object. In this fashion, the poem reveals that versification can both simplify and complicate the task of parsing a sentence. Lineation may facilitate—misleading—connections between some phrases while emphasizing the isolation of others. Perhaps most confounding is the suggestion that inferences based on the fact that one sentence element is next to or follows another are not necessarily any more reliable than anything else.

Cameron proposes that "Dickinson's poetry dramatizes the impossibility of wholeness understood as boundedness. It does so in its almost incomprehensible adherence to piecemeal utterance, in the refusal of the syntax to endorse resolutions marked by conventional grammatical pauses, connections or punctuated units of sense."[61] On this basis, she concludes that "Dickinson's

60. Christopher E. G. Benfey, *Emily Dickinson and the Problem of Others* (Amherst: University of Massachusetts Press, 1984), 74. See also Sharon Cameron, *Lyric Time: Dickinson and the Limits of Genre* (Baltimore: Johns Hopkins University Press, 1979), 161.

61. Cameron, *Choosing Not Choosing*, 182.

language is language that is broken."[62] One might respond that Cameron underestimates the power of these so-called "piecemeal utterances," which are highly functional phrases and clauses. The poems do betray an unmistakable sense of their constructed quality—they are overtly made up of parts—but if anything each part does too much rather than too little. There is certainly no shortage of eloquence or potential profundity in the text we have been examining. Propositions such as "A nearness to tremendousness an agony procures" or "Affliction's location is illocality" could easily stand alone as aphorisms.

It would be equally plausible, however, to maintain that Dickinson's poems reveal Cameron to be overly optimistic in her assumption that syntax ever "endorses resolutions" in the straightforward sense she implies, since the relationships between the parts of a sentence are always more fragile than this would allow. Word to word, phrase to phrase, or clause to clause, the various elements of a grammatical construction never sum like terms in an arithmetic problem. An irreducible element of the provisional, the unstated, or the implied will invariably under- or overshoot any synthesis for which a given formulation may aim. "A Nearness to Tremendousness" depicts these tensions graphically. At one moment, it may appear that we can summarize it in a simple sentence, as Miller tries to do; the next, we may feel that we are looking at eight distinct lines whose so-called "connections" are more a factor of their haphazard juxtaposition with one another on the page than anything else. The poem's own name for this verbal randomness bordering on chaos is "illocation," which suggests "illocution," presumably the opposite of "elocution." In this discourse of articulation and disarticulation, the boundaries we draw in an effort to grammatize the strings of words will never prove sufficient. In the manuscript version of the poem, the third metrical line is written: "Affliction ranges Bound - / lessness -", as if to underscore that any act of delimitation is as much a subtraction as an addition.[63] Unable to demonstrate that any given phrase or clause is in its proper location, the reader is left unsure whether this poem is best treated as if it were composed of sentences or of something else.

In "A Nearness to Tremendousness," problems arise because the phrases are alternately too labile or too static, either aligning themselves with one another too readily or not having anything to do with each other at all. In other texts, there is a tendency for parts of the different lines to fuse with one another across the line breaks, working against both the versification and the sentence

62. Cameron, *Choosing Not Choosing*, 182–83.

63. For a facsimile of the manuscript page, see Franklin, *The Manuscript Books of Emily Dickinson*, vol. 2, 980.

grammar and further complicating our sense of what it means that one group of words is near to or follows another. This poem is presented to show the manuscript lineation, which introduces breaks in the first and third metrical lines:

Except the Heaven had come
so near -
So seemed to choose My Door -
The Distance would not
haunt me so -
I had not hoped - before -

But just to hear the Grace depart -
I never thought to see -
Afflicts me with a Double loss -
'Tis lost - and lost to me - [64]

Thematically the two stanzas of this poem present a simple back-and-forth motion as "the Heaven" draws near and departs. Far from enigmatic, the text is practically pedantic in its efforts to explain what it means, with the fourth line of the first stanza clarifying the first three lines, and the last line fleshing out the phrase "Double loss." The result is a lucid account of a profound experience, a brush with the godhead.

Formally, the text is balanced, with the lines and sentences appearing to work in perfect tandem. The segmenting of the phrases and clauses is not disruptive, and there are no obvious points at which the reader makes an assumption about the grammar only to have it unravel shortly thereafter. The relationships between the metrical lines are supplemented by no punctuation save for the dashes that appear at the end of each. While in some poems these marks heighten the sense that the different pieces of the text simply do not cohere in the ways we customarily expect the elements of a sentence to do, here they feel curiously superfluous.[65] If we read the eight metrical lines of the poem

64. For a facsimile of the manuscript page, see Franklin, *The Manuscript Books of Emily Dickinson*, vol. 2, 789. Franklin's version of this poem (Fr. 702) is identical to what is presented here save for the absence of the breaks in metrical lines one and three.

65. Like Dickinson's tendency to capitalize words for emphasis, dashes were not uncommon punctuation marks in the mid-nineteenth century, although she uses them with unusual frequency. The 1844 edition of Webster's *An American Dictionary of the English Language*,

as distinct rhythmic structures partially organized by a rhyme scheme—as true verse, as it were, rather than as sentences split up into verses—then these two stanzas could arguably get by without any punctuation whatsoever.

The only overt complexity in this otherwise stable set-up is the element of indirection present in the poem's first word, "Except," which opens things with a somewhat contorted counterfactual logic ("Were it not for this fact, this would not be the case"). This negative moment informs the entire text, since what is ultimately lost is both proximity to the divine and the absence of any expectation of enjoying such proximity. The speaker ends by saying that she has lost the state of not hoping for something, that she has lost her lack of hope. An expectation that one never had is thus created in being destroyed.

---

which Dickinson had in her personal library, offers the following definition: "dash (n.) A mark or line in writing or printing, noting a break or stop in the sentence; as in Virgil, quos ego—: or a pause; or the division of the sentence." Noah Webster, *An American Dictionary of the English Language*, 2 vols. (Amherst, MA: J. S. & C. Adams Brothers, 1844). A grammar book that Dickinson probably used in school explains that "the dash is used where a sentence is left unfinished; where there is a sudden turn, or an abrupt transition; and where a significant pause is required." William Harvey Wells, *A Grammar of the English Language for the Use of Schools* (New York: Mark H. Newman, 1846), 194.

Critics have made so many different claims for Dickinson's dashes that one wonders what they cannot do. The dashes are said to bind or divide; to invite prospective glances at future lines or prompt retrospective glances at those that have just been read; to speed the rhythm up or slow it down; to lengthen pauses or shorten them; to make the text more solemn or render it more playful. Ellen Louise Hart maintains that the "dashes serve multiple, sometimes oppositional purposes, as critics have shown: making syntactic connections, letting meaning resonate, allowing sound to echo, introducing silence acting as a musical rest, or permitting a breath." Ellen Louise Hart, "Alliteration, Emphasis, and Spatial Prosody in Dickinson's Manuscript Letters," *Reading Emily Dickinson's Letters*, ed. Jane Donahue Eberwein and Cindy MacKenzie (Amherst: University of Massachusetts Press, 2009), 218. Scholars' accounts of the dashes are often quite colorful, as if each were striving to surpass the next with the vividness of his or her imagery. Martha Nell Smith writes that the dashes "sashay across the page" and "dance up or down" as "giddy punctuation." Martha Nell Smith, *Rowing in Eden: Rereading Emily Dickinson* (Austin: University of Texas Press, 1992), 10. In contrast, Beth Maclay Doriani describes the dashes as adding "slowness and solemnity" to the "homiletical rhetoric" of the "poetic prophet." Beth Maclay Doriani, *Emily Dickinson: Daughter of Prophecy* (Amherst: University of Massachusetts Press, 1996), 48. Focusing on a few specific poems, Roseanne Hoefel writes that the marks indicate "stuttering tenseness." Roseanne Hoefel, "Emily Dickinson Fleshing Out a New Word," *Emily Dickinson Journal* 1, no. 1 (1992): 57. Kamilla Denman notes parallels between the dashes, "stretching stitches of the tugging bodice," and "the erratic beat of the speaker's bursting heart." Kamilla Denman, "Emily Dickinson's Volcanic Punctuation," *Emily Dickinson Journal* 2, no. 1 (1993): 38, 39.

Rereading the first stanza with this complication in mind, we see that the emphasis is not on the immediacy of the here and now, but on the intractable opposition between the near and the distant, while in the second stanza the potential disjunction between hearing and seeing stands out as discordant rather than harmonizing. Apparently things do not cohere as solidly as one might have supposed. The poem is like "A Nearness to Tremendousness" after all, for its words linger uncomfortably close and yet not quite close enough to one another.

In the poem's first sentence, we are never far from the word "so," each of whose three iterations has a different meaning, as if the opening lines were a vocabulary exercise. This effect is mirrored at the end of the second stanza with the repetition of the words "loss" and "lost," both of which contain *s-o* in reverse. If this lexical connection appears fanciful, Dickinson writes in another contemporaneous poem about the curious negativity of "A loss or so," a formulation in which "or" at once makes "loss" vaguer and yet more precise while laying the groundwork for the word with which "so" will rhyme in that poem, "no."[66]

In a poem about something being unexpectedly nearby, it is striking that the first two instances of the word "so" are held apart yet brought together. If we follow the metrical lineation, they are separated by the word "near" along with the dash and line break: "so near - / So seemed. . . ."; on the manuscript page, they are even closer to one another, as the "so" in the "runover" of the first metrical line appears right above the "So" at the start of line two. Formally, the line break interrupts neither the phrasal structure nor the rhythm—to the contrary, it works smoothly with both. This is certainly not an instance of enjambment. Nonetheless, the repetition of the word "so" becomes an invitation to read against the sentence grammar and isolate the three-word sequence "so near so" as an independent statement. For the sentence structure to yield to such alternative syntacto-semantic pressures is by no means necessarily a recipe for chaos, although putting the status of "nearness" as an organizing principle in play may have some unexpected consequences. If nothing else, we may begin to suspect that the poem is also suggesting that words and phrases that do appear side by side within a line of verse are not necessarily more intimately connected with one another than those divided by breaks of any sort on the page: "So near! So?"

Several years earlier, Dickinson wrote a series of three poems in which she experimented with the signifying capacities of "so," and in each case, the word

66. Fr. 538.

was directly associated with figures of underdetermination and loss. One of the texts, only four lines long, reads:

> By such and such an offering
> To Mr So and So -
> The web of life is woven -
> So martyrs albums show! (Fr. 47)[67]

It was not until the end of the nineteenth century that "so and so" became commonly used as a term of dismissal. Just as "such and such" refers to an unspecified thing, here "so and so" refers to an unspecified person, someone whose identity for whatever reason does not need to be or will not be made explicit. Like Whitman's ellipses, these two phrases flaunt their laziness by defaulting on their obligation to refer or signify, and the resulting imprecision impacts every noun in the text. Depending on how one interprets the various motifs, "Mr So and So" may be God, a specific individual to whom the poem or the collection of which it is a part is dedicated, or a generic reader. If anything, the very notion of writing a poem to or for someone is parodied, as if to show how empty a gesture it is.

As underdetermined as "so and so" and "such and such" may be, they are merely a prelude to the pure emptiness of the third instance of the word "so" in the text ("So martyrs albums show!"), which is genuinely content-free, functioning only to point back to what has just been said. As an adverb and a conjunction, "so" is a versatile word that is eminently capable of facilitating all sorts of syntactic and semantic relationships, yet Dickinson's short poem seems to empty it of these powers. Returning to "Except the Heaven had come so near" with these dynamics in mind, we note that the word "so" appears three times before the first-person pronoun makes an entrance. When the "I" is explicitly articulated, it is in a sequence that comes into relief only when we once again read against the alignment of the grammar and lineation and group another trio of words that emerges at the end of the third and the beginning of the fourth line: "me, so, I."[68] The poetic subject, we might say, is inflected—or infected—by "so," perhaps even to the point of risking the loss of its own speci-

67. For a facsimile of the manuscript page, see Franklin, *The Manuscript Books of Emily Dickinson*, vol. 1, 24.

68. The word "so" is derived from the Proto-Indo-European third-person reflexive pronominal stem, the root of the modern German *sich* or the French *se*, meaning that this reads not "me, myself, I" but "me, herself, I."

ficity and becoming just another "Mr So and So."[69] Rudyard Kipling's "Just So Stories" got their name from having to be told in precisely the way that the author's daughter stipulated. In this "So Story," however, the poetic self receives at best a so-so welcome in her own poem even as she appears to be on the verge of becoming the leading spokeswoman for the word "so."[70]

In "The Bible is an antique Volume -" proper nouns threatened to demonstrate their independence of grammar, flaunting their capacity to signify in the absence of any structure of predication. As a word, "so" could not be more unlike divine names such as "God" or "Satan." Its significance necessarily depends on what it connects or modifies; absent a syntactic structure, it has no chance of being meaningful. In this poem, however, the word "so" does assert some degree of autonomy, not because it malfunctions in any given instance, but because its repetition across the space of three short lines serves to foreground the power of sequence, prompting us to disregard the line breaks and the divisions of phrases and clauses that should keep the "so" of "so near" and the "so" of "so seemed" apart.

In equally creative ways, Dickinson's and Whitman's texts break the sense of naturalness surrounding the linearity of sentences, foregrounding their inherently hierarchical structure. At the same time, they caution us that revealing sequence to be less than all-powerful is not tantamount to subordinating it to other dynamics. The model of language that emerges in their work is first and foremost defined not by a particular structure or form, but by tensions that no single syntactic or semantic paradigm can resolve. Both writers experiment with the leveling of grammatical hierarchies, or at least they attempt to allow verbal elements to coexist in parallel in unusual ways. Whitman's texts systematically isolate a dimension of the classical sentence and then exaggerate it, whether this means connecting impossibly many elements by juxtaposing them in sequence, allowing the brute repetition of words or phrasal structures to substitute for alignments of subjects and predicates, or introducing punctuation marks that take on a life of their own and potentially suspend or displace the verbal formations around them. Dickinson's poems present themselves as

69. We could go further and treat the second "so" in "Except the Heaven had come so near - / So seemed to choose My Door -" as a noun and thus as the subject of a sentence: "the heaven came so near that *so* seemed to choose my door." Only in being chosen by "so" is there a "me"—here a "my"—at all. On this reading, *so* usurps the ultimate chooser, God.

70. Anne-Lise François has argued that the poetic self in Dickinson exists in a "subdued" self-relation such that it is not imperative that any given experience prove meaningful or worthy of being related. See her *Open Secrets: The Literature of Uncounted Experience* (Stanford, CA: Stanford University Press, 2007), esp. 136–37.

schematic arrays of phrases and clauses that may or may not submit to the synthetic operations on which we rely when we suppose that a series of words can be read as a statement, question, wish, or command. In pitting the authority of grammar against other discursive dimensions, whether diction or versification, her texts reveal an instability at the heart of the sentence form that may be both a source of its power and a clear limit to it.

The results of Dickinson and Whitman's experiments are less agrammatical formations than texts that are parasitic of normal linguistic structures. The conventional paradigms of syntax and semantics never entirely recede into the background and are always on the verge of reasserting themselves. Nonetheless, both poets afford us a glimpse of a language in which there is nothing self-evident about the sentence, meaning that it is no longer the default norm from which other patterns will deviate and that we can no longer read with the sole or even principal goal of identifying its logics in action.

CHAPTER 3

Sentences Terminable and Interminable

To mistake the rhythm of a sentence is to mistake the very meaning of the sentence.

FRIEDRICH NIETZSCHE

But what philosophy and the philosopher find difficult is stopping.

SØREN KIERKEGAARD

While our most accomplished authors rarely speak of having perfected an essay, poem, or short story, even the inexperienced wordsmith occasionally has the sense, if only briefly, of having gotten a sentence just right. For the most part, however, writing is a mixture of anticipation and disappointment, since a composition rarely feels worthy of the impulses that brought it into being. No matter how many times one tells oneself that one's nascent thoughts were probably not the proto-wonders one fancies them to have been, the conviction that one is not doing justice to one's original ideas proves impossible to escape. This sense of failure can manifest itself at the level of individual sentences—Why does this proposition not sound as profound as it did in my head?—or with the relationships between sentences, which somehow never follow from or build upon one another as smoothly or forcefully as one hoped.

As much as we try to be upbeat about our sentences, we tend to look upon them with disquiet, even trepidation. Writing presents boundless possibilities—one genuinely has the opportunity to do an unlimited number of things with words—and yet with this freedom comes self-doubt, as we are haunted by the awareness that however we shape a particular statement, there are countless other, possibly superior forms it might have taken. We are also nagged by the suspicion that if our writing is probably not as bad as we fear, we are nonetheless incapable of making a sober judgment about it. Even when optimism prevails, it is all too easy to second-guess oneself. One of the basic maxims of writing guides is that "most of us think our writing is clearer than it really is.

We know what we mean, so we see it in what we write."[1] The moment we start feeling good about our text may be precisely when we need to be most skeptical about it.

In most circumstances, writers are blessed with the opportunity to revise. The sense of disappointment one may feel upon assessing a new composition is ameliorated by the chance to reword, excise, or expand, although there is no guarantee of making things better rather than worse. The freedom to tinker with one's sentences also raises the vexing question of how to know when to stop.[2] One is forever tempted by the prospect that just a little more work will improve things, yet perfection remains maddeningly elusive. In the end, one does not finish a given sentence so much as one tries to make peace with its imperfections and move on. We might suppose that we can be freed from this particular brand of self-torture by a time limit imposed from without, but many authors take it for granted that their work will still be in draft form long after its publication. In the most extreme cases, a sentence is something with which one is never done, an abiding companion that can be tweaked to the end of one's days.

In the midst of the many self-recriminations writing inspires, it is worth asking whether our exasperating relationship with our sentences is less a product of our relative strengths and weaknesses as writers than a symptom of the degree to which our understanding of composition is informed by mutually incompatible paradigms. On the one hand, we continue to display an uneasy loyalty to the notion of genius that assumed its modern form with Kant and the Romantics. Distinguished by inspiration, intoxication, and mania rather than by systematic, self-regulating labor, the spontaneity of the imagination is regarded as a marvelous, albeit enigmatic power that ensures that there will always be a steady stream of exciting innovations to enjoy. On the other hand, we are equally convinced of the importance of method, believing that writers, whatever their aims, must construct their sentences like artisans or engineers, respecting established principles of formalization and employing compositional tactics whose practical virtues have a solid track record. In these terms,

1. Michael Harvey, *The Nuts and Bolts of College Writing* (Indianapolis: Hackett Publishing, 2003), 10.

2. The sense that writing is a process with no obvious terminus is potentially augmented when working with a computer, which, as Jacques Derrida has observed, makes further correction "so quick and easy, [that] one is led to believe that revision could go on indefinitely." Jacques Derrida, "Word Processing: An Interview with Jacques Derrida," *Oxford Literary Review* 21, nos. 1–2 (1999): 8.

good sentences are not pennies from heaven, but products of sustained effort, which means planning, calculation, and skilled execution.

To write as a genius is to pursue a praxis that can at best be only partially understood, and what we create may not be worthy of serious consideration unless it stands over and against us as mysterious, even threatening, in its otherness. In contrast, to write as a verbal craftsman is to imagine that one is in control of one's language, with the luxury of reflecting on the felicity of every clause, phrase, or word as one patiently tries out different options until everything is just right. Unlike the genius, the methodical, disciplined writer can explain what she is attempting to do and offer educated guesses as to why a particular compositional gambit is or is not succeeding. Since she is not at the mercy of the muse's caprice, she is also spared the inconvenience of having to wait for inspiration to strike.

It is easy enough to cite lines from the Romantic poets in which they seem to embrace some notion of creativity as the spontaneous outpouring of the imagination, but such gestures are more often than not complicated invocations, if not ironizations, of an ideal whose practical implications will be murky at best. Even in the heyday of the cult of genius, with seventeenth- and eighteenth-century doctrines of method in full retreat, authors expressed trepidation about the prospect of relying entirely on inspiration rather than calculation. Nowhere is this clearer than in Samuel Taylor Coleridge's preface to his fragmentary poem "Kubla Khan," where he purports to relate the circumstances surrounding this famously unfinished composition. These introductory prose remarks are arguably better known than the verses that follow, and they are often treated by editors as part of the text proper and numbered as if they were the opening lines.

Writing about himself in the third person, Coleridge explains that this incomplete work is being published at the request of an unnamed author of renown (Byron), although it is a "psychological curiosity" rather that something with "*poetic* merits."[3] The psychological phenomenon in question is dreams, or more specifically the relationship between the experience of dreaming and the experience of trying to reconstruct the details of that experience when one wakes up, which in this case means remembering the lines of verse we claim to have penned in our sleep. Coleridge relates that he dozed off in his chair "at the moment he was reading the following sentence, or words of the same substance, in Purchas's *Pilgrimage*: 'Here the Khan Kubla commanded a palace

3. Samuel Taylor Coleridge, "Kubla Khan," *Major British Poets of the Romantic Period*, ed. William Heath (New York: Macmillan, 1973), 474.

to be built, and a stately garden thereunto. And thus ten miles of fertile ground were inclosed with a wall.' "[4] In the ensuing hours of unconscious activity—or opium reverie, as Coleridge elsewhere suggests—he maintains that he wrote "from two to three hundred lines; if that indeed can be called composition in which all the images rose up before him as things, with a parallel production of the correspondent expressions, without any sensation or consciousness of effort."[5] Coleridge is adamant that it should have been possible to preserve this dream text for posterity in its entirety, insisting that when he awoke he had "a distinct recollection of the whole."[6] As he began to put pen to paper, however, he was interrupted by a visitor, and when he returned to his desk, almost everything had faded from memory, forcing his readers to content themselves with the fifty-four lines that exist today.

In the process of debunking the empirical veracity of virtually every detail of this story, scholars have tended to overlook its multiple ironies. Coleridge's (tall) tale is predicated on the notion that the sentences that sparked his poetic vision were so compelling that they put him to sleep, suggesting that the line between the inspirational and the stupefying is razor thin. That his story about "Kubla Khan" may have a more complex relationship to its source material than one might initially suppose is further evident from his very need to begin with a "quotation" whose precision is immediately disavowed (and rightly so, it turns out, since Coleridge does not come even close to reproducing the sentence from Purchas's text accurately). Although the poet is apparently convinced that he could have remembered hundreds of lines of his "composition," he is unable to reconstruct two short clauses from the history book he was just perusing, and he cannot even be bothered to look them up afterward, as if the details were unimportant, despite the fact that this narrative is supposedly all about the glorious specificity of what he was attempting to get down on the page.

These tensions suggest that Coleridge's preface is less an account of being in the fickle grips of the muse than a description of the anticipation and excitement that comes with the all-too-familiar feeling that for once one's ideas are effortlessly taking written shape, only to have the most genial turn of phrase or perfectly modulated line become utterly ordinary the moment it is set down on the page, or in this case when one wakes up. As Freud said of our ability to recount our own dreams, revision of the "primary" version has always already begun even as we are in the midst of the oneiric experience. Every text is a

4. Coleridge, "Kubla Khan," 474.
5. Coleridge, "Kubla Khan," 474.
6. Coleridge, "Kubla Khan," 474.

"Kubla Khan," haunted by the idea of a primal incarnation that proves forever irretrievable, a collection of lines we are sure we "wrote" even as we acknowledge that "writing" may not be the correct verb. Fated to be interrupted by forces from the external world that will confound our efforts to turn our fantasy composition into reality, we are condemned to keep trying to pick up the pieces and like Coleridge, himself an inveterate reviser of his own texts, to continue tinkering with our sentences in an attempt to revive their lost splendor.

Throughout the nineteenth century, writers were preoccupied with the question of what it means to be done with a sentence, assuming this is ever possible. To a large extent, this involved trying to reconcile discordant models of composition or dispensing with one or more of them altogether. One way of dispelling the oppressive, even paralyzing fantasy of a primal draft that can never be recovered is to abandon the notion that our compositions begin as inchoate proto-thoughts or visions that gradually give rise to complete sentences and instead pursue a process in which one sets out with a clearly defined goal for one's text and then takes deliberate steps to craft it in order to realize that end.

Such a reembrace of method emerges, albeit in idiosyncratic form, in the work of Edgar Allan Poe. In "The Philosophy of Composition," Poe outlines a technical procedure in which inspiration and accident are to be entirely excluded from the creative process. Instead, the author is to begin by deciding what impact she wants her piece to have on its reader and then work backward, shaping each individual part to ensure that the language serves in "the construction of the [intended] effect."[7] From the text's length, theme, and motifs to the repetition of specific vowels or consonants, every detail will come into play in an engineering of affect that is to have the rigor of a mathematical calculus. With every vestige of the inscrutable banished, there can no longer be any sense of disappointment that one's sentences are not living up to the chimerical proto- or prelinguistic thoughts and visions they were supposed to capture. In fact, what one's story or essay "represents" will be of secondary or tertiary importance, since content, traditionally understood, is relevant only insofar as it serves the larger goal of eliciting the desired response in the reader.

Poe initially sets out his method in general terms, invoking a novel by William Godwin as an example of why a writer should know precisely how the plot concludes before beginning to write anything down, in order to be able to tailor every section to culminate in the predetermined conclusion. However,

7. Edgar Allan Poe, "The Philosophy of Composition," *Essays and Reviews* (New York: Literary Classics of the United States Inc., 1984), 14.

because a work's "unity of effect or impression" is partly dependent on the unity of the reading experience—Poe maintains that the piece has to be capable of being consumed comfortably in a single sitting—a poem is the ideal forum for the display of writerly prowess, followed closely by the short story.[8] The bulk of Poe's essay sees him endeavoring to demonstrate the finer points of his doctrine by explaining how he wrote "The Raven" in the manner he prescribes, refining the diction, tone, and structure in order to instill in his reader the feeling of beauty, the "excitement, or pleasurable elevation, of the soul" to be realized through a presentation of the melancholia experienced by the first-person speaker as he reflects on the death of his beloved.[9]

The pièce de résistance of this verbal construction is the infamous refrain "nevermore," which is repeatedly voiced by the raven in the speaker's chamber until it gradually becomes interwoven with his own remarks, as if the human being and his avian visitor were engaged in a genuinely dialogical exchange. Poe maintains that in order for this word to do the work being asked of it and produce melancholia in the reader, it must be repeated in exactly the same way each time, monotonously, like a mechanical death knell. Any indication that the entity enunciating the "nevermore" is altering its articulations in response to the remarks of the poet interlocutor risks sentimentalizing the scene and blunting the sense of finitude and irrecoverable loss being imparted. To avoid the appearance of some "exercise of reason on the part of the creature repeating the word," an animal was chosen to voice these syllables, although it could just as well have been an automaton, as in an E. T. A. Hoffmann story; today the personal assistant on a cell phone could also do the job nicely.[10]

From the time of the essay's publication, Poe's readers have searched for evidence that his argument is all a big joke. Surely this cannot really be how he wrote his texts, much less a guide for how we should write ours. A glance at Poe's oeuvre does not suggest that this matter can easily be resolved. While his writings are notoriously preoccupied by grave, even grisly topics such as the fear of losing one's sanity or being buried alive, an unmistakable element of play coexists alongside these weighty concerns. As insistent as the uncertainty and terror may be, such elements of pathos often feel like tokens in a game that have been deployed in calculated ways, exactly as "The Philosophy of Composition"

8. Poe, "Nathaniel Hawthorne," *Essays and Reviews*, 571. Poe offers Hawthorne as an example of a writer who has excelled at his craft because he respected the dictates of "The Philosophy of Composition" avant la lettre.

9. Poe, "The Philosophy of Composition," 18, 16.

10. Poe, "The Philosophy of Composition," 18.

prescribes. This is most evident in the verse texts. Thanks to their light meters and rhymes, coupled by an at times almost parodic indulgence in repetition, the somber subjects tend to be presented in a lively tone that is forever on the verge of tipping over into the frivolous, as if these were exercises in treating particular themes rather than meditations on serious issues.

Things become even more complicated in Poe's stories, which are the centerpiece of his legacy. The originality of these narratives seems so obvious that one is reluctant to characterize them as the product of a calculus, as if we could simply run a Poe algorithm and generate a few more. Surely the author celebrated as the father of modern detective and horror fiction has to be lauded for his innovations, even if he does maintain in "The Philosophy of Composition" that creativity is a means to an end rather than an end in itself. Perhaps the truth is that Poe did follow his own method, but only to a degree. Given the extent to which the distinctive power of many of his stories hinges on their shocking and in most cases unpredictable final scenes, it is quite plausible to imagine that they were constructed in reverse, working backward from the punchline so that every detail helps build toward a conclusion that retrospectively gives the preceding events their full significance. The sense that these texts were the product of painstakingly systematic design is heightened by their self-reflexivity, as Poe's narrators routinely comment on the dilemmas they face in trying to relate their tales, to the point that the very distinction between Poe's fiction and his essays threatens to break down. Maybe, as some readers have suspected all along, "The Philosophy of Composition" is the scary story, while "The Tell-Tale Heart" and "The Fall of the House of Usher" are the critical commentaries.

If "The Philosophy of Composition" was composed according to the doctrine it preaches, it may have been with the specific intention of frustrating its audience with the implausibility of its proposals.[11] As readily as we acknowledge the limits, if not the inherent mystification, of the Romantic conception

11. While Poe inveighs against the mystifications of intuition and inspiration, his argument is by no means free of conceptual baggage. No less than Kant, he arrives at his conclusions on the basis of far-reaching claims about the workings of the human mind. In the course of replacing the authority of genius with a compositional calculus, he implicitly takes a position on a number of the most hotly debated topics of nineteenth-century philosophy, including the common nature of aesthetic experience, the relationship between affect and interest, and beauty's status as "the most intense, the most elevating, and the most pure" of pleasures, which supposedly makes it such a reliable resource for the writer who wants to be sure that solid cause-and-effect relationships ground her text's ability to impact the reader as intended ("The Philosophy of Composition," 18).

of genius, we are likely to be uncomfortable embracing a compositional methodology that posits such a profound degree of control over the function and reception of a piece of writing. Almost all conceptions of literature accord some element of spontaneity or contingency, however minimal, to a text's language or to the processes whereby it is read. Surely something unforeseeable or unpredictable that will escape Poe's calculations is at work in every poem or story, something about which it makes no more sense to maintain that the author designed it than to say that the muse delivered it fully formed. In this regard, even the vaunted "nevermore" may not be manageable in the way Poe outlines. While he ultimately claims that it instills melancholia in the reader in virtue of its status as a collection of particular sounds rather than as a signifier linked to one or more signifieds, the semantic features of the word are irrepressible, and the utterance is forever on the verge of tipping over into "more never," which in "The Raven," in which there is always another "never" to come, is ironically never "never" enough.

Before concluding that Poe is too optimistic about the prospects of making language do his bidding, we should ask ourselves whether we are any less confident on this score. Although Poe avers that authors want their readers to believe that their texts came to them via ecstatic intuition, very few writers would deny that there is a conscious, calculated, deliberate aspect to their craft, and there are relatively few contexts in which it is a slur to refer to someone as a "wordsmith." Even Poe's claim that much-celebrated "originality" is merely a tool for getting people interested in one's texts so that they can work their magic is far from blasphemous in contemporary culture, where it is widely accepted that whatever zany exploits allow one to draw the reader in are fair game given how many blurbs and taglines are constantly competing for our attention.

When it comes to designing individual sentences, Poe's assumptions about the possibility of controlling words dovetail closely with guidelines with which we are all familiar. Stanley Fish gives no indication that he is saying something ambitious, much less controversial, when he declares: "People write or speak sentences in order to produce an effect, and the success of a sentence is measured by the degree to which the desired effect has been achieved."[12] Many style manuals likewise follow Poe in insisting that an author should proceed by considering the goal of a sentence and fashioning it accordingly. Such compositional prescriptions are usually buttressed by explications of sample sentences,

12. Stanley Fish, *How to Write a Sentence: And How to Read One* (New York: HarperCollins, 2011), 37.

and from the casual to the highly technical, these demonstrations follow the lead of "The Philosophy of Composition" in relying on a host of assumptions about cognition, perception, and memory in predicting how given features of form and content will affect a hypothetical reader or listener.

Some go further and argue that our alleged ability to make individual sentences do our bidding has far-reaching consequences for our capacity to make much longer sections of text function in the ways we want. Fish proposes that if we understand writing well as a process of articulating logical relationships with predicative statements, it follows that someone who can produce a clear, precise sentence "can, by extrapolation and expansion, write anything: a paragraph, an argument, an essay, a treatise, a novel."[13] We may balk at the vagueness of "by extrapolation and expansion." It is hard to see how paragraphs and chapters, let alone plots or arguments, are simply expanded versions of individual grammatical structures. If nothing else, the limitations that the rules of syntax impose on a writer's choices in ordering the elements of a sentence have no analog on a larger scale, where there is seemingly a much broader array of options. Still, Fish might rejoin that the new rhetorical and stylistic considerations that impose themselves once we move beyond the level of sentence grammar do not fundamentally alter the need for a clarity and precision that only a facility with subject-predicate forms can facilitate. Like countless authors of style manuals before him, he believes that the organizational principles of the sentence are an important and possibly even essential resource for successfully giving shape to entire texts.

One may nonetheless insist that the ability to fine-tune the effects of an individual sentence is a necessary but hardly sufficient condition for writing essays or stories in the way Poe envisions. While many famous authors are renowned for their intricate syntax and the rhythms of their prose, there are others whose novels have delighted tens of millions of readers with their plots and characters despite the fact that their individual sentences rarely inspire emulation, except when they are parodied. As Adam Gopnik observes of binging on Philip K. Dick novels, "At the end of a Dick marathon, you end up admiring every one of his conceits and not a single one of his sentences."[14] Moreover, if the functional unit of composition is the paragraph or the chapter rather than the sentence, a writer who fusses too much over individual grammatical structures is at risk of neglecting the broader patterns of her composition. In the Romantic era,

13. Fish, *How to Write a Sentence,* 8.

14. Adam Gopnik, "Blows against the Empire: The Return of Philip K. Dick," *New Yorker*, August 20, 2007, https://www.newyorker.com/magazine/2007/08/20/blows-against-the-empire.

Andrew Elfenbein argues, "good sentences made bad novels."[15] In this vein, the literary and art critic Herbert Read characterizes Ralph Waldo Emerson as "an example of an author who was so concerned with the aphoristic quality of his sentences that he forgot the rhythmical life of his paragraphs."[16] Read likewise mentions Conrad as someone not writing in his native language who therefore worked diligently, and by and large with extraordinary success, to form fantastic sentences, but in the process neglected the pace and structure of his paragraphs. Peter Elbow, the former director of the writing programs at the University of Massachusetts–Amherst and Stony Brook University, acknowledges that composition teachers and style manuals inevitably focus on sentences because they are the "basic building blocks of energy in words," but he quickly cautions, "I ruin my writing experience and drive students crazy if I am too preoccupied with sentences alone. For we can read long passages of well-energized sentences and still experience a serious lack of organization. Whole texts need larger global pieces of energy."[17]

This basic question of how the construction of successful sentences relates to the construction of successful paragraphs, chapters, or books is a nagging concern for writing pedagogy at all levels of instruction. In the still canonical *The Elements of Style*, Edmund Strunk and E. B. White expend considerable effort explaining how to produce good sentences, only to summarily declare, with virtually no clarification, that the paragraph is the real "unit" of composition.[18] Attempts to further detail the internal logics of the paragraph are often contradictory. At one moment, it is characterized as the presentation of a single thought whose formal boundaries should create a break "between one idea and the next," that is, as virtually indistinguishable from the sentence; at the next, it is presented as a multi-step argument, possibly a microcosm of or model for the text in which it appears.[19] In *The Sense of*

15. Andrew Elfenbein, *Romanticism and the Rise of English* (Stanford, CA: Stanford University Press, 2009), 158.

16. Herbert Read, *English Prose Style* (London: G. Bell & Sons, 1928), 53. According to Read, "rhythm . . . is an affair of the paragraph, and rhythmically the sentence is subordinate to the paragraph" (51).

17. Peter Elbow, "The Music of Form: Rethinking Organization in Writing," *CCCC* 57 (2006): 627.

18. William Strunk Jr. and E. B. White, *The Elements of Style*, 4th edition (New York: Pearson, 2000), 15.

19. Andrew P. Johnson, *A Short Guide to Academic Writing* (New York: University Press of America, 2003), 55. On the internally conflicted nature of paragraph theory, see Elfenbein, *Romanticism*, 212–13. In his 1977 *The New Sentence*, Ron Silliman describes a mode of writing

Style, the linguist Steven Pinker argues that the detailed instructions on how to build a paragraph found in many writing manuals are "misguided, because there is no such thing as a paragraph," which is to say that there is "no unit of discourse that consistently corresponds to a block of text delimited by a blank line or an indentation."[20] Pinker acknowledges the existence as well as the importance of paragraph *breaks*, but he suggests that they are appropriate for all sorts of different kinds of divisions within blocks of prose and that offering a formal account of the paragraph as such, as if it were governed by a set of rules that even remotely approximated the precision of the rules of syntax, is folly.

In discussing "The Raven," Poe argues that the entire text is designed to make a single word, "nevermore," realize its destiny as the *ne plus ultra* of poetic words by instilling a profound sense of melancholic beauty in the reader. He does not suggest, however, that if we hit on just the right core word for a poem, the rest will "naturally" follow. Accepting that the whole is to be in the service of one key part is by no means the same thing as understanding how to organize the whole to best foreground the power of its central element. With Poe's prose, the situation is slightly different, since many of his stories appear to have been written for the sake of a single *sentence*, whether to make a particular proposition credible or in an effort to keep an utterance's pernicious logic from destroying the surrounding narrative. One of the most graphic illustrations of these difficulties is "Never Bet the Devil Your Head: A Tale with a Moral." The story opens with the narrator observing satirically that since the critics can and do find a lesson in every narrative put in front of them, it must follow that "no man can sit down to write without a very profound design."[21] Curiously, the narrator himself is routinely accused of failing in this regard and writing stories in which the critics can find no deeper meaning. Eager to refute the charge, he announces that he will preempt this story's critical reception by relating "a history about whose obvious moral there can be no question whatever, since he who runs may read it in the large capitals which form the title of the tale" (*PT*, 459). What ensues is a brief account of an individual who

---

peculiar to some prose poets of the San Francisco Bay Area in which the paragraph, conceived of as a quantitative unit rather than a unit of "logic or argument," "organizes the sentences in fundamentally the same way a stanza does lines of verse"—"grammar has become . . . prosody." Ron Silliman, *The New Sentence* (New York: Roof, 2003), 91, 89, 88.

20. Steven Pinker, *The Sense of Style: The Thinking Person's Guide to Writing in the 21st Century* (New York: Penguin, 2014), 145.

21. Edgar Allan Poe, *Poetry and Tales* (New York: Literary Classics of the United States Inc., 1984), 458 (hereafter cited in text as *PT*).

is decapitated in the course of an encounter with a mysterious small man in a dark suit.

Thematically, this text appears to be entirely faithful to the polemics of "The Philosophy of Composition." The narrator repeatedly disparages vague intimations of profundity as characteristic of the flightiness of "transcendentalism," insisting that the world, like his story, should be read as something that takes place on the surface and that there is no need for us to be forever on the lookout for allegory. As in many of Poe's tales, however, it is difficult to decide whether the polemical, all-knowing tone bespeaks a seriousness of purpose or the presence of an underlying joke whose parameters are not fully articulated. There is definitely an element of parody in the too-perfect coordination of message and medium inherent in the opening proclamation that the story will demonstrate the truth of its own title. At the level of the plot, this spills over into something approximating buffoonery. The central figure is one Toby Dammit. As his surname suggests, this veritable allegory of exclamation is afflicted with a kind of speech disorder, for he cannot utter "a sentence without interlarding it with a proposition to gamble," ranging from "I'll bet you what you please" to "I'll bet the Devil my head" (*PT*, 460). As speech acts, such claims are stillborn and do not actually result in Toby risking anything on the outcome of a future event. In fact, the narrator insists that "with [Toby] the thing was a mere formula—*nothing more*," adding that "his expressions on this head had no meaning attached to them whatever. They were simple if not altogether innocent expletives—imaginative phrases wherewith to round off a sentence" (*PT*, 460, my italics). In this perversion of the Romantic doctrine of genius, the imagination is praised for producing empty utterances rather than beautiful lines of verse.

Foreshadowed by the narrator's comment that Toby's bets were "not altogether innocent," one of these "mere formulas" ultimately does become a real wager, and with no less than the real Devil. Like a broken clock that is right twice a day, a perfect context for the performative utterance springs to life, the mechanical expostulation becomes a felicitous speech act, and the unfortunate Toby loses both the bet and his head. At the beginning of the tale, the narrator avers that the critics will manage to unearth some hidden meaning in any story, but he insists that this story's moral will be spelled out in its title in order that no further hermeneutic excavations will be required. In the same way that "The Raven" was written for "nevermore," "Never Bet the Devil Your Head" was written for the sake of a sentence, which is apparently the only way to write if one wants to ensure that one's readers will not pervert one's plans and discover the allegedly "deeper" truth of one's text.

Stanley Fish proposes that we can write a story if we can write a sentence. Poe suggests that if we write a story, it had best include a sentence that entirely encapsulates its significance, or someone else will write such a sentence for us, turning our narrative into the illustration of their decisive statement. The moral of this "Tale with a Moral" is that you must not let the reader beat you to your own punchline. Entirely consistent with "The Philosophy of Composition," the author is to have the last word from the start, in this case by making the opening injunction—"Never bet the devil your head"—the first and last word on the words that follow.

Is this to say that Poe's tale has not one moral, but two? Strictly speaking, the narrator wrote it not in order to prevent others from unlocking its putatively hidden secrets, but in an attempt to refute the charge that he writes stories without morals, an impossible achievement if he is correct that the critics can find a deeper significance in anything they read. The story crafted for the sake of a single sentence was designed to show that the narrator is not Toby Dammit, that is, that he is not capable of producing a string of empty formulas with no meanings attached. As for the single sentence in question, the beauty of "Don't bet the Devil your head" is that the injunction is almost impossible to take at face value and will always be read as if it has some sort of symbolic or allegorical content. Moreover, when we reread the title—and subtitle—from the perspective of the story's conclusion, we must ask whether the moral being set out at the start in black and white is that one should not bet the devil one's head, or the tautological proposition that this "tale with a moral" has a moral. Either way, we find ourselves condemned to do precisely what the narrator mocks and begin some hermeneutic digging in order to look "deeper" to find the narrative's real meaning, possibly something along the lines of "There's no such thing as a *mere* formula" or "Warning: Finishing a sentence may be lethal!" Rejecting the story's attempts to inoculate itself against external interpretation, we put ourselves in the position of the reviled transcendentalists by beginning to write our own versions of the narrator's opening line, which was supposed to be an untouchable punchline.

The question is whether this is a game we want to play. The narrator closes with a bitter detail, commenting that when the transcendentalists refuse to pay for the unfortunate Toby's funeral, he has him "dug up at once" and "sold . . . for dog's meat" (*PT*, 467). This gruesome conclusion suggests that the meat of the matter may be that the distinction between a meaningful sentence and a sentence that has "no meaning attached" is not as clear-cut as the difference between a complete body and one with no head attached. In the end, then, it is not certain whether the goal of writing a story for the sake of a sentence is best served if we decide that the sentence is substantial or empty. Did the narrator construct an entire fictional milieu in order to conjure up a situation in which the tale's opening claim could have some significance or in an effort to render that claim nonsensical? Writing a story "for" a sentence turns out to be an exercise in writing against every sentence insofar as any statement that threatens to reveal itself to be more than "a mere formula [and] *nothing more*" is at risk of obscuring the integrity of the perfect coincidence between message and meaning posited in the narrative's opening paragraph.

Poe's "The Facts in the Case of M. Valdemar" presents us with a similar scenario in which an entire world is constructed for the sake of a single lethal sentence. The story is narrated by a mesmerist who undertakes the unprecedented step of hypnotizing an individual on the brink of death. As all signs of vitality fade, the subject improbably retains the ability to speak from his trance, answering the question of whether he still sleeps: "Yes;—no;—*I have been* sleeping—and now—now—*I am dead*" (*PT*, 840). Having made this declaration, the body miraculously lies in a state of suspended animation for seven months without decaying; the only sign of life is a quivering of the tongue when the mesmerist passes his hands over it. When the narrator and his associates finally summon the courage to try to wake the "sleeper," they hear: "For God's sake!—quick!—quick!—put me to sleep—or, quick!—waken me!—quick!—*I say to you that I am dead!*" (*PT*, 841). With "ejaculations of 'dead! dead!' absolutely *bursting* from the tongue and not from the lips of the sufferer," the entire body dissolves into a putrid organic mess (*PT*, 842).[22]

This story is ostensibly written for the purpose of making the impossible possible and allowing the utterance "I am dead" to be, for once, a literal statement. The complication is that this sentence, which appears to contravene its own content by virtue of being uttered, is actually quite ordinary. If the notion of a dead being that can speak runs counter to our understanding of life and consciousness, it is a commonplace among those who study language that any utterance must be capable of functioning in the absence of its "author," whether she is in the next room or in the grave. In other words, the

22. For an analysis of premortem and postmortem speech in modern poetry, see Diana Fuss, *Dying Modern: A Meditation on Elegy* (Durham, NC: Duke University Press, 2014). For a study of scenes of death in modern narrative, see Garrett Stewart, *Death Sentences: Styles of Dying in British Fiction* (Cambridge, MA: Harvard University Press, 1984).

vitality of the entity that supposedly thinks, speaks, or writes "I am alive" or "I am dead" is irrelevant and furthermore *must* be irrelevant for signification to be effected.[23] It is less that the speaker or writer of such an utterance needs to be dead in order to say it than that he or she is dead to the utterance the moment it is articulated. If it stands to reason that a dead person cannot say "I am dead," one's sentences, whatever they say, need to be able to function in one's absence, not least in the event of one's death, or else they are not sentences. The putatively impossible "I am dead" is thus the condition of possibility of any sentence thought to have an author. Every sentence is a death sentence, because a sentence becomes a sentence only by confirming its independence from its mortal creator and implicitly underscoring the inevitability of his or her death. In this respect, Poe's story is not first and foremost about supernatural forces but about a feature of language that we wittingly or unwittingly accept as ordinary every time we open our mouths or pick up a pen.

To realize the goal of having a figure utter "I am dead" in a "meaningful" fashion, "The Facts in the Case of M. Valdemar" hollows out the interiority of the hypnotized man to the point that there is no "inside" left to express itself any more than there is in the case of the raven in the poet's chamber who repeatedly cries out "nevermore." Just as the word "I" must separate itself from the fiction that it is the sole provenance of the entity that employs it in any given self-referential gesture, so the mesmerist's dead subject has to become little more than an animate tongue—a reduction of the human body to a single organ of articulation that also takes place in several other Poe stories.[24]

Strikingly, the triumph of the statement "I am dead" is also its demise, for in the story's last moments, the sentence collapses into a stutter—"dead! dead!"—in a manner reminiscent of other instances of repetition in Poe, be it "nevermore," "the bells" in the poem of the same name, or the refrain of

23. For discussions of these philosophical issues and their significance for Poe's story, see Roland Barthes, "Textual Analysis of a Tale by Edgar Poe," trans. Donald G. Marshall, *Poe Studies* 10, no. 1 (June 1977): 1–12; and Jacques Derrida, *Voice and Phenomenon: Introduction to the Problem of the Sign in Husserl's Phenomenology*, trans. Leonard Lawler (Evanston, IL: Northwestern University Press, 2001), 82.

24. In "The Man That Was Used Up," the remarkably captivating individual who is the focus of the narrator's—not to mention all of polite society's—attention is revealed to be 99 percent prosthesis, the only remnant of his original body being one-eighth of his tongue. Trading only on this fleeting trace of his corporeal existence, he becomes not just a full-fledged linguistic entity, but the driving force behind social discourse.

madness at the end of "The Tell-Tale Heart" ("louder! louder! louder! *louder*!") (*PT*, 842, 559).[25] If this death sentence of sentences can be ellipsed to the point that only a single word remains, it may be that it is this truncated subject-predicate construct rather than "nevermore" that is the melancholy echo behind every utterance, as if any sentence, no matter what it appears to be saying, were really just calling out: "[I am] dead! [I am] dead!" The narrator stresses that if this moment of raw self-expression is an instance of mechanical iteration, the mechanicity at work is supernatural because the ejaculations of "dead! dead!" burst "from the tongue and not from the lips of the sufferer" (*PT*, 842). At the point at which the automaticity of language—the inexorable power of "I am dead" to signify in the absence of a conscious being who would say or write it—is most directly asserted, the body parts that allow for the production of the signifying phonemes are absent. The speech of the entranced subject is a physical impossibility even as the animation of a dead body is evidently not.

In "Never Bet the Devil Your Head," the narrative fails to protect the injunction at the start of its title from the charge of meaning something other than what it says. "The Facts in the Case of M. Valdemar" is arguably more successful in making "I am dead" into a literal utterance, although at the cost of revealing that this death sentence lurks in every sentence. Even at this extreme juncture, however, we continue to approach these sentences, and by extension all sentences, as if one could ask why they were spoken or written and expect a coherent answer. While the prospect of controlling any given sentence may appear tenuous, it is still possible to explain, at least retrospectively, a sentence's "function," irrespective of the degree to which its mission is ironized in the course of being realized. What would it mean to conceive of a sentence wholly outside such a technocratic model, treating it as an instance of language that was neither a means to an end nor an act designed to produce a particular effect? Is some notion of a sentence's use or design integral to its very identity as a verbal construct?

Poe's "The Imp of the Perverse" is driven by such questions. The story opens with a first-person narrator explaining how he committed a murder to considerable financial advantage and got off scot-free, with everyone convinced that his victim died of natural causes. A few years later, a mysterious

25. In Poe, a word never comes into its own until the possibility of its repetition is confirmed with its second appearance, almost as if in its first manifestation any word were under suspicion of being an inscrutable sign from a private language.

impulse drives the narrator to confess, and he recounts his experiences to the reader from his cell only hours before his execution. Toby Dammit constantly bets his life yet does not "really" bet his life until his fateful last wager. In contrast, the defining speech act of this tale, a confession, is articulated only once, but it works perfectly the very first time.

The story proves to have been written less to explain the confession itself than to explain the sentence that made the confession possible, or rather inevitable. As is often the case in Poe, a linguistic problem is initially characterized with a mixture of philosophical and psychological jargon. If there is a cause of his self-damning act, the narrator tells us, it is a "radical, primitive, irreducible sentiment" that is universal to our species, "an innate . . . principle of human action, a paradoxical something, which we may call perverseness, for want of a more characteristic term" (*PT*, 827). The narrator maintains that "this overwhelming tendency to do wrong for the wrong's sake" will not "admit of analysis or resolution into ulterior elements," and in this respect, it cannot be grasped by our customary explanatory paradigms (*PT*, 827). Like the critics in "Never Bet the Devil Your Head" who find a moral for every story, we invariably understand a series of events by attributing an agent's behavior to the motives we retrospectively posit he or she must have had. This is the flip side of the process described in "The Philosophy of Composition" in which we give a plot "its indispensable air of consequence, or causation" by looking to the end and seeing how we can get there, step by incontrovertible step.[26] In contrast, this primitive sentiment, which compels us to act "for the reason that we should *not*" and "to do wrong for the wrong's sake," pushes the very notion of self-interested agency into the background (*PT*, 827). Indeed, the narrator insists that the existence of this "perverse" drive has never been recognized because it serves no need or goal. To the extent that it cannot be ascribed any utility, it is not there.

No less than "I am dead," perverseness turns out to have been there all along as the other side of language—an inverted language, a corrupt language, or simply language that does not do the work it should. From the Latin *perversus* ("turned away from what is right"), "perverse" did not acquire the sense of "sexually deviant" until decades after Poe wrote his story; but it already had a long history as a linguistic concept, sharing an etymological root with "verse" in the Latin *versus*, "a turn of the plow" or "a line of writing."[27] In postclassical Latin, a *perversio* names the reversal of words in a sentence; in medieval Latin,

26. Poe, "The Philosophy of Composition," 13.

27. The Latin *vertere*, "to turn," has the sense of "to translate" as well as "to transform."

it denotes a falsification, an erroneous inversion of terms, or even a corruption of the text such as a copyist's error.

The prime example of being beset by the imp of the perverse involves a "usually curt, precise, and clear" individual who gives in to the desire to "tantalize a listener by circumlocution" (*PT*, 828). As the story continues, the narrator reveals that this circumnavigation of one's own statements is less the decision of an individual to do wrong for wrong's sake than a manifestation of the ever-present possibility that any sentence may turn against itself without a single word or punctuation mark changing. A *per-version* is a turning (troping) of words that has gone all the way around, as it were, such that this twisted language becomes indistinguishable from its nonperverse counterpart, the most straightforward sentence now existing in parallel with its deviant alter ego, a para-phrasis. This is why the most innocent-looking sentence can prove to be the most lethal.

Perversion does not manifest itself as formal negation—it is not a matter of inserting "not" into an affirmative proposition. This becomes clear when the narrator relates his internal musings as he went about town, enjoying the fact that he had killed with impunity: "I would perpetually catch myself pondering upon my security, and repeating, in a low undertone, the phrase, 'I am safe'" (*PT*, 831). Together, these three one-syllable words become an ungovernable sentence, or in the first instance, "a haunting and harassing thought" that the narrator could "scarcely get rid of . . . for an instant" (*PT*, 830). Vexed by what we would today call an earworm ("the ringing in our ears, or rather in our memories, of the burthen of some ordinary song, or some unimpressive snatches from an opera"), he cannot escape this refrain of "I am safe," which proves no less annoying than "I am dead" (*PT*, 830–31). The narrator soon finds himself murmuring the sentence over and over, but far from producing a sense of security, this intimate expression of self-affection becomes increasingly foreign with each iteration and ultimately confronts him as a menace in its own right, more like a traumatic symptom than a reassuring gesture.

At this point, the narrator has no choice but to attempt to intervene in the sentence that is uncannily his and yet not his, although this only sees one speech act perverted into another:

> One day, whilst sauntering along the streets, I arrested myself in the act of murmuring, half aloud, these customary syllables. In a fit of petulance, I remodeled them thus; "I am safe—I am safe—yes—if I be not fool enough to make open confession!" No sooner had I spoken these words, than I felt an icy chill creep to my heart. . . . And now my own casual self-suggestion that I might possibly be fool enough to confess the murder of which I had been guilty, confronted

> me, as if the very ghost of him whom I had murdered—and beckoned me on to death. (*PT*, 831)

The narrator seeks to halt the onslaught of this haunting sentence not by negating it, but by affirming it—"yes"!—and then appending to it one of its essential conditions: it will remain true as long as I do not say, "I confess!" Unfortunately, once the integrity of the repetition of "I am safe" has been broken by the interjection, it becomes impossible to return to the original formulation. If these three words are ostensibly designed to serve as a kind of performative utterance—safety is assured as long as one can keep saying that one is safe—they are constitutively open to perversion by a counterperformative, "I confess," whose inevitable appearance is facilitated through "casual self-suggestion." When the narrator does bare his soul, then, he delivers the announcement in a "passionate hurry, as if in dread of interruption before concluding the brief, but pregnant sentences that consigned me to the hangman and to hell" (*PT*, 831). The truly perverse feature of his dilemma is that each decisive utterance is made in total disregard for both the past and the future, as if all that mattered were that the speaker not be interrupted in getting out these two ("I confess") or three ("I am safe") words *this* time, even though in this case to finish one's sentence is literally to finish oneself.

Poe's tales complement the commonplace view that the moment we speak or write a sentence it is no longer ours with the uncomfortable suggestion that we can never be done with any of our sentences, especially when they are no longer ours. If "The Facts in the Case of M. Valdemar" suggests that every sentence is a death sentence, "The Imp of the Perverse" proposes that every sentence is equally a life sentence, a companion that will plague one for the duration of one's natural existence. In revealing that the simplest subject-predicate construction may be the most unstable, Poe's stories cast doubt on our ability to make any sentence produce the results we desire. "I am safe"; "I am dead"; "I bet the devil my head"—in each case, the misfiring of a clause demands an entire narrative to explain it, as if Poe wrote his tales not to give his readers nightmares but to reassure them that language still worked.

Literary history suggests that many of Poe's inheritors were not reassured. His great admirer Charles Baudelaire translated—and thereby presumably perverted—"The Imp of the Perverse" into French, calling it "Le Démon de la perversité." This demon returned in "Le Démon de l'analogie" ("The Demon of Analogy"), a prose poem by another of Poe's ardent admirers, Stéphane Mallarmé. Written in 1864, shortly after Mallarmé had begun translating Poe into French, it has been identified by a number of scholars as a version—revision, or perversion—of Poe's original story. Although it is not immediately obvious why analogy should be perverse, its transformative powers are on exhibit in every sentence of Mallarmé's text. In a tribute to—or parody of—Baudelaire, symbolic correspondences proliferate to the point that the alignment of any two terms becomes potentially meaningful. Various sensory and intelligible orders stand in for one another metonymically and metaphorically, ensuring that the dynamics of perception, memory, and language become hopelessly intertwined.

From the opening words of the prose poem, we are also dealing with a ghostly sentence. The trials and tribulations of the first-person speaker center on his attempts to reconcile the powers of sentences and analogies as he tries to understand and take control of his relationship with this phantom:

> Have unknown words ever played about your lips, the haunting and accursed fragments of an absurd sentence?
>
> I went out of my apartment with the distinct sensation of a wing sliding along the strings of some instrument, languid and light, which was replaced by a voice that, with a downward intonation, pronounced the words: "The Penultimate is dead," in such a way such that
>
> *The Penultimate*
>
> ended one line and
>
> *Is dead*
>
> broke off from the fateful suspension more uselessly in the void of signification. I took a few steps down the street and recognized in the "nul" sound the tight string of a forgotten musical instrument . . .[28]

In contrast to Poe's narrator, for whom "I am safe" is never quite absurd enough, Mallarmé's poet immediately decides that there is something wrong with this four-word formulation. Most commentators have followed the speaker in agreeing that "the Penultimate is dead" is a mysterious and possibly nonsensical sentence, a rush to judgment that is surprising given that the word "penultimate" is not particularly unusual, especially in this context. As the poet helpfully explains, it "is a lexical term signifying the next-to-last syllable of a word"; and "its appearance," he adds, "[is] merely the unwanted

28. Stéphane Mallarmé, *Divagations*, trans. Barbara Johnson (Cambridge, MA: Harvard University Press, 2007), 17 (translation modified).

residue of the linguistic labor through which my noble poetic faculty daily sobs to see itself interrupted."[29] From this perspective, the manifestation of the ghostly sentence is not a symptom of a horrific crime but an ordinary feature of the psychopathology of everyday life. A milder version of the refrain that haunts the narrator-murderer in "The Imp of the Perverse," this detritus of the unconscious drifts into the thoughts of a writer who, like Poe's character, is loath to be interrupted and cannot bear to put his work aside even as he walks through the city.

Like "I am safe," there is nothing grammatically puzzling about "the Penultimate is dead," but whereas this proposition is first presented to the reader as a compact four-word statement, this is not how it initially appears to the poet. The mysterious voice that articulates the words pronounces them as part of two distinct lines of a poem; or rather, based on the intonation, the first two words constitute the end of a line of verse, then the turn (*versus*) into the next line is deferred as the last two words break off for no obvious reason. The interruption of the poet's routine is itself an instance of interruption, albeit one that is in turn interrupted, for if versification invades and begins to pervert the prose poem, prose quickly reasserts itself. In the process, the word "Penultimate" is subject to considerable violence, pulled first one way and then another. Both here and later in the text, the poet takes advantage of the resulting instability at the level of the letter and perverts the word's syllabification as he fashions a new syllable and a new word: *n-u-l* ("no," "nil," "no one").

For better or worse, building a word with which to comment on the vexingly meaningful instances of meaninglessness with which the poet is confronted fails to assist him in escaping the utterance that stalks him and the incomprehensibility that comes with it:

> The sentence came back, a virtual reality, detached from any previous stroke of plumes or palms, heard henceforth only through the voice, until finally it articulated itself all alone, animated by its own personality. I walked along (no longer contenting myself with mere perception), reading it at the end of a line, and, having once adapted it as an experiment to my voice, soon pronounced it with a pause after "Penultimate," in which I felt a painful pleasure: "The Penultimate," then the taut forgotten string, stretched over the *nul* sound, which broke, no doubt, and I added, in the manner of a funeral oration, "Is dead."[30]

29. Mallarmé, *Divagations*, 18.
30. Mallarmé, *Divagations*, 17–18 (translation modified).

Although he can rationalize why the word "penultimate" belongs to him, the poet continues to be tormented by this sentence that is not his own. At the same time, he does appear to win some control over it, moving from "perceiving" the statement, to "reading it," to pronouncing it as he sees fit, ostensibly co-opting the articulation of the utterance in the very instant that it confronts him as autonomous. To be sure, the power he exercises over the ghostly formulation by repeating it only goes so far. If the poet can pause between the first and the last two words, he must finish, the mechanics of his speech becoming interwoven with the physical logic of the string motif that runs throughout the text. Like Poe's narrator, he is beset by linguistic compulsion. The phantom sentence will be heard.

A sentence that is not quite a sentence; a section of two lines of a poem that is not quite a section of two lines of a poem; an utterance with straightforward grammar comprising four eminently definable words whose literal and metaphorical meanings are nonetheless mysterious—surely "the Penultimate is dead" begs for exegesis. Mallarmé's poet is content to recite it and then reword it, as if this will neutralize its insistent haunting: "I resolved to let the sad words wander on my lips, and I walked on, murmuring comfortingly, as it offered condolences, 'The Penultimate is dead, she is dead, really dead, the poor desperate Penultimate,' thinking that . . . by expanding the speech, I might bury her once and for all."[31] Like the narrator in "The Imp of the Perverse," the speaker's instinct is to domesticate the line by revising or expanding it. It would appear that it is the simplicity and compactness of the spectral formulation that must be combatted, as if the Penultimate can never truly be dead and buried if all one can say about it is that it is dead and buried. No matter how diligently the poet tries to inter the specter, this ghostly sentence is not listening. Melancholia emerges in the final line of the text, as he declares that despite his best efforts to come to terms with the linguistic phantom, he is "condemned forever to wear mourning for the inexplicable Penultimate."[32] As in "The Philosophy of Composition," melancholia is a purely formal affect. Evacuated of any relationship to the sensuous, it manifests itself in the endless repetition of an inescapable death sentence that is indifferent to all attempts to enliven it.

Perhaps the mistake lies in treating the sentence about the Penultimate as an autonomous unit, since the concept of penultimacy implies a subordination to an ordering logic that the term, that is, the penultimate term, does not entirely control. Considered in isolation, the "next-to-last" inevitably appears as a kind

31. Mallarmé, *Divagations*, 18.
32. Mallarmé, *Divagations*, 18.

of ghost, an apparition that hints at the former presence of a larger series that may be invisible or have been lost. Having raised this problem in the form of a sentence that comes out of nowhere, Mallarmé's prose poem ends with the Penultimate as its last rather than its second-to-last word, which one might read as the poem's attempt to kill off the ghost. The logic, however, cuts both ways, since the gesture of closing with the next-to-last risks negating the authority of the poem's last word as "last," thereby leaving open the possibility that there may be more to come, if only in ghostly form, in which case the falsely final word of the text would affirm the continued supremacy of the Penultimate's haunting.[33]

We might surmise that it is imperative for the poet that the Penultimate not have the last word, even if it is the last word of the poem and if this last word concludes a pithy pronouncement of the Penultimate's death. In fact, this does not turn out to be the central concern. As the poet tells it, the truly shocking aspect of the experience he is relating is not the prospect of interminable mourning, which he associates with sorrow or resignation. The real horror arises in the penultimate paragraph of the poem when the poet realizes that the voice that has been articulating the sentence plaguing him is actually his own. This uncanny instance of linguistic self-recognition as self-alienation is followed by a second shock in the final paragraph, when the poet notices that he is standing outside a shop that sells string instruments. A complex web of wing, plumage, and string motifs runs throughout the text and is perverted into all manner of sensible and intelligible forms. When this forest of symbols is suddenly instantiated in a collection of physical objects, the poet is confronted with a signifying field in which analogism has been generalized to such a degree that it elides the very distinctions that allow for comparisons, and resemblances lose their capacity to signify. The possibility of aligning two terms in a meaningful way is suspended, and he is left gawking at a display of concrete strings that may or may not point to anything more than the raw fact of their own physical existence.

Mallarmé's poet is haunted by a sentence about the death of a lexical term for a word's next-to-last syllable, a sentence that seems to be at once as literal and as figurative as the host of different motifs that he stumbles upon in the course of his day. The poet cannot claim the four phantom words as his own, nor can he disavow them completely, as if they were a graffito he passed on a wall that could be safely put behind him as soon as he turned the corner. No matter how many times a new iteration of the mysterious sentence puts

33. On the question of this poem's "last" word, see Claire Lyu, "The Poetics of the Penult: Mallarmé, Death, and Syntax," *MLN* 113, no. 3 (April 1998): 561–87.

the word Penultimate to rest, the death sentence for the Penultimate never becomes the object of a death sentence. The resulting prose poem is a kind of requiem for our ability to be done with any sentence, as if every writer were condemned to be forever stuck on the next-to-last step of whatever section of a composition she were struggling with.

A poignant reading of Poe's story, this prose poem is only one moment in the protracted struggle with the concept of the sentence that continues throughout Mallarmé's oeuvre. In many of his verse texts, which are commonly alexandrine sonnets, the traditional formal structure serves as a promise of intelligibility, creating a semblance of order that vanishes as soon as one starts reading. As in "The Demon of Analogy," a dense concatenation of motifs of uncertain provenance quickly imposes itself, like the pieces of a puzzle with no accompanying picture to assist us in putting them together. As Alain Badiou writes, "There is a certain element of the detective novel in the Mallarméan enigma: an empty salon, a vase, a dark sea—what crime, what catastrophe, what enormous misadventure is indicated by these clues?"[34] Some scholars have compared the intermittent manifestations of these different motifs to the movements of a musical score in which multiple elements present themselves as significant over a span of time without any simple resolution of their meanings or relative priority, forcing the reader/listener to contend with various parallel "open threads."[35]

Mallarmé is notorious for the ways in which his verse exploits the flexibility of French syntax, bending the rules of grammar to the point just before they break. In some cases, the reader must look forward several lines to find a subject, object, or verb that one would expect to encounter much earlier in the sentence. In other poems, words are positioned in ways that make it difficult if not impossible to know what parts of speech they are; they can also seem to be simultaneously pointing back to terms that have already appeared and forward to elements yet to be encountered. The potential for ambiguity is augmented by a liberal reliance on different kinds of participles and the routine intermingling of active and passive voices. Sometimes entire sentences unfold with nothing that quite constitutes a finite verb to anchor them.

Already in "The Demon of Analogy," we encountered an ambivalence that leaves its mark on Mallarmé's most traditional as well as his most experimental works, including the notorious "A Roll of the Dice Will Never Abolish

34. Alain Badiou, *Being and Event*, trans. Oliver Feltham (New York: Continuum, 2007), 191.

35. On music and Mallarmé's poetry, see Jacques Rancière, *Mallarmé: The Politics of the Siren*, trans. Steven Corcoran (New York: Continuum, 2011).

Chance," which he was still correcting on his deathbed. In his texts, the sense that we are dealing with the wreckage of language is always accompanied by the suggestion that the sentence may be poised to return as more dynamic and powerful than ever before, be this a resurrection of past verbal triumphs or the appearance of a new linguistic form that remains as yet unthinkable. There is, however, no timetable for this renaissance. Mallarmé leaves us surrounded by sentences that may be traces of a bygone glory or portents of one yet to come, but in either case, we can neither count on them nor be confident of our ability to be done with them.

In the verbal landscape laid out by Coleridge, Poe, and Mallarmé, phantoms lurk in every clause. What does it mean to start a sentence, much less finish one, when its status as a ghost of the past or a specter of the future is preordained from the start, inspiration has taken the form of a capricious daemon, and method has become an uneasy negotiation with technical terms that tirelessly aver their own finitude? The clash between the compositional philosophies of genius and method that is enacted in these authors' works offers a vision of writing as an interminable, arguably even futile process.

At this juncture, an obvious question imposes itself. Whatever one may say of nineteenth-century letters, a shortage of great works was not one of its afflictions. How, then, can the theory and practice of writing be so at odds with one another? Why should such extraordinarily successful authors be the ones to lament the impossibility of their craft? This contradiction reaches its apex with the oeuvre of Gustave Flaubert. Often heralded as a novelist of virtually unsurpassed achievement, Flaubert's reflections on his own compositional praxis put the crowning touches on the notion of writing as an endless labor of revision, canonizing the modern conviction that the crucial stumbling block in our struggle with words is the inherent fallibility of the sentence itself.

While tales of Flaubert's epic revisionary processes are legion, it is worth recognizing that such stories, not unlike Coleridge's account of the writing of "Kubla Khan," were actively propagated by Flaubert himself. As literary history has it, he lived a sort of obsessive-compulsive nightmare, often working on a single paragraph for days in a maniacal effort to get everything just right. In an 1888 essay, Walter Pater quotes Guy de Maupassant's account of these labors:

> Possessed of an absolute belief that there exists but one way of expressing one thing, one word to call it by, one adjective to qualify, one verb to animate it, [Flaubert] gave himself to super-human labor for the discovery, in every phrase, of that word, that verb, that epithet. In this way, he believed in some mysterious

> harmony of expression, and when a true word seemed to him to lack euphony still went on seeking another, with invincible patience, certain that he had not yet got hold of the *unique word*. . . . A thousand preoccupations would beset him at the same moment, always with this desperate certitude fixed in his spirit: "Among all the expressions in the world, all the forms and turns of expression, but *one*—one form, one mode—to express what I want to say."[36]

Maupassant takes the liberty of speaking for Flaubert's spirit in the first person, as if he can do a better job than Flaubert himself of saying exactly what Flaubert wanted to say about saying exactly what he wanted to say. The doctrine Maupassant describes appears to lurch between collapsing form and content, the what and the how, such that they cannot be separated, even provisionally, and bifurcating medium and message, as if the latter existed independently of the forms it takes in any given verbal incarnation, a kind of semantic ideal waiting to be instantiated in words. Maurice Blanchot attributes this inconsistency to Flaubert himself, who vacillates between "trying to write well in order to think well and trying to think well in order to write well."[37]

Although Flaubert's name was indelibly linked to the notion of *le mot juste* from an early stage, he penned nothing of length on the subject, using the phrase or similar ones only a few times in his letters. To this day, authors frequently describe the experience of setting out to read everything Flaubert had to say about choosing "the right word," only to discover that there is very little to speak of. *Le mot juste* has come to be the name for a methodological doctrine that does not actually exist, at least not in any sustained form, and for better or worse, the concept continues to inform almost every discussion of Flaubert. In Walter Pater's reading of Maupassant's account of the novelist, Flaubert is said to be seeking "the unique word, phrase, sentence, paragraph, essay, or song absolutely proper to the single mental presentation or vision within," and thereby reuniting "the world of thought" and "the world of language" like "body and soul."[38] In the face of these attacks on the enemies of exactitude, ambiguity persists. In writing about writing, Flaubert has no trouble conveying his sense—intuition, conviction—that what currently stands on the page is not what he wants to say. It is by no means obvious, however, that he shares Pater's

36. Walter Pater, *Appreciations: With an Essay on Style* (London: Macmillan, 1913), 27.

37. Maurice Blanchot, *Infinite Conversation*, trans. Susan Hanson (Minneapolis: University of Minnesota Press, 1993), 333.

38. Walter Pater, *Selected Writings of Walter Pater*, ed. Harold Bloom (New York: Columbia University Press, 1974), 117.

confidence that "the single mental presentation or vision within" exists in the present rather than as something past that is almost forgotten—like Coleridge trying to remember the verses in his dream—or as something in the future with which Flaubert's language may ultimately hope to catch up.

What is not ambiguous is Flaubert's investment in the idea that there exists one version of a sentence that will be palpably superior to all the others. In the history of rhetoric, some of the most influential purveyors of style have held a very different view. In a classical example, Erasmus offers a virtuoso demonstration of compositional flexibility when he takes a "not particularly fertile" sentence—"Always, as long as I live, I shall remember you"—and pens two hundred variations of it; he then complements this tour de force with 195 variations on the sentence "Your letter pleased me mightily."[39] In confirming that any statement can take myriad forms, Erasmus hopes to give the fledgling writer a sense of the many possibilities on offer, in effect reassuring him that there are countless paths to success. While Flaubert would not necessarily be troubled by the idea that one could produce so many variants of a given sentence, he would be horrified by the notion that one might not have any way of deciding which among them was the best.

Unlike Poe, who teases us with the suggestion that if we really understand what he is saying about composition, we too will be able to write something like "The Raven," Flaubert appears to formulate his remarks on writing primarily for himself. One notices right off that he has no anxiety about the possibility of being viewed as an artisan or engineer. No less than Poe, he is suspicious of appeals to genius, averring that we should "not trust that sort of overheating which is called inspiration, and into which there enters more nervous emotion than muscular strength."[40] In some cases, he writes almost as if his clauses emerged from an assembly line. "When my novel is finished, in a year," he tells the poet Louise Colet, "I will bring you the entire manuscript, for curiosity's sake. You'll see the complicated machinery [*mécanique compliquée*] I used to make a sentence."[41]

The overarching conceit of Flaubert's reflections on his work is that he has put more energy into his compositions than is humanly possible, becoming, as

39. Desiderius Erasmus, *De Copia: Foundations of the Abundant Style, Collected Works*, vol. 24, trans. Betty I. Knott (Toronto: University of Toronto Press, 1978), 348–65.

40. Cited in Tony Williams, "The Writing Process: Scenarios, Sketches, and Rough Drafts," *The Cambridge Companion to Flaubert*, ed. Timothy Unwin (New York: Cambridge University Press, 2004), 166.

41. Cited in Williams, "The Writing Process," 166.

Pater says, "the martyr of literary style."[42] Flaubert believes that technical facility or a clarity of purpose only gets one so far without a willingness to devote potentially endless effort to one's task. "One achieves style," he writes, "only by atrocious labor, a fanatic and dedicated stubbornness."[43] Alongside—if not displacing—both genius and method, we have a compositional doctrine on the order of *No pain, no gain*. Maupassant says that Flaubert is guided by his belief in "some mysterious harmony of expression," although the ensuing quest takes, and will inevitably take, the form of a process that is anything but harmonious. Something is out of proportion in the relationship between production and product, resulting in a kind of fanaticism that acquires a life of its own and all but demands the sacrifice of the author. As James Wood puts it, "style became religious with Flaubert."[44]

Crucially, this religiosity is informed by materialist impulses as much as by spiritual ones. In Flaubert's accounts of producing his novels, Roland Barthes locates nothing less than a new aesthetic in which the value of writing lies in "the work it has cost. There begins now to grow up an image of the writer as a craftsman who shuts himself away in some legendary place."[45] If Poe focuses on the use-value of a text, its utility in creating a particular impact on its readers, Flaubert presents us with a labor theory of literary value. This is not an ideal system in which inputs are perfectly mirrored by outputs or the time and energy expended on any given sentence is directly reflected in its quality. Even when the result of Flaubert's exertions is a book on the order of *Madam Bovary*, a sense of loss, if not outright futility, prevails. For Flaubert, writes Barthes, style is "absolute suffering, infinite suffering, useless suffering," and it is useless because no matter how hard he works, he can never be convinced that he has arrived at the perfect harmony of expression—in fact, he is often unsure as to whether his efforts are making things better rather than worse.[46] Flaubert's sentences can never look just right to him, no matter what generations of future readers may say to the contrary. More than any particular feature

42. Pater, *Appreciations*, 27.

43. Cited in Roland Barthes, "Flaubert and the Sentence," *A Barthes Reader*, ed. Susan Sontag (New York: Farrar, Straus & Giroux, 1982), 297.

44. James Wood, "How Flaubert Changed Literature Forever," *New Republic*, December 12, 2014 (originally January 18, 1999), https://newrepublic.com/article/120543/james-wood-flaubert-and-chekhovs-influence-style-and-literature.

45. Roland Barthes, *Writing Degree Zero*, trans. Annette Lavers and Colin Smith (New York: Hill & Wang, 1968), 63.

46. Barthes, "Flaubert and the Sentence," 296.

of his prose, the cornerstone of his legacy as a writer may be his conviction about the impossibility of perfecting one's texts.

Thanks to the numerous surviving drafts of Flaubert's works, his labors of revision can be followed blow by blow as individual sentences are subject to countless transformations, taking shape and being altered time and again in a process whose stages begin to resemble the stills making up a cinematic sequence. Unsurprisingly, his oeuvre has become a key test for the possibilities of so-called "genetic criticism," where the aim is to "recover material that has . . . been overlaid by the definitive version. The genetic editor . . . attaches significance to what the writer himself has cleared away in favor of a final version deemed to be superior."[47] Taking only a few iterations of a given clause to compare and contrast, the interpretive possibilities are exponentially magnified, and one can draw all kinds of inferences about any and every emendation. Less legible in such comparisons is the degree to which the onslaught of revision undermines the claim of any given incarnation of one of Flaubert's sentences to stand alone as a syntactic construct or sequence of terms, that is, to be a sentence, however provisional.

As certain as Flaubert is that sentences—life's "adventures," as he called them—are his bread and butter, he also views them as daunting challenges, if not outright adversaries.[48] In a well-known letter to Colet, he wrote of his ambition "to give prose the rhythm of verse (keeping it distinctly prose, however)."[49] His process of revision was nonetheless designed to purge his prose of one of the features most common to poetry: repetition. In his correspondence with George Sand, Flaubert describes spending his "life trying to write harmonious sentences, avoiding assonances," the repetition of vowel sounds close enough to one another for the echo to be heard.[50] While this is ostensibly a circumscribed activity, it is not clear how far one has to go in expunging such acoustic flaws, and when one moves to the trans-sentential level, the possibilities for error grow exponentially. Whatever *le mot juste* meant for Flaubert, it was never simply a matter of selecting, say, the right adjective for a word (the *obdurate* man, the *inflexible* man, the *intransigent* man), because in fine-tuning one's diction, one must simultaneously assess all of the surround-

47. Williams, "The Writing Process," 171.

48. Cited in Barthes, "Flaubert and the Sentence," 302 n. 16.

49. Gustave Flaubert, *The Letters of Gustave Flaubert: 1857–1880*, ed. and trans. Francis Steegmuller (Cambridge, MA: Harvard University Press, 1980), 182.

50. *The Correspondence of Gustave Flaubert and George Sand*, trans. Francis Steegmuller and Barbara Bray (London: Harvill Press, 1999), 27.

ing words in order to avoid inadvertently repeating phonemes in too close proximity to one another. This entire exercise seems to run parallel to the ambition to find the one single word that is absolutely appropriate for what one wants to say, if not to clash with it insofar as the effort to avoid the repetition of particular sounds or words by inserting synonyms risks unsettling any lexical precision that has been achieved.

Referring to three pages of *Madame Bovary*, Flaubert comments, one hopes hyperbolically: "I will doubtless discover in them a thousand repetitions of words which I'll have to get rid of. At this moment, late as it is, I can see virtually none."[51] Once discovered, an error of the kind that vexes Flaubert will stand forth as gloriously inappropriate, but until it is identified, such a repetition can be maddeningly elusive, there being no obvious way to systematically unearth it or others like it. As Flaubert elaborates his "linguistics of correction," writes Barthes, he

> manages to introduce the vertigo of an infinite correction: the difficulty for him is not correction itself (actually limited), but discernment of the place where it is necessary. Certain repetitions appear, which had not been noticed the day before, so that nothing can guarantee that the next day new "mistakes" will not be discovered; thus, there develops an anxious insecurity, for it always seems possible to *bear* new repetitions. The text, even when it has been meticulously worked over, is somehow *mined* with risks of repetition.[52]

Before it is a series of signifying elements or the articulation of one or more logical relationships, a sentence is defined by the possibility that each and every word in it may be a mistake, and for reasons that have nothing to do with grammar. Most troublingly, refinements in syntax and diction, no matter how extreme, can never hope to inoculate a sentence against such mistakes, to which it remains constitutively open. One consequence is that any given word, as much as it may seem to be exactly the right element for the place in the sentence in which it appears, is under suspicion of representing the premature return of an earlier word or syllable. Every word is potentially the ghost of a prior lexical entity that needs to be suppressed, a hypothetical revenant whose mere potential to effect repetition can terrorize its author. Before it can connote or denote, represent or refer, a word gives rise to the fear that it or parts of it have recently been used.

51. Cited in Barthes, "Flaubert and the Sentence," 301 n. 11.

52. Barthes, "Flaubert and the Sentence," 298, 301.

If purging one's composition of unwanted repetitions remains a formidable—and possibly endless—task, Flaubert also faces the question of how to decide when one has realized a Ciceronian "stream of eloquence" (*flumen orationis*) and perfected the articulations between sentences.[53] In the first instance, this involves a stylistic conundrum that most of us will have wrestled with, consciously or unconsciously: How long should any given sentence be? Perusing his manuscripts, it appears that Flaubert has no simple answer. As Tony Williams explains, scholars "have noted a pattern of expansion and contraction: the first rough draft, typically, is still fairly short, but is expanded in the next rough draft, only to be pared down in the third. The removal of superfluous detail and the generally more concise expression contribute to the characteristic ambiguity of the final version."[54] Despite the exacting integrity of Flaubert's revisionary efforts, he proceeds in a classical fashion, entirely in line with Erasmus's prescription that one "first compress the subject to such an extent that you can subtract nothing, and then enrich and expand it so that nothing can be added."[55] One problem is that with concision may come ambiguity. Once "shorter" cannot simply be valorized as "clearer," the question of why less is better than more becomes more difficult to answer.

Flaubert does not conceive of the movement through his texts from sentence to sentence in terms of a logical development, as if he were drawing up one large argument or formulating strings of syllogisms. His stated aim is rather to realize the rhythms of verse in prose, although he is painfully aware that there are no pre-established metrics, in particular no syllable counts, with which to regulate his clauses, which in the most immediate sense would mean telling him where they should stop. As a unit of discourse, a sentence is by

53. Flaubert offers many elegant accounts of the sort of language he aspires to produce, as when he declares that he can conceive of

> a style that would be beautiful, that someone will create one day, in ten years, or in ten centuries, and which would be as rhythmical as verse, as precise as the language of science, and with the undulations, the humming of a cello, plumes of fire, a style which would enter your mind like a rapier thrust, and on which finally your thoughts would slide as if over a smooth surface, as when one glides along in a boat with a good tailwind. (Cited in Williams, "The Writing Process," 167)

54. Williams, "The Writing Process," 170–71.

55. Erasmus, *De Copia*, 298. Making a difficult chore sound far too easy, Erasmus describes what he hopes he is teaching us: "The purpose of these instructions is to enable you so to include the essential in the fewest possible words that nothing is lacking, or so to enlarge and enrich your expression of it that even so nothing is redundant" (*De Copia*, 301).

definition finite. Grammatically speaking, it must end because its hierarchical structure is organized by subordinations and superordinations of terms that remain unstable until the whole is fully realized. The possibility that a sentence might not conclude threatens not just the completeness of the thought being expressed, but the relationships between words, phrases, and clauses that make such an expression possible. Rhetorically speaking, a sentence must end as well because much of its authority—its claim to say or do something—rests on its status as a putatively stand-alone formation with a defined beginning and end, its semblance of autonomy giving it the aura of a consequential judgment.

The problem is that syntactically a sentence has no inherent limits beyond the contingencies of space and time, memory, and the author or reader's patience. It is always hypothetically possible to add another phrase or clause, if only by tacking it on at the end. Flaubert's sentences unfold in the grips of this irreducible tension between the inevitably bounded form that they will have to assume and the unbounded potential they threaten to actualize. Every one of them implicitly says: "this sentence will never be done," and "this sentence must be brought to a close, for if one cannot be finished, all sentences may be exposed as equally interminable, unrealizable projects." One consequence is that the rhythm of an individual sentence can never offer a model for the rhythmic modulations between sentences, and vice versa—although this fact will not and perhaps should not keep the inveterate stylist from attempting to reconcile clausal and transclausal patterns.

The sentence turns out to be challenging for Flaubert not because it is too rigid or restrictive, but because it is not restrictive enough. Whether on its own or as part of a larger sequence of similar constructions, the briefest subject-predicate statement presents an author with innumerable decisions that often appear to be resolved arbitrarily rather than systematically. As Flaubert says, "The simplest sentence, like 'he closed the door,' 'he went out,' requires incredible artistic ruses."[56] If, as Blanchot argues, "Flaubert is forever trying to master the formlessness" that constantly threatens the sentence, his writing method is not a neurotic fine-tuning of details in a quest for a chimerical perfection, but a "search for [a] form" that would make it possible to say definitively that a given incarnation of an utterance is superior to the hundreds of other shapes it could take.[57] Every sentence implicitly makes a case for its peculiarities, offering itself up as a model to be emulated, but this only heightens the sense that the problem with sentence style is a dearth rather than an abundance of rules.

56. Cited in Blanchot, *Infinite Conversation*, 335.

57. Blanchot, *Infinite Conversation*, 333, 334.

If the sentence is often regarded as an inherently conservative paradigm that cries out to be superseded by more radical forms of signification, Flaubert reveals it to be an infinitely complex interplay of possibilities governed by ordering principles that have yet to be enumerated, much less understood. In this vein, Blanchot casts skepticism on the image of Flaubert the artisan, insisting that whatever technical knowledge he possesses, it is a knowledge of the implausibility of there ever being a systematic process for creating sound sentences. Thinking along similar lines, Barthes draws a remarkable conclusion from Flaubert's compositional dicta: "Because the sentence is free, the writer is condemned not to search for the *best* sentence, but to take responsibility for *every* sentence."[58] Until she can confirm the paradigmatic exemplarity of her own sentences, until she can definitively show us how a sentence should look, a writer is accountable for what is lacking in each and every sentence, whether she wrote it or not. Flaubert does not labor tirelessly on his texts simply in an effort to perfect his prose; rather, he works in the hope that the very idea of perfecting a sentence will not be revealed as incoherent. For him, the sentence is a kind of ideal, but it never becomes a fully-fledged metaphysical entity, forever retaining the status of an object that resists being reduced to one or more concepts, rules, or principles, as if the obstacles to good writing were physical as much as anything else.[59]

Flaubert never renounces his conviction that there should be a "right answer" for any given sentence, an organization of phrases and clauses that is best in itself as well as for the series of sentences in which it appears. We should not, however, conceive of his labors in terms of a Romantic striving after an ideal that one approaches asymptotically but can never reach. The goal is at once more modest and more daunting, for all Flaubert is trying to do is to write a sentence, but his attempts to do so reveal that whether it is the ravings of a genius or the refined product of a skilled craftsman, no sentence ever validates its own form, that is, no sentence ever serves as a satisfactory argument for itself. When Flaubert declares, "I would like to make books in which it would only be a matter of *writing* sentences [his emphasis]," he is lamenting the fact that he cannot write a sentence without calling the very possibility of writing a sentence into question.[60]

It is no small irony that Flaubert, the inventor of a labor theory of sentence value, pursued a compositional praxis that few could hope to have the time

58. Barthes, "Flaubert and the Sentence," 304 (translation modified).

59. In Flaubert, argues Barthes, the sentence becomes a "thing" ("Flaubert and the Sentence," 303).

60. Cited in Blanchot, *Infinite Conversation*, 336.

or luxury of imitating, especially since the likelihood of failure is almost absolute. That one might spend days trying to perfect a single sentence is one thing; that one would assent a priori to the judgment of this sentence and every other one as "flawed" or "constitutively incomplete" is quite another. From an early age, we are taught that in speech and writing, being able to finish our sentences is a prerequisite for substantive participation in almost any social process. In fact, it would be no exaggeration to state that what we—casually and technically—call "the subject" is almost invariably an entity that is presumed to have the power to speak in complete sentences. Invoking Julia Kristeva's declaration that "every ideological activity is presented in the form of compositionally completed utterances," Barthes proposes that we reverse this proposition and recognize that "any completed utterance runs the risk of being ideological."[61] From the perspective of our discussion of Flaubert, we might say that the conviction that a sentence *can* be completed is the ideological conceit par excellence. Although it is outside the scope of this discussion, one could think further about the extent to which different forms of political power are predicated on the right to decide what does and does not count as a finished sentence.

If our goal is to finalize our sentences, Flaubert does not give us much cause for optimism about our prospects for success. What, however, if the very intention to write in complete sentences is misguided or a symptom of the degree to which we are unwittingly subjecting ourselves to constraints whose authority is far from obvious? Like the narrator of "The Imp of the Perverse" who rushes to spit out "I confess" before he can be interrupted, we may routinely operate under a demand for verbal closure whose very existence we rarely, if ever, recognize. One contemporary of Flaubert who did not have the luxury of ignoring such restrictions was Daniel Paul Schreber (1842–1911), a German judge diagnosed with dementia praecox—what would today be called schizophrenia. Schreber was made famous by Sigmund Freud, who wrote a second-order case history based on Schreber's *Memoirs*. In their intertextual conversation, Freud plays the straight man to Schreber's excesses, at least insofar as the authority of complete sentences is concerned. In the course of his analysis, Freud makes his infamous claim that "the core of the conflict in cases of paranoia among males is a homosexual wishful phantasy of *loving a man*."[62]

61. Barthes, *The Pleasure of the Text*, 50.

62. Sigmund Freud, *Psychoanalytic Notes on an Autobiographical Account of a Case of Paranoia (Dementia Paranoides), The Standard Edition of the Complete Psychological Works of Sigmund Freud,* vol. 12, trans. James Strachey (Toronto: Hogarth Press, 1981), 62 (Freud's italics).

More specifically, he insists that the principal forms of paranoia can all be represented as contradictions of a single sentence: "I (a man) love him."[63] As this sentence is never consciously articulated by the patient in this form, the analyst must show how this central maxim is to be inferred from the analysand's expressions of persecution, delusion, and erotomania.

While Freud insists that he is relying on empirical observations drawn from his practice in reaching these conclusions, he is clearly taken with the rhetorical power of this simple *I love him* and the different guises it can assume. Like Erasmus reviewing the manifold incarnations of a statement, he spends a significant amount of time rehearsing the various negative forms in which it is indirectly expressed by the male paranoid: "I do not *love* him—I *hate* him"; "I do not love *him*—I love *her*"; "It is not *I* who loves the man—*she* loves him"; "*I do not love at all—I do not love anyone*."[64] Reading these different formulations as instances of inversion, reversal, or irony, the interpretively adroit analyst should be able to show without great difficulty that all of them unfold within a closed field of well-organized affirmations and negations and constitute the same expression of homosexual desire.

Stepping back to admire this elegant elucidation of the various permutations of the paranoid's core dictum, we cannot help but notice that the entire set-up is at odds with Schreber's own relationship to language, since unlike Freud, he rarely enjoys the luxury of beginning his reflections from the standpoint of a complete sentence. Writing about Schreber, Jacques Lacan proposed that "if the neurotic inhabits language, the psychotic is inhabited, possessed, by language."[65] For Schreber, this possession is a predicament in which he, like the narrator of "The Demon of Analogy," is constantly struggling to finish sentences he cannot escape even as they are decidedly not his own. In his *Memoirs*, Schreber exhaustively describes his battles with the "divine rays" that assail his nervous system and play it like an instrument: "My nerves are influenced by the rays to vibrate corresponding to certain human words; their choice is therefore not subject to my own will, but is due to an influence exerted on me from without."[66] Schreber presents these verbal intruders as the

63. Freud, *Psychoanalytic Notes,* 63.

64. Freud, *Psychoanalytic Notes,* 63–65 (Freud's italics).

65. Jacques Lacan, *The Seminar of Jacques Lacan (Book III): The Psychoses 1955–56*, trans. Russell Grigg (New York: W. W. Norton, 1993), 250.

66. Daniel Paul Schreber, *Memoirs of My Nervous Illness*, trans. and ed. Ida Macalpine and Richard A. Hunter (New York: New York Review of Books, 2000), 197 (hereafter cited in text as *MS*). Freud declared that Schreber's divine rays are nothing more than a projection of libidinal cathexes. In this respect, he concluded, "they lend Schreber's delusions a striking conformity

product of forces entirely beyond his control, but despite their evident power over him, they haunt him with fragments rather than complete sentences, creating what he calls "the system of not-finishing-a-sentence" (*MS*, 197).

Schreber maintains that the fragmented nature of these intrusive sentences would not be such a problem except for the fact that the human nervous system instinctively responds to such stray pieces of language: "It is in the nature of nerves that if unconnected words or the beginnings of phrases are thrown into them, they automatically attempt to complete them to finished thoughts satisfactory to the human mind" (*MS*, 197–98). According to Schreber, our mental reflex is to "finish the sentence," and crucially, he insists that the psyche does this not out of any allegiance to communication or semantic integrity, but instinctively, without thought. If in most circumstances we would hesitate before treating the content of a psychotic's pronouncements as anything more than part of the illness, in this case we may be reluctant to infer that the desire to make fragments into sentences is symptomatic of pathology. Schreber's impulse to turn phrases into independent clauses may even be a sign of health rather than sickness.

Over time, the divine rays give Schreber increasingly cursory formulations, often offering him nothing more to work with than a stray conjunction or adverb and finally just pairs of one-syllable interjections: "O ja" (*MS*, 198). Against all odds, he valiantly manages to craft finished sentences from even the merest scraps, although this does not mean that he is simply filling in the blanks as one would in a Mad Lib game, putting a noun of his choice in the noun slot, a verb of his choice in the verb slot, etc. On the contrary, Schreber insists that he restores the sentences to their original state, although the status of this primal version becomes increasingly vague as he moves from suggesting that the divine light rays are giving him fragments of sentences he has already heard or said himself to musing that he knows how to finish the sentences because he feels the answers on his body.

Lacan claims that the beginnings of the sentences with which Schreber wrangles tend to break off at the point at which a crucial word is about to appear, implying that these interruptions are symptoms of unconscious censorship. If a review of Schreber's examples does not readily substantiate this observation, he does offer some that threaten to ironize the entire set-up by clouding the distinction between a complete and an incomplete sentence. In a

with our own theory" (*Psychoanalytic Notes*, 78). One could ask whether it is Freud who is projecting here. For his part, Lacan wryly observed that "the voices that preoccupy Schreber with their continuous discourse are psychologists," in particular behaviorists (*The Psychoses*, 114).

couple of cases, he presents as a fragment something that looks like an entirely respectable sentence, then proudly announces that he has finished it by adding the adverb that was "missing" at the end. Taking Flaubert's revisionary machinations to the next level, Schreber hints that once a few words are there, all the words are potentially there, as if every time a sentence tried to come to an end it had to struggle to stave off one more addition that could emerge from anywhere in the lexicon of the language.

However he does it, Schreber leaves no doubt that he finds finishing all these sentences exhausting. To attempt to spare himself the verbal wrangling, he gradually trains his mind not to respond automatically to the fragments imposed on him, and he does so by incessantly repeating the words and phrases he has been given by the divine rays, turning them into what he calls "not-thinking-of-anything-thoughts" (*MS*, 201). Rather than prompts for a complete statement to follow, the initial words of the sentences-to-be are transformed into nonstarters, leaving Schreber spinning in curious refrains of "If only my . . ." (*MS*, 201). Over time, the divine rays begin to speak to him increasingly slowly, to the point that it takes them up to sixty seconds to say something as short as "but naturally," each syllable emerging in a slow-motion stutter: "B.b.b.u.u.u.t.t.t. n.n.n.a.a.a.t.t.t.u.u.u.r.r.r.a.a.a.l.l.l.y.y.y." (*MS*, 202). Here the prospect of a sentence finishing or being interrupted is restaged at the level of the word or syllable, with each individual letter threatening to be both part of an infinite string of characters and the very last one.

To block out this kind of fragment, Schreber memorizes poems from Goethe, Schiller, and some lesser-known writers, then recites them to himself, one set of someone else's sentences serving to keep another set at bay. In "The Imp of the Perverse," the narrator does not have to recite "I am safe" for very long before realizing that the sentence is all too meaningful, albeit not in the way he had anticipated. In contrast, Schreber steadfastly deems the content of the poems he mobilizes as verbal shields to be irrelevant. His defense against the compulsion to complete incomplete sentences is a language emptied of significance, pure sound, which is exactly what Poe argues that the raven's "nevermore" should be. In the most extreme case, Schreber quietly counts to himself (1, 2, 3, 4 . . .), moving from words to integers and leaving grammar completely behind so that he can enjoy some semblance of discursive "freedom" in the form of rote articulation.

As foreign as the nerve language that torments him may sound, Schreber allows that we all have a sense of what its intrusions are like, since we have all had the experience of inadvertently reciting to ourselves things we have memorized, the only difference being that Schreber takes these autodiscursive experiences and their implications a little more seriously than the rest of us. This comment drives home just how similar his "solution" to his problem is to the problem itself. Surely there is much in a Goethe or Schiller poem that might torment one, especially if one cannot remember how to complete some of the lines and finds oneself finishing them automatically in one manner or another.

Anticipating this objection but still reluctant to acknowledge that his psyche may have good reasons for not wanting to know what the rays are saying to him, Schreber ultimately deems all their remarks to be nonsensical, despite evidence to the contrary. The best example—arguably the archetypal self-reflexive moment in his text—is when the divine rays ask him: "What are you thinking of now?" (*MS*, 55). The question incenses Schreber, who deems it ludicrous and vigorously attacks it with what Freud elsewhere calls "kettle logic." Under what circumstances, he fumes, could one ever hope to respond to such a preposterous query, for one is not always thinking, one is always simultaneously thinking about thousands of things, and besides, one is often thinking about nothing. Even when the divine rays speak in syntactically and morphologically sound sentences, our linguist Schreber is not content. "All nonsense cancels itself out," one of his divine beings tells him, which reassures Schreber, who wants to apply the claim to all sentences (*MS*, 273). Asked at one point by the rays whether he is ashamed in front of his wife, Schreber's reply is that he is ashamed not for himself, but for language. He rues the way in which fragments insist on becoming something complete, he is embarrassed by sentences that boast of being complete, and above all, he cringes at statements that have the audacity to imagine that they are more meaningful than the rote recitation of verse.

Compelled by forces beyond his control to finish sentences he has no sense of having begun, Schreber offers a compelling picture of the demands language makes on us and the madness that may ensue when we attempt to resist them. At the height of the Romantic period, Friedrich Schlegel, perhaps anticipating the conflicts between genius and method that would preoccupy subsequent generations, proposed that in order to speak or write freely, one must be liberated from the imperative to finish what one starts. In terms that would no doubt have appealed to Schreber, he maintained that "even a friendly conversation that cannot freely break off at any moment, completely arbitrarily, has something intolerant or restrictive about it."[67] Schlegel asks us to envision

67. Friedrich Schlegel, *Philosophical Fragments*, trans. Peter Firchow (Minneapolis: University of Minnesota Press, 1991), 5 (translation modified).

a discourse in which every word or syllable is completely informed by and yet utterly indifferent to the fact that it may be the last. The spontaneity of expression, or silence, would thereby be pitted against grammatical, logical, and rhetorical or narrative dictates, each of which in its own way lays down expectations for how a given sentence, if not a given paragraph or chapter, must continue. For the twentieth-century inheritors of Flaubert's interminable sentences and Poe's terminal—and lethal—ones, Schlegel's suggestion lingers as a tantalizing reminder of the possibility of truly abandoning traditional sentential forms, although it leaves us with a nagging sense that the language he is describing may be the one that we already have.

CHAPTER 4

The Democratic Sentence

Write the truest sentences that you know.

ERNEST HEMINGWAY

If you ask yourself how you would be able to tell a page of Hemingway if it were unexpectedly placed before you, you would be compelled to answer: *Because it would be like Miss Stein!*

WYNDHAM LEWIS

In 1897, three years after his infamous announcement at Oxford that someone had been tampering with the rules of verse, Stéphane Mallarmé declared that literature was "undergoing an exquisite and fundamental crisis."[1] At issue was not simply a loosening of the rules of prosody or the waning authority of the alexandrine form that had dominated French poetry for centuries. Mallarmé sought to highlight a more fundamental disturbance, a challenge to the horizontal line as the core organizing principle of a text, and with it an unsettling of the most foundational premises about syntax and its relationship to semantics. Basic linguistic norms appeared to be in retreat, whether as a prelude to discursive collapse or in anticipation of the emergence of new, as yet unimagined linguistic forms.

Mallarmé's remarks may seem less earth-shattering and more grandiose when we realize that he was largely speaking about his own writing. Nonetheless, the text he was working on at the time and would still be correcting on his deathbed would almost single-handedly inaugurate a new crisis of the sentence, subjecting grammatical and compositional conventions to a profound shock.[2] Virtually all subsequent experimental poetry owes a debt to "A Roll of the Dice Will Never Abolish Chance," a work in which the freedom

1. Stéphane Mallarmé, "Crisis of Verse," *Divagations*, trans. Barbara Johnson (Cambridge, MA: Harvard University Press, 2007), 201.

2. For a discussion of the provocations of "A Roll of the Dice," see R. Howard Bloch, *One Toss of the Dice: The Incredible Story of How a Poem Made Us Modern* (New York: W. W. Norton, 2017).

of free verse runs amok. Twenty pages in length, the consecutive facing pages constitute ten compositional units or panels with text flowing back and forth between them; the font size varies, and italics come and go. One reads from left to right, but the verses do not all begin flush-left or even at the same distance from the left-hand side of the page, and they range in length from a single word to a dozen or more. Line breaks, single or multiple, are abundant but hardly systematic in their appearance, meaning that from a distance the pattern of words on any given panel may look like a shape demanding interpretation in its own right. Sometimes pieces of language appear to have been haphazardly scattered about; at other moments, a "line" will cascade downward in the shape of a descending staircase, with each word or phrase a step. Unexpected gaps can appear in the middle of phrases ("*The lucid and lordly crest   of vertigo*"), with two vertical columns of words emerging when this occurs on several successive strips of the page.[3] This adds to the general sense of precariousness, since one has to read across, if not simply disregard, the resulting gap in order to follow the unfolding of the clauses, although it seems odd not at least to attempt to account for its glaring presence.

As the spaces between words, letters, and lines become an increasingly prominent feature of the textual field, the authority of conventional grammar begins to abate. The syntactic placement of any given noun or verb still reveals something about its function in the clause in which it appears, but the novel typography creates relationships between words that are organized by less obvious but potentially no less forceful or precise principles. Semantic coherence does not vanish completely. One can parse the sentences and identify at least the specter of traditional versification, but the verbal landscape is decidedly unsettled. No less polemical than any of Mallarmé's formal pronouncements about the state of verse in his age, "A Roll of the Dice" declares that the dawn of the century will see new kinds of signifying constellations displace, if not outright dismantle, the authority of predicative structures.[4]

Acknowledging that his reader is likely to become preoccupied with, not to mention unnerved by, the abundance of blank spaces in his poem, Mallarmé observes that stanzas have traditionally been surrounded by a great deal of empty space, most printed lyrics taking up only a fraction of the page on

3. Stéphane Mallarmé, *Collected Poems*, trans. Henry Weinfield (Los Angeles: University of California Press, 1994), 138.

4. On the unique challenges of Mallarmé's language, see Jacques Derrida's masterful "The Double Session," in *Dissemination*, trans. Barbara Johnson (Chicago: University of Chicago Press, 1981), 173–286.

which they appear. All he has done is to fold these spaces into his poem. "I don't transgress against this order of things," he explains; "I merely disperse its elements."[5] By simultaneously increasing and decreasing the speed with which its sentences can be scanned, if not demanding that each of its pages be treated as an image as well as a collection of words, "A Roll of the Dice" blurs the line between seeing and reading, or perhaps reveals that it was never very stable in the first place. The enormous impact of these graphematic experiments is readily evident if one considers Futurist poetry, Wyndham Lewis's *Blast*, or Dadaist collage, projects whose experimental typographies have been subject to countless imitators.

In the preface to "A Roll of the Dice," Mallarmé declares that henceforth the "basic unit" will be neither the sentence nor the paragraph, neither the line of verse nor the stanza, but the page.[6] Walter Benjamin proposed that in this respect Mallarmé was "the first to incorporate the graphic tensions of advertisement" into poetry, an observation that begins to complicate any simple distinction between the so-called "high" and "mass" culture of the era.[7] Today, it may appear that we have moved even further into uncharted waters thanks to the advent of digital interfaces that all but remove any sense of a "top" or "bottom" to the page. In fact, these newly emergent forms of the textual field may constitute a regression from Mallarmé. As we scroll through articles or entire books, we embrace a more conventional model of language in which the sentence is the exclusive thread organizing our processing of the material, irrespective of any unexpected line breaks or of how long or short the horizontal strings of words may be. Far from further heightening the tension between signifiers and blank space, the latter tends to be disregarded altogether—when there is no longer a page, there is no longer an unutilized part of the page, either.

In the decades following Mallarmé's death in 1898, the sense of aesthetic upheaval heralded by his work scarcely abated as European and American modernism came to be defined by tumultuous transformations in literary practices whose effects continue to be felt. As writers pursued the experiments in radical typography and free verse begun in the previous century, they produced texts that bore little resemblance to what earlier generations would have recognized as exemplars of traditional genres. Even those that could still be

5. Mallarmé, *Collected Poems*, 121.

6. Mallarmé, *Collected Poems*, 121.

7. Walter Benjamin, *One-Way Street*, *Selected Writings*, Vol. 1: *1913–1926*, ed. Marcus Bullock and Michael Jennings (Cambridge, MA: Harvard University Press, 2004), 456.

classified as lyrics or dramas had highly unconventional features; hybrids were the new norm.

No less than the poetry, much of the prose of the first decades of the twentieth century was distinguished by far-reaching formal and stylistic innovation, perhaps most notoriously in the work of James Joyce, whom Umberto Eco termed "the anarchist of language."[8] *Ulysses* was designed as a wholesale assault on literary conventions, and it wreaks havoc with standard syntactic schemas when it is not ignoring them altogether. The novel concludes with Molly Bloom's infamous soliloquy in which the "sentences" are thousands of words in length, with scarcely a punctuation mark to be found, a verbal extravaganza that would be surpassed by *Finnegans Wake*, in which multiple dialects and instantiations of various languages from different historical periods blend into a dazzlingly confusing idioglossia.[9] Anthony Burgess has observed that in this novel the only character is language. Words are constantly breaking down into syllables and recombining into new terms whose precise significance can be difficult to pin down.[10] As in "A Roll of the Dice," grammar still plays an important role, but it has some competition.

Despite the prominence of these and similarly unorthodox practices, it would be misleading to conclude that the archetypal modernist sentence is necessarily a monstrous run-on amalgamating dozens of independent and dependent clauses as it unfolds with near total disregard for conventional compositional practices. One of the most successful authors of the period, Ernest Hemingway, fashioned short, often austere sentences that have rarely been deemed stylistically "difficult," much less "alternative," and continue to be upheld as models worthy of emulation. Marcel Proust, Robert Musil, and Thomas Mann all wrote notoriously long sentences, but as intricate as their hypotactic constructions may be, they epitomize lucidity and rhythmic elegance rather than discordance and confusion. If only the most intrepid fan would dare imitate such precise, dynamic prose, it has impressed countless readers with its rhetorical and representational powers. Far from challenging

8. Cited in Adrian Tahourdin, "Is *Finnegans Wake* Unreadable?," TLS Blogs, *Times Literary Supplement,* July 9, 2014, https://www.the-tls.co.uk/is-finnegans-wake-unreadable/.

9. The literary figures of this period hardly had a monopoly on the concoction of new languages. In 1887, Ludovic Lazarus Zamenhof published a booklet describing his Esperanto, which would become the most widely spoken constructed tongue in the world. Explicitly designed to help peoples and nations transcend their differences and coexist peacefully, Esperanto has clearly not enjoyed the influence its founder hoped it would, but it certainly represented a major effort to reshape the rules of the verbal landscape.

10. Cited in Tahourdin, "Is *Finnegans Wake* Unreadable?"

the sentence form, these oeuvres testify to its nearly unlimited powers and to the extraordinary range of striking shapes it can assume in the hands of an author content to respect grammatical norms.

To be sure, the inability of some modernist writers to bring their gargantuan novels to a close suggests that the structural openness of the sentence may be inherently destabilizing when it is taken as a model for a larger narrative, which proves to be incapable of emulating the clear stopping point of a terminal punctuation mark. Proust notoriously did not live long enough to finish his ever-expanding magnum opus, while Musil is said to have wanted to end his lengthy but unfinished *The Man Without Qualities* in the middle of a sentence, with a comma. Above all, then, what distinguished this era of European and American literature was a constant interplay of classical and avant-garde impulses that ensured that conventional grammatical and representational paradigms and challenging innovations marched side by side, often in the same text. The crisis of the sentence announced by Mallarmé was equally a carnival of the sentence that celebrated the authority of existing rules and norms even as it raised the prospect of altering them to the point of unrecognizability. In this festival of tradition and experimentation, even the most unassuming text could ultimately betray the contingency of its own style, as if on another day it might well have assumed an entirely different form.

Whatever their stylistic orientation, many modernists shared an interest in publicizing their opinions about their craft. The most programmatic aesthetic statements tended to be made by figures whose positions on key issues underwent multiple metamorphoses over the course of their careers, and the concepts informing specific pronouncements were often presented as if their significance was self-evident when in fact it was anything but. Even in calls for precision, polemic was typically privileged over exactitude, and the shock value of a grand proclamation frequently seemed more important than its implications. Further complicating matters, the most formally or stylistically innovative authors could be the least confident that their interventions constituted true shifts in the language. The perception of the need to make something "new" out of the sentence did not necessarily bring with it a reliable plan for how to do so or a surefire way of deciding whether or not one had been successful.

The best-known modernist challenge to the traditional sentence form may be the so-called "stream of consciousness" made famous by Joyce, William Faulkner, and Virginia Woolf. It is an attempt to represent the inner workings of the mind as a flow of impressions, intimations, and musings that manifest themselves verbally as strings of words that may or may not respect conventional grammatical, logical, or rhetorical paradigms. Henri Bergson's account of the flux of time and his emphasis on life as "unceasing creation" is generally invoked as the philosophical model for this kind of writing, which seeks to capture the inherent dynamism of thought and self-perception and attempts to liberate our concepts of the mind and language from the static forms in which they have traditionally been mired.[11] In this spirit, stream of consciousness can be distinguished from interior monologue, which presents a character's reflections in a comparatively stable fashion, relying on conventional morphology and syntax in the course of articulating more accessible semantic relationships.[12]

From its inception, stream of consciousness was a subject of debate. Although modernist fiction is often said to democratize its subject matter, the promise—or threat, depending on one's perspective—of this narrative mode seems to be that it democratizes language itself, leveling or at least reconfiguring the traditional hierarchies ordering the parts of a sentence. That this might constitute a provocation to entrenched cultural interests was not lost on the era's foes of democracy. As Anne Fernihough explains: "Bergsonian flux was rejected by *Action Française* and by modernist legislators like Pound, [T. E.] Hulme, and Wyndham Lewis on account of its Romantic, progressive overtones. These writers scorned so-called stream-of-consciousness writing as a 'feminine,' bodily type of writing, even when used by male authors such as Joyce."[13] In a gesture that illustrates the complex interplay of stylistic pronouncements, sexual politics, and the philosophy of consciousness that defined the period, Lewis "attacked the way in which *Ulysses* 'imposes a softness, flabbiness and vagueness everywhere in its Bergsonian fluidity.' "[14]

As a fan of democracy, Virginia Woolf drew similar conclusions about this mode of writing, but saw them as cause for celebration. She praised the inclusiveness and dynamism of Dorothy Richardson's stream-of-consciousness prose as a form of *écriture féminine* and credited Richardson with creating a new kind of sentence: "She has invented, or, if she has not invented, developed and applied to her own uses, a sentence which we might call the psychological sentence of the feminine gender. It is of a more elastic fiber than the old, capable of stretching to the extreme, of suspending the frailest particles, of

11. Cited in Paul Douglass, *Bergson, Eliot, and American Literature* (Lexington: University Press of Kentucky, 1986), 122.

12. Gerald Prince, *Dictionary of Narratology* (Lincoln: University of Nebraska Press, 2003), 94.

13. Anne Fernihough, " 'Go in Fear of Abstractions': Modernism and the Specter of Democracy," *Textual Practice* 14, no. 3 (2000): 493.

14. Fernihough, "Go in Fear of Abstractions," 493.

enveloping the vaguest shapes."[15] Taken together, Woolf's and Lewis's arguments indicate the degree to which stylistic questions *were* political questions in modernist aesthetics.

From this perspective, modernism is progressive because it liberates language from traditional sentence forms. In a radio address, Woolf describes the importance of fashioning texts in which words, "highly democratic" by nature, manifest themselves in such a way that we see clearly that "one word is as good as another" and that "there are no ranks or titles" in the lexical realm.[16] If larger ideological questions are at stake, so are one's personal prospects as an author. To have any hope of writing well, one must constantly remind oneself that words "are the wildest, freest, most irresponsible, most unteachable of all things" and that we err insofar as we suppose that these "irreclaimable vagabonds" will respect the laws we lay down for them.[17] Only by accepting that our "few trifling rules of grammar" are barely adequate to the task of controlling verbal forces can we hope our own texts will benefit from their full—albeit ungovernable—powers.[18]

Is stream of consciousness, of which Woolf was among the most celebrated practitioners, a form of writing—perhaps the quintessential form—that respects the wild, even anarchic nature of words? The term comes from William James, also a reader of Bergson, who in his 1890 *The Principles of Psychology* declared: "Consciousness does not appear to itself chopped up in bits. Such words as 'chain' or 'train' do not describe it fitly as it presents itself in the first instance. It is nothing jointed; it flows. A 'river' or a 'stream' are the metaphors by which it is most naturally described. *In talking of it hereafter, let us call it the stream of thought, of consciousness, or of subjective life*."[19] James invokes

15. Woolf, "Romance of the Heart," *Times Literary Supplement*, May 19, 1923, reprinted in *Women and Writing*, ed. Michèle Barrett (New York: Harcourt, 1979), 191. In "Women and Fiction," Woolf elaborates on this idea: "In a novel, which covers so wide a stretch of ground, an ordinary and usual type of sentence has to be found to carry the reader on easily and naturally from one end of the book to the other. And this a woman must make for herself, altering and adapting the current sentence until she writes one that takes the natural shape of her thought without crushing or distorting it." Cited in Pamela J. Transue, *Virginia Woolf and the Politics of Style* (Albany: SUNY Press, 1986), 9.

16. Fiona Macdonald, "The Only Surviving Recording of Virginia Woolf," *BBC–Culture*, March 28, 2016, http://www.bbc.com/culture/story/20160324-the-only-surviving-recording-of-virginia-woolf.

17. Macdonald, "The Only Surviving Recording."

18. Macdonald, "The Only Surviving Recording."

19. William James, *The Principles of Psychology*, vol. 1 (New York: Dover, 1950), 239.

moving water in an effort to characterize the consciousness of consciousness. The flowing figures do triple duty, representing the sum of one's thoughts and feelings, one's sense of oneself as an embodied being, and one's intimations of semiconscious and unconscious processes and impulses. May Sinclair was the first to deploy James's term in a literary context when she used it to describe Richardson's novels, although Richardson herself rejected the label, condemning the "borrowing . . . by Miss May Sinclair from the epistemologists, of this more than lamentably ill-chosen metaphor, long since by them discarded but still, in literary criticism, pursuing its foolish way."[20] Such protests notwithstanding, the label "stream of consciousness" acquired a life of its own and has become a mainstay of discussions of the modernist novel.

Given how frequently James's term is referenced, there has been curiously little discussion about whether his work supports the application of this concept to the literary field. James does go out of his way to aver that no linguistic depiction of consciousness can do justice to the "numberless" relationships making up the currents of the mind, implying that any form of experimental prose one pursues will be at best only an approximation of the dynamic it seeks to depict.[21] At the same time, his river never becomes a maelstrom. In retaining the rudimentary features of a unidirectional vector, it remains a viable figure for strings of words unfolding in a sequence.

Whether James anticipated that the resulting constructions would look anything like passages from Joyce or Faulkner is another question. Several decades after he published *The Principles of Psychology*, he made some comments about representations of the workings of the mind that are very different from the accounts of his thinking typically offered in literary discussions: "When we take a general view of the wonderful stream of our consciousness, what strikes us first is the different pace of its parts. Like a bird's life, it seems to be an alternation of flights and perchings. The rhythm of language expresses this, where every thought is expressed in a sentence, and every sentence is closed by a period."[22] What predominates here is neither disorganization nor obscure connections, but a coherence predicated on definite beginnings and ends. In

20. Dorothy Richardson, "Novels," *Life and Letters To-Day* 56 (March 1948): 189. For Sinclair's observation, see May Sinclair, "The Novels of Dorothy Richardson," *The Egoist* 5, no. 4 (April 1908): 57. It is uncertain whether Sinclair took "stream of consciousness" directly from James. Suzanne Raitt argues that the term was already in wide circulation in the early twentieth century. See Suzanne Raitt, *May Sinclair: A Modern Victorian* (Oxford: Clarendon Press, 2000), 219.

21. James, *Principles of Psychology*, 245.

22. William James, *Psychology: The Briefer Course* (New York: Dover, 2001 [1920]), 27.

giving his stamp of approval to language as an appropriate model for characterizing the patterns of consciousness, James does not describe paragraphs devoid of capitalization and punctuation, but the ordinary beat and tempo of distinct propositions, that is, a string of statements clearly delineated from one another. The movement of water turns out to be of only secondary significance, since what actually gives shape to our self-awareness is not the rhythms of processes in the natural world but the rhythms of language. The so-called "stream" of consciousness is a series of orderly sentences rather than run-ons, and the precise starts and stops that coordinate these sentences with one another are a crucial feature of the "flows" that define the workings of the mind.

The fact that James ultimately throws his lot in with such conventional grammatical constructions may be a symptom of his linguistic conservatism. Surely the traditional sentence has done little to quell suspicions that it is too stable, static, or outright stuffy, not least because it seems to force all mental dynamics to conform to a standard schema of logical predication. In contrast, the stream-of-consciousness sentence promises something prelogical or preformed, a level of improvisation in which one is constantly presaging the advent of a new linguistic order while graphically exposing the limits of the old. Disorientation should not, however, be confused with structural radicality. The reader ploughing through a stream-of-consciousness passage may struggle to follow the rapid jumps in perspective, the appearance of pronouns with no obvious antecedents, and the frequent shifts between topics. Nothing about the language will be easy to digest. Taken individually, the clauses of such prose can nonetheless be quite simple, even primitive, the opposite of the hypotactic marvels that abound in Mann or Proust. Molly Bloom's soliloquy at the end of *Ulysses*, for example, is essentially a series of straightforward subject-predicate constructions set side by side, sometimes without separating punctuation, at other times linked by *and*s. Far from revealing that the workings of the mind cannot be captured by traditional logico-grammatical forms, her ruminations bespeak a fairly ordinary conception of thought as a string of easily digested propositions; and despite what James would predict, the paucity of punctuation does not result in an absence of rhythm. Like many other sections of *Ulysses*, one need only read a small part of this sequence aloud to hear the distinctive tempo, which regularly approaches the melodic or sing-song.

While stream of consciousness is perhaps the most familiar stylistic innovation of modernist writing, other experiments with the sentence were no less influential. Eschewing monstrous constructions that sprawled across pages, some authors crafted minimalist forms of only a few syllables. Implicitly or explicitly, many of these projects took their cue from Ezra Pound's 1913 injunction: "Go in fear of abstraction."[23] Widely used in many contexts, often with little clarification, the abstract is usually contrasted with the concrete in a dichotomy of intangible concepts, forces, or laws and tangible persons, places, or things. What this potentially obscures is the fact that an abstraction (e.g., "the murderer") is the product of an operation or series of operations by which a subject comes to be identified with only one of its predicates ("the man is a murderer"), while the subject's countless other features are forced into the background (the man may also be a father, a lover, etc.). From this perspective, a sentence is by nature a kind of abstraction machine because it tears its subject from the rich network of determinations that shape its identity; and only an impossibly long sentence that enumerates all of a given subject's features seems to have any hope of avoiding the charge of privileging one or more attributes over the others. Given this, stream-of-consciousness prose might be considered a form of resistance to this "limitation" of traditional discourse, an effort to undercut the assumption that in any autonomous grammatical construction, one or at most several predicates must, if only fleetingly, reign supreme over the rest.

In his Imagist phase, Pound did not follow Joyce in attacking abstraction through syntactic expansion, but instead tried to strip away the trappings of established rhetorical figures and emblematic codes in the belief that what remained would be concrete.[24] Here words, considered independently of their

23. Ezra Pound, "A Few Don'ts by an Imagiste," *Poetry* 1, no. 6 (March 1913): 201. Only slightly less well known than his "Make It New," Pound's warnings about abstraction preoccupied many of his contemporaries. Modernist thinkers at both ends of the political spectrum argued against democracy precisely because it was seen to be "a process of *abstraction*, abstraction of the uniqueness of the individual into a mere cipher or statistic" (Fernihough, "Go in Fear," 488 [emphasis in original]; see also 493). Carried to the extreme, the result would be a society of "dead and mechanical individuals incapable of independent thought." Rachel Potter, *Modernism and Democracy: Literary Culture 1900–1930* (New York: Oxford University Press, 2006), 84.

24. Pound wrote repeatedly about the imperative to avoid "convention and cliché." Ezra Pound, "A Retrospect," *Literary Essays of Ezra Pound*, ed. T. S. Eliot (New York: New Directions, 1968), 11. Terminologically confusing though it may be, the campaign against abstraction waged by modernist poets was informed by some of the same impulses that were fueling the rise of what we today call "abstract" art. The Cubists and the Imagists shared an interest in capturing the concrete, singular dimensions of individual perceptual experiences in ways that would challenge the stability of traditional representational paradigms. As Daniel Albright argues, Pound was not opposed to abstract art; to the contrary, he liked the fact that abstract art "*almost* annihilated representation." Daniel Albright, *Quantum Poetics: Yeats, Pound, Eliot, and the Science of Modernism* (New York: Cambridge University Press, 1997), 136. Writing about Gertrude Stein,

status as parts of larger verbal constructions, were a central concern. As the most famous Imagist manifesto instructs: "Employ always the exact word, not the nearly-exact."[25] Pithy though the injunction may be, exactly what notion of exactitude is under consideration and how it will manifest itself is far from obvious. We all have a sense of what this may mean, because we have all had the frustrating experience of hunting for the best adjective to modify a particular noun, and we know all too well the aggravation of having the perfect word right on the tip of our tongue. Such intuitions, however, seem like a flimsy basis for a poetic doctrine, especially when the issue is precision.

The Imagists' efforts to develop a precise notion of precise diction were informed by their complex relationship with Romanticism. Crediting Ford Madox Ford with the observation that William Wordsworth was "so intent on the ordinary or plain word that he never thought of hunting for *le mot juste*," Pound appears to ally himself with the abiding lore about Gustave Flaubert, who allegedly labored for hours, if not days, over every word he wrote.[26] Of course, in attempting to break with the poetic languages of the past, including what they regarded as established—and now thoroughly clichéd—Romantic idioms, Pound and his cohort were well aware that the Romantics had set out to do the very same with the clichés of their day and apparently failed. In the "advertisement" at the start of the first edition of his *Lyrical Ballads*, Wordsworth declared that his poems were experiments to ascertain "how far the language of conversation in the middle and lower classes of society is adapted to the purposes of poetic pleasure."[27] In the various prefaces and addendums that appear in subsequent editions of the book, Wordsworth tries time and again to detail precisely what the language of the middle and lower classes is, but he struggles to find the appropriate words with which to talk about the appropriate and inappropriate words for his verses. "The real language of men" seems

---

who regularly hosted Pound in her salon, Cynthia Ozick argues that Stein and Pound both "wanted to invent Cubism—not in oils but in words, where refraction produces not abstraction but subtraction." Cynthia Ozick, "A Prophet of Modernism: Gertrude Stein," *New York Times Magazine*, November 24, 1996.

25. Preface to *Some Imagist Poets* (1915), in *Modernism: An Anthology of Sources and Documents,* ed. Vassiliki Kolocotroni, Jane Goldman, and Olga Taxidou (Chicago: University of Chicago Press, 1998), 269.

26. Pound, "A Retrospect," *Literary Essays of Ezra Pound*, 7. A condemnatory, even contemptuous tone lurks in Pound's reference to the "ordinary." To this day, his positions on the arts are routinely referred to as elitist or aristocratic, accusations that are not easily dismissed.

27. William Wordsworth and Samuel Taylor Coleridge, *Lyrical Ballads*, ed. R. L. Brett and A. R. Jones (New York: Routledge, 1968), 7.

to be a more abstract, or at least more unruly, concept than one might suppose, although clarifying the term "poetic diction," the name for the language being rejected, proves no less vexing a task.[28] Wordsworth writes that he is "anxious to give an *exact* [my emphasis] notion of the sense in which [he] use[s] the phrase *poetic diction* [Wordsworth's emphasis]."[29] Before he can comment on the qualities of his poems' vocabulary, he needs to find a way to comment, precisely, on his word choice for word choice.

Ultimately, Wordsworth's position is that poetic diction is not a natural, spontaneous coordination of feeling and expression, but something artificial. It allows the writer to align whatever terms or imagery he likes with any given emotion, which is to say that poetic diction is "arbitrary, and subject to infinite caprices upon which no calculation whatever can be made."[30] Far from a weakness, however, this whimsy is what frees poetic language from external determinations and allows it to foster true creativity, while the language of ordinary people, despite ostensibly being grounded in spontaneous acts of expression, turns out to be eminently stable and unresponsive, to the point of indifference, to the specific contexts in which it emerges. "Ordinary" or "natural" language is a code, a collection of established lines, and in its predictable modulations, it betrays the very immediacy and particularity it is entrusted to impart, whereas the artificiality of poetic diction gives it the capacity to facilitate unique verbal interventions in any and every situation.

Mindful of these tensions and concerned that the call for exactitude should itself be exact, the unsigned 1915 Preface to *Some Imagist Poets* attempts to clarify its own vocabulary: "The 'exact' word does not mean the word which exactly describes the object in itself, it means the 'exact' word which brings the effect of that object before the reader as it presented itself to the poet's mind at the time of writing the poem."[31] While the intent is to convey conviction, the quotation marks and the need to repeat the word "exact" a second time reveal that when it is used to describe other words, the word "exact" can never be exact—or be qualified exactingly—enough. If the goal is to write something concrete and precise, more than word choice will have to be taken into account, not least because "word choice" is itself an abstraction, as if creating sentences were ever simply a matter of leafing through the thesaurus. If nothing else, the—possibly phantasmagoric—scenario whereby an author struggles

28. Wordsworth, *Lyrical Ballads*, 233.

29. Wordsworth, *Lyrical Ballads*, 311.

30. Wordsworth, *Lyrical Ballads*, 244.

31. Peter Jones, ed., *Imagist Poetry* (Harmondsworth: Penguin, 1988), 136–37.

to find the "right word" presumes a preexisting structure, if not a precise place in a sentence, into which the desired verbal element is to be plugged.

Skeptical of enthusiasm for *le mot juste*, Woolf attacked the very notion that pieces of language can be considered independently of the syntactic formations in which they appear, insisting that "a word [is] not a word indeed until it is part of a sentence."[32] In a similar vein, she emphasized that words resist "being lifted out on the point of a pen and examined separately," for "they hang together, in sentences, in paragraphs, sometimes for whole pages at a time."[33] Predictably, the result is that there is considerable disagreement about what the fundamental compositional unit in Woolf's own work is. Pamela J. Transue claims that "like a poet, who for the most part is also trying to impart a vision, Woolf's unit is the phrase. 'Moments of being' [instances of shock or revelation] are too evanescent to be contained within sentences, paragraphs, or chapters."[34] In contrast, Harvena Richter maintains that in Woolf "the base upon which rhythm and vocabulary are set is . . . the sentence"; whereas James Wood argues that Woolf believed that novelists should work in paragraphs and chapters, not sentences.[35] The coexistence of these disparate claims suggests that to approach a text solely from the perspective of its words, sentences, or paragraphs may be to embrace the very abstractions that both Woolf and the Imagists seek to avoid.

Isolated citations from Imagist manifestos notwithstanding, Woolf's demand that we treat words as parts of sentences was not foreign to Pound and the writers associated with him in the early 1910s. As in Flaubert, the search for just the right adjective or verb is only a small part of the labor that goes into perfecting a given sentence, the quest to find the "exact word" proving to be shorthand for a host of different ambitions. For all his concern with diction, Pound also privileges rhythm conceived independently of the meaning of the sentence being articulated, going so far as to recommend that we learn to write by studying the sounds and cadences of languages with which we are unfamiliar. He also stresses that in rejecting traditional poetic meters, he is concerned to find not *les mots justes* but "a rhythm . . . which corresponds exactly to the

32. Macdonald, "The Only Surviving Recording."

33. Macdonald, "The Only Surviving Recording."

34. Transue, *Virginia Woolf*, 135.

35. Harvena Richter, *Virginia Woolf: The Inward Voyage* (Princeton, NJ: Princeton University Press, 1970), 145; James Wood, "A Novel Brings Israel's Conflicts to New York," *New Yorker*, July 24, 2017, https://www.newyorker.com/magazine/2017/07/24/a-novel-brings-israels-conflicts-to-new-york.

emotion or shade of emotion to be expressed."[36] In these respects, he sounds remarkably like Woolf when she scoffs at the idea that writers should labor to find exactly the right word, declaring: "Style is a very simple matter: it is all rhythm. Once you get that, you can't use the wrong words," whereas attempting to go from words to sentence rhythm is bound to end in failure.[37]

Rhythm itself is a notoriously ephemeral concept, an irreducibly material phenomenon at one moment, an entirely abstract one the next. Mindful of this complication, Pound elaborates a notion of "efficient writing" as a paradigm for a dynamic yet concrete model of language.[38] As Jonathan Rose observes, the embrace of efficiency "was one of the shibboleths of the Edwardian period."[39] Under its aegis, texts were to take the form of an economy in which excess expenditure was avoided as every word contributed vigorously, doing its part for the larger process.[40] In his essay series "I Gather the Limbs of Osiris," Pound relies on the vocabulary of industrial technology, declaring that facts "govern knowledge as the switchboard governs an electric circuit" and that to look at a new poem is to enter "into the engineering laboratory" and see "successively an electric engine, a steam-engine, a gas-engine, etc."[41] Above all, poetic language must "act without waste."[42] Force, energy, and intensity are to be realized by the poet-engineer through text-machines governed by a perfect, that is, thermodynamically impossible, system that experiences no friction and produces no by-products. No less than with the notions of the exact word and

36. Ezra Pound, "A Retrospect," *Literary Essays of Ezra Pound*, 9. In the unsigned preface to *Some Imagist Poets*, we are told that "in poetry, a new cadence means a new idea" and that the goal is "to create new rhythms—as the expression of new moods—and not to copy old rhythms, which merely echo old moods" (Jones, *Imagist Poetry*, 135).

37. Virginia Woolf, *The Letters of Virginia Woolf*, ed. Nigel Nicolson and Joanne Trautmann (New York: Harcourt Brace Jovanovich, 1975–1980), III: 247. Woolf also writes: "All writing is nothing but putting words on the backs of rhythm. If they fall off the rhythm, one's done" (*The Letters of Virginia Woolf*, IV: 303).

38. Ezra Pound, "Mr. Hueffer and the Prose Tradition in Verse," *Poetry* 4, no. 3 (June 1914): 120.

39. Cited in A. Walton Litz and Lawrence Rainey, "Ezra Pound," *Modernism and the New Criticism, The Cambridge History of Literary Criticism* (vol. 7), ed. Litz, Louis Menand, and Rainey (New York: Cambridge University Press, 2000), 63.

40. Pound's injunction "to use absolutely no word that does not contribute to the presentation" is a mainstay of style manuals to this day. Pound, "A Retrospect," *Literary Essays of Ezra Pound*, 3. Similarly, Pound enjoins the writer to "use no superfluous word, no adjective which does not reveal something" ("A Retrospect," 4).

41. Cited in Litz and Rainey, "Ezra Pound," 63. Pound also writes about words being "charged with a force like electricity" (Litz and Rainey, "Ezra Pound," 63).

42. Litz and Rainey, "Ezra Pound," 63.

rhythm, such a model threatens to take on a life of its own and start working against the very quest for concreteness that gave rise to it. If abstraction was the enemy, mechanical production was an odd paradigm for Pound to embrace, since for his contemporaries it was one of the prime figures for the abstractions that shape life in democratic capitalist society.

What kinds of sentences emerge when a writerly praxis informed by such considerations tries to put its "machines" to work? Although it did not appear in any of the Imagist collections, Pound's "In a Station of the Metro" is frequently invoked as the quintessential Imagist poem, if not one of the defining works of the modernist period. Ubiquitous in anthologies, it is usually printed:

IN A STATION OF THE METRO

The apparition of these faces in the crowd;
Petals on a wet, black bough.[43]

From its first publication, Pound went to considerable lengths to craft a detailed origin story for the text that presented it as an effort to capture a specific experience that occurred at a particular point in space and time: "Three years ago in Paris, I got out of a 'metro' train at La Concorde, and saw suddenly a beautiful face, and then another and another, and then a beautiful child's face, and then another beautiful woman, and I tried all that day to find words for what this had meant to me, and I could not find any words that seemed to me worthy, or as lovely as that sudden emotion."[44] According to the first half of the account, the putative concreteness of this brief piece was a product of its status as the expression of a singular moment of perception. It was, as Pound wrote, "testimony . . . of the eyewitness," and hence a realization of the basic Imagist aim to impart "an intellectual and emotional complex in an instant of time."[45] Such a forceful immediacy, declared Pound, was to be a "constation of fact. It presents. It does not comment. It is irrefutable because it doesn't present a personal predilection for any particular fraction of the truth."[46]

43. Ezra Pound, "In a Station of the Metro," *The Penguin Anthology of Twentieth-Century American Poetry*, ed. Rita Dove (New York: Penguin, 2013), 54.

44. Ezra Pound, "Vorticism," *Fortnightly Review*, September 1, 1914, 467.

45. Pound, "A Retrospect," *Literary Essays of Ezra Pound*, 11; Pound, "A Few Don'ts by an Imagiste," 200.

46. Ezra Pound, "The Approach to Paris, V," *New Age* 13, no. 23 (1913): 662.

In contrast, the second half of Pound's account—"I tried all that day to find words for what this had meant to me, and I could not find any words that seemed to me worthy, or as lovely as that sudden emotion"—describes not a direct documentation of immediacy without intervening reflection or interpretation, but rather the irreducible gap between the perceptual experience, the thoughts and feelings it inspired in the poet (his experience of his experience), and his attempts to capture all of this in a verbal form. Continuing his story, Pound writes that his first effort to find words that were "worthy" of his moment in the Metro was a "thirty-line poem" that he discarded; six months later, he took another stab at it and came up with something half that length; and finally, a year after his initial effort to get this "moment" down on paper, he settled on the now famous "*hokku*-like sentence."[47]

This commentary makes it clear that what was published as "In a Station of the Metro" was not the spontaneous coordination of a feeling and its expression, but the product of a long process of revision in which supposedly extraneous layers of representation were stripped away to leave only an essential core. "Imagism," writes Daniel Albright, "was a movement dedicated to elimination."[48] Far from being instantaneously fashioned by circumstance, Pound's poem is the result of a series of negations, each of whose determinateness is supposed to imbue the remaining language with additional concreteness. As Daniel Tiffany argues, a "regime of elimination and prohibition" is "fundamental to the 'objectivity' of Imagist poetics."[49] When everything deemed expendable has been discarded, all that is left is the title and fourteen words, each of which now enjoys a special status by virtue of having made the cut.[50] The question is whether these negative forces leave their mark on what

47. Cited in Bartholomew Brinkman, "Making Modern 'Poetry': Format, Genre, and the Invention of Imagism(s)," *Journal of Modern Literature* 32, no. 2 (Winter 2009): 34. Randolph Chilton and Carol Gilbertson describe another of Pound's accounts of the text's emergence: "After seeing beautiful faces in the Paris Underground, he says, he tried to articulate his experience and ended with 'nothing but spots of color' until, months later, he remembered the Japanese tradition, 'where sixteen syllables [sic] are counted enough for a poem if you arrange and punctuate them properly.'" Randolph Chilton and Carol Gilbertson, "Pound's '"Metro" Hokku': The Evolution of an Image," *Twentieth Century Literature*, 36, no. 2 (Summer 1990): 228.

48. Albright, *Quantum Poetics*, 136.

49. Daniel Tiffany, *Radio Corpse: Imagism and the Cryptaesthetic of Ezra Pound* (Cambridge, MA: Harvard University Press, 1995), 156.

50. In *The Work of Revision*, Hannah Sullivan argues that writers in the modernist period broke with the Romantic ideal of spontaneous production and "revised more than their

we now know as Pound's text, or whether the genetic assumptions underlying the account of the relationship between process and product are themselves misleading.

In a further demystification of the poem's aura, several scholars have shown that Pound's story of its emergence, the notion that it was occasioned by an experience in the Paris underground, is simply not true, because its two lines are actually a revision of part of a stanza of another poem that he wrote in 1909.[51] As a reworking of existing verses, "In a Station of the Metro" is a representation of another text as much as of an individual's state of mind at a specific point in space and time. Recalling Pound's vision of the poet-engineer, we might say that this short piece is the product of a larger textual machine driven by an as-yet-undetermined set of formal and thematic principles. Among other things, this makes it more difficult to defend the individual images in the poem against the charge of being symbols with, in Pound's words, "an ascribed or intended meaning," a damning judgment since to his mind such elements usually "produce very bad art."[52]

Acknowledging these complexities and accepting that the Imagist understanding of the exact word is only to some extent about words as such, one might rejoin that Pound's poem, the signature text of a doctrine if not of an era, is nothing if not a striking collection of words. The exceptional elegance with which its terms are sonorically, rhythmically, and semantically coordinated with one another is hard to overlook. In reading and rereading its two lines, one cannot help but admire how well chosen each noun or adjective is while reflecting on how difficult, if not impossible, it would be to replace them with comparably distinctive substitutes.[53] Or at least this is the conclusion at which the poem and the entire aesthetic ideology surrounding it wish us to arrive.

---

predecessors in several senses: more frequently, at more points in the lifespan of the text, more structurally and experimentally (rather than through lexical substitution alone), and more self-consciously, often leaving traces of the revision in the final product." Hannah Sullivan, *The Work of Revision* (Cambridge, MA: Harvard University Press, 2013), 22. That revision was treated highly self-consciously by authors such as Pound seems indisputable, but this may not be peculiar to the modernists in the way Sullivan describes.

51. See K. K. Ruthven, *A Guide to Pound's "Personae," (1926)* (Berkeley: University of California Press, 1969), 153.

52. Ezra Pound, *Gaudier-Brzeska* (New York: New Directions, 1970), 86.

53. An inheritor of this strand of modernist poetics, Hans-Georg Gadamer lauds the work of Paul Celan for affirming that it is "obligatory" that a poem "not contain a single word standing for something in such a way that another word could be substituted for it." Hans-Georg

In two manuscript drafts of the poem that Pound ended up crossing out, he put the word "Metro" in quotation marks, perhaps because the French transportation system was still a novelty for this Idaho-born writer. Interpretations of the text tend to treat the figure of the Paris underground as a metonymy for modern metropolitan life, and hence as the basis for an opposition between the culture of the poem's first line and the natural order that predominates in the second. Putting quotation marks around this one word, however, suggests that the term is being used with reservation, not least because it constitutes the presence of an intruder from a foreign language in Pound's English. If one has to follow Wordsworth in being even more exact than the word "exact" itself allows, a degree of mediation is introduced that may irremediably compromise the putative precision, not to mention immediacy, of the whole work.

The fact that Pound removed the punctuation marks in later versions of the poem only makes matters worse, since it implies that at some stage in the composition process there may—literally or figuratively—have been scare quotes around any or every word in the text, and there is, moreover, no guarantee that some of the figurative ones are not still there. This would mean that each term in the poem would be distinguished not by its singular perfection as the ideal choice for the role it fills, but by its status as the product of a selection process that may have spawned many misgivings and cannot easily be brought to a close. In effect, a word becomes exactly the right word for the verses in which it appears by gesturing toward all the words that it beat out to get there or by which it has not yet been replaced, which is to say that the discarded alternatives are present "in spirit," like ghosts haunting the fourteen words one actually reads—arguably an appropriate predicament for a text about apparitions. As Hugh Kenner says of the people the poet encounters in the Metro, "this is a crowd seen underground, as Odysseus and Orpheus and Koré saw crowds in Hades. And carrying forward the suggestion of wraiths, the word 'apparition' detaches these faces from all the crowded faces."[54] Taking this a step further, we might say that Pound's poem is composed of word wraiths, specters of a language that is most exact—and perhaps only exact—about its own incorporeality, insubstantiality, and flux.[55]

Gadamer, *Gadamer on Celan: "Who Am I and Who Are You?" and Other Essays*, trans. Richard Heinemann and Bruce Krajewski (Albany: SUNY Press, 1997), 130.

54. Hugh Kenner, *The Pound Era* (Berkeley and Los Angeles: University of California Press, 1971), 184.

55. Tiffany characterizes the Imagist poem in terms of its "resistance to language" and argues that in this particular text "the remains of Victorian poetry assume the haiku form as a cipher of

No matter how powerful we find the poem's juxtaposition of terms, ghostly or otherwise, it is important to remember that if this text is not overtly made up of sentences, it is not an agrammatical jumble of words, either. The articles and adjectives are correctly situated to modify the nouns, and the prepositional phrases respect standard syntactic conventions. There are no verbs of any form, yet it is possible to mull over these verses for quite some time without noticing their absence, perhaps indicating that the verbs are implicit and do not need to be written out. In this regard, it is typically supposed that the two lines are linked by an implied "is" or "is like," creating a metaphor or simile in which the apparition of the faces is compared to petals on a bough.[56]

The question is whether formalizing the presence of this rhetorical figure by making the presence of the copula explicit amounts to normalizing what is taking place, particularly since a metaphor is itself necessarily an abstraction, isolating as it must one or two specific predicates of the petals and the faces in order to draw a connection between them. Pound's claim that "we no longer think or need to think in terms of monolinear logic, the sentence structure," invites us to consider whether "In a Station of the Metro" is distinguished by the way in which it resists assimilation into conventional logico-grammatical paradigms.[57] The earliest printed version of the poem points in this direction, for

---

ritual death" (*Radio Corpse*, 49). On this account, Imagism is an encounter with the belatedness of experience, not its expressive priority, and Imagist poems are an irremediably haunted terrain.

56. In the earliest versions of the poem, the first line ended with a colon, but in the fall of 1916, Pound replaced it with a semicolon, which is how it has been printed since. On the details of this emendation, see Chilton and Gilbertson, who note that in one 1914 variant, the poem's first line ended with a period ("Pound's '"Metro" Hokku,'" 229, 233 n. 6). In closing with a colon, the first line seems to introduce the second more directly, intensifying the sense that this is a statement of identity, a "this is that." The semicolon by no means disqualifies such a reading, but the change in punctuation underscores the possibility that the two lines coexist in a way that is less explicit than a simple predicative assertion of "x is (like) y." In his 1916 book on French sculptor Henri Gaudier-Brzeska, Pound attempted to describe what an alternative to a conventional metaphor or simile might be. Citing "the pine-tree in mist upon the far hill looks like a fragment of Japanese armor," he argued that neither the tree nor the armor is beautiful because of its resemblance to the other, but "because their diverse planes overlie in a certain manner" (*Gaudier-Brzeska*, 120–21). In these terms, "In a Station of the Metro" produces not one image but two, if not three (an image of two overlapping images), further confounding its own claim to expressive immediacy and augmenting the sense that the poem is a puzzle composed of distinct pieces rather than intrinsically interdependent, much less fused, elements.

57. Quoted in Vincent Sherry, *Ezra Pound, Wyndham Lewis, and Radical Modernism* (New York: Oxford University Press, 1993), 179.

its most distinctive feature is not its grammar or imagery, but its Mallarméesque typography:

IN A STATION OF THE METRO

The Apparition   of these faces   in the crowd :
Petals   on a wet, black   bough .

Ezra Pound[58]

The extra spaces in the first line threaten to transform it into a string of independent units: a noun phrase, followed by two distinct prepositional phrases. Highlighting the tension between the text's grammar and imagery, this shifts the focus away from the appropriateness of any given word and reminds us that it is only as a member of a group of words that any of the terms comes into its own, perhaps indicating that "the" or even the colon at the end is just as arresting as the "apparition." One can and perhaps must ignore the gaps and read the words as a line of verse that unfolds with an elegant rhythm, but the very need to synthesize the phrases with one another is thereby exposed as something artificial, if not violent. Even the punctuation aspires to a sort of "stand-alone" status, as if the poem were not a testimony to a unity of representation and experience but a demonstration of the precariousness obtaining between parts of speech in even the simplest coordination of words. If Joyce or Faulkner exploit the expansive potential of syntax, which can continue indefinitely without any mandated stops, Pound's poem appears to respect the constraints of grammar at a subsentential level, although it remains ambiguous whether the resulting minimalist construction is the ruin of a former sentence, a proto-sentence on its way to becoming a fully-fledged one, or a gesture toward a different kind of textual unit that is no longer defined by its obedience to or defiance of sentence grammar.

In the second line of the first printed version of the poem, the gaps created by the extra spaces no longer respect the integrity of the individual grammatical units. The verse begins with a single noun standing alone in its putative

58. Ezra Pound, "In a Station of the Metro," *Poetry: A Magazine of Verse* 2, no. 1 (April 1913): 12. Two manuscript drafts that Pound crossed out were arranged slightly differently. They read:

The apparition of these faces in the crowd :
Petals on a wet black bough .

The apparition   of these faces   in the crowd :
Petals   on a wet   , black bough .
(Cited in Brinkman, *Making Modern Poetry,* 38 n. 11)

exactitude, but things immediately become more complicated as the words in the prepositional phrase that follows spread apart. Rather than augmenting any sense of disorder, the idiosyncratic layout drives home how powerful subsentential grammar is, since even in the absence of a finite verb to anchor the formation, it is all but impossible not to read "Petals   on a wet, black   bough ." as "Petals on a wet, black bough." At the same time, the status of these words as parts of a sentence, past or future, becomes ever more uncertain. Whereas Mallarmé's typography sought to unsettle the power of the horizontal line, Pound's poem signals a return to it, albeit in a language in which each element—definite article, noun, even punctuation mark—potentially acquires an independence it would not otherwise enjoy, flaunting its resistance not simply to the sentence form, but to any unit of text larger than itself, in effect shaking off the very designation of "part of a whole." In this respect, "In a Station of the Metro" confirms Woolf's observation about the way in which words resist "being lifted out on the point of a pen and examined separately," although it does so by staging one version of just such a putatively impossible extraction.

It is not clear to what extent Pound still had control over the typography of "In the Station" as it was republished in various venues; whatever the case, the spacing of the text gradually became standardized to the version we know today, possibly with his blessing.[59] What does not vanish is the sense that the power of this minimalist form stems in part from the fact that its brevity does not foster ambiguity and if anything actively negates it. In her reflections on the unruliness of words, Woolf is keenly aware that even the most pragmatic verbal construct can have many unintended resonances, her own caution about imagining that one could treat the words in a text in isolation from one another notwithstanding. Describing, as it so happens, the experience of passing the time while waiting for a train on an Underground platform, she details just how far-reaching the act of reading and rereading the sign "Passing Russell Square" can be. "Passing," she writes, suggests "the transiency of things, the passing of time and the changes of human life"; "Russell" invokes "the rustling of leaves

59. On the history of the different versions of Pound's poem, see Chilton and Gilbertson, "Pound's '"Metro" Hokku,'" 225–36; and Steve Ellis, "The Punctuation of 'In a Station of the Metro,'" *Paideuma* 18 (Winter 1989): 205. The gradual re-imposition of a more conventional typographic scheme (and possibly also the shift from a colon to a semicolon at the end of the first line) is sometimes described as Pound transforming the text from an Imagistic to a Vorticist work (see Brinkman, *Making Modern Poetry*, 34). The problem with this argument is that the vocabulary and imagery Pound uses to describe the vortex—"mechanics," "maximum energy," "the greatest efficiency"—were already prominent in his 1911–12 essays. Ezra Pound, "Long Live the Vortex!" *Blast* 1, ed. Wyndham Lewis (London: John Lane, The Bodley Head, June 20, 1914), 153.

and the skirt on a polished floor; also the ducal house of Bedford and half the history of England"; and "Square" conjures up "the sight, the shape of an actual square combined with some visual suggestion of the stark angularity of stucco."[60] In this account, the various denotations and connotations of the three words making up an ostensibly banal participial phrase have the power to lead the casual reader into a dense sociopolitical, literary-historical, and philosophical forest that may prove to be even more labyrinthine than the London Tube map.

Pound's poem does not lend itself to such a reading, extending no invitation to its reader to extract its individual words one by one and explore them as a lexicographer might. Importantly, this may have less to do with the precision of the text's diction than with the way in which the novel grammar of its non-sentential sentences reveals powers inherent in minimal forms that do not stem from the semantic fecundity of vocabulary. Arguably no contemporary of Pound discerned the potential of such formations more clearly than William Empson. In the final chapter of *The Seven Types of Ambiguity*, he observes that there appears to be a growing consensus that the English language is becoming more ambiguous; fewer words are being used, and those more loosely and hence with ever-greater possibilities for confusion. Empson sees things differently, and to make his point, he considers one of the most commonplace instances of compact diction, the newspaper headline. Like the title of a book or movie, a headline is designed to intrigue the potential reader, although just getting people to remember the blurb well enough to repeat it to others may suffice.

Empson's memorable example comes from a British newspaper:

ITALIAN ASSASSIN BOMB PLOT DISASTER.[61]

60. Virginia Woolf, "Craftsmanship," *Collected Essays*, vol. 2 (New York: Harcourt, Brace & World, 1966), 247. Remaining, intriguingly enough, with the theme of transportation, Woolf offers another similar example:

> Written up opposite us in the railway carriage are the words: "Do not lean out of the window." At the first reading the useful meaning, the surface meaning, is conveyed; but soon, as we sit looking at the words, they shuffle, they change; and we begin saying, "Windows, yes windows—casements opening on the foam of perilous seas in faery lands forlorn." And before we know what we are doing, we have leant out of the window; we are looking for Ruth in tears amid the alien corn. The penalty for that is twenty pounds or a broken neck. This proves, if it needs proving, how very little natural gift words have for being useful. If we insist on forcing them against their nature to be useful, we see to our cost how they mislead us, how they fool us, how they land us a crack on the head. (Woolf, "Craftsmanship," 246)

61. William Empson, *The Seven Types of Ambiguity* (London: Chatto & Windus, 1949), 236.

These five words are not a sentence in any conventional sense. There is no clear subject-verb agreement, for as Empson observes, a number of the words may be nouns, verbs, or adjectives, and these ambiguities raise a host of questions about what modifies what. Considerable creativity will be required to treat this headline as the core of a larger sentence, some of whose elements have been ellipsed. If one were to attempt to write out the hypothetical "complete" statement, the result might take the form of five separate sentences. Similarly, it would be difficult to summarize the content by rephrasing the headline in different words. If the arrangement of these five terms vis-à-vis one another does not readily facilitate their classification as parts of speech, a reader may have no choice but to assign specific roles to them by fiat, in effect imposing a grammar where there is no discernible syntax.

To say that this headline is not a conventional proposition is by no means to judge it to be meaningless. To begin his account of its signifying peculiarities, Empson introduces a contextual detail, explaining that as best he can recall, the assassin was not Italian. This would suggest that the word "Italian" modifies the whole event, the "Italian Disaster," and that we should therefore resist the temptation to scan the line as if there were a caesura (Italian Assassin / Bomb Plot Disaster). Empson's point, however, is that this is a powerful piece of writing irrespective of how little we know about the circumstances to which it refers. In this respect, he is celebrating the "fluidity" of the English language, but only insofar as we recognize that this is not a claim that everything is up for grabs. Situated neatly in the center, the word "bomb" stands out, no matter what one determines the rhythm of the line to be, and Empson declares that the five-word sequence is, metaphorically speaking, an explosion: "It conveys [its point] with a compactness which gives the mind several notions at one glance of the eye, with a unity like that of metaphor, with a force like that of its own *favorite* bombs."[62]

Empson's own comments give the mind several notions at one glance of the eye, any of which may themselves prove to be explosive. His first simile—"a unity like that of metaphor"—may be damning with faint praise, since he would readily allow that metaphors divide as much as they unite. His account of the headline thus foregrounds what Pound will only begrudgingly acknowledge, namely that multiplicity precedes unity in the poetic image.[63] Empson's

62. Empson, *Seven Types*, 237.

63. While Empson does not say as much, one could go further and argue that this headline comments on the way in which any title or heading must to some degree "shake things up" where grammar is concerned. Headlines have to earn their right to be lead-ins by sharply

second simile—"a force like that of its own *favorite* bombs"—appears to literalize the discussion of metaphors in proposing that the word "bomb" is in this instance a bomb, or at least part of a bomb. The "disaster" is thereby recuperated as something to celebrate as we are encouraged to take stock of our own favorite verbal explosives. Far from recommending that formulations such as the Italian Assassin line be rationed, Empson stresses that he does not feel "that it will be a *disaster* if other forms of English literature adopt this fundamental mode of statement."[64] Obscurities be damned—bombs away!

Empson's more sober conclusion is that "the grammatical sentence is not the only form of statement in modern English" and that "the machinery [he has] been using upon poetry is going to become increasingly necessary if we are to keep the language under control."[65] Like Woolf, who is all too aware of the propensity of words to do more or less than one intends, Empson believes that diligence will be required to keep abreast of such explosive verbal dynamics, although he leaves no doubt that we are much in need of such volatile forces. His invocation of "machinery" throughout *The Seven Types of Ambiguity* may be reminiscent of Pound's industrial vocabulary, but while Pound enjoins his poet-engineer to strive for aesthetic equilibrium, in Empson the appearance of the mechanical signals an unavoidable imbalance between a desire for control and the recognition that it would be best to let the powers of language run their course without outside interference.[66] Empson thus takes pains to acknowledge the destabilizing, even violent potential of this particular headline even as he lauds it as an example of a new kind of linguistic formation that offers the prospect of reenergizing English, "at present a rather exhausted language."[67]

While Empson was following Pound's lead in searching for minimalist sentences with which to reinvigorate the discursive realm, a very different kind of minimalism was winning fame for an author whose work would soon come to enjoy a unique status in the canon of English-language prose. Regardless of

---

distinguishing themselves from the more conventional constructions to follow, although in the process they may become models for further compositional excess, corrupting the article they introduce.

64. Empson, *Seven Types*, 237 (emphasis added).

65. Empson, *Seven Types*, 237.

66. In *The Seven Types of Ambiguity*, Empson refers to "the machinery of interpretation" (144), "grammatical machinery" (196), the "machinery of analysis" (222), "intellectual machinery" (238), and "the machinery of description" (254).

67. Empson, *Seven Types*, 257.

whether one has read any of Ernest Hemingway's novels or short stories, one has almost certainly been apprised of the virtues of his simple, direct prose, which elegantly straddles the boundaries between fiction, personal memoir, and journalism; and Hemingway's tips on how to write like he does remain core maxims of compositional instruction at all levels.[68] As Stanley Fish summarizes the injunctions for which "Papa" has become famous: "Use short sentences, write clearly, use simple Anglo-Saxon words, don't overwrite, avoid adjectives . . . and leave yourself out of it. The result [is] a style that has been described as realistic, hardboiled, spare, unadorned, minimalist, and lapidary."[69] In contradistinction to the para-sentential forms explored by Pound and Empson or the syntactic soup of Faulkner and Joyce, Hemingway's prose is considered ideal for emulation by writers of all ages, stages, and aims. One cannot reasonably encourage students to take their compositional cues from most of the major figures of early twentieth-century European and American letters, but surely everyone can profit from a dose of this unique brand of linguistic parsimony.

As he did with many authors, Pound lent Hemingway considerable support in his career, and the mentee would appear to have done his benefactor proud by realizing his vision of a textual economy in which not so much as an ounce of power is wasted. Still, there is something slightly excessive, even comical, about the Hemingway phenomenon. The reliance on "Papa" as a fount of writing advice is so exaggerated that every note he made on a scrap of paper is treated as holy writ, as if it would be a crime to squander a single morsel of wisdom such as: "You can phrase things clearer and better"; "You can remove words which are unnecessary and tighten up your prose."[70] Hemingway himself was evidently in on the joke. As Ian Crouch relates, he "was

68. For an account of the canonization of Hemingway's poetics of "show, don't tell" in American writing programs after the Second World War, see Mark McGurl, *The Program Era: Postwar Fiction and the Rise of Creative Writing* (Cambridge, MA: Harvard University Press, 2009), 99.

69. Stanley Fish, *How to Write a Sentence: And How to Read One* (New York: HarperCollins, 2011), 73. In the event that we forget about some of Hemingway's edicts when pursuing our own writing projects, there is an online *Hemingway Editor* (www.hemingwayapp.com) that will assist us in making our prose "bold and clear," principally by identifying instances of the passive voice and sentences that are too long or dense, as well as by offering suggestions for replacing longer words with shorter ones and for eliminating qualifiers, especially adverbs. The lower the reading level of a piece of prose, the more likely it is to pass muster with the algorithm.

70. Cited in Charles McGrath, "A Mutable Feast: Batch of Hemingway Ephemera from Cuba is Digitized," *New York Times*, February 10, 2014.

able to see the humor in the public's sense of his work; [*New Yorker* writer] Lillian Ross caught him, at times, playacting a kind of Indian-speak version of his characters' reticence: 'He read book all way up on plane.' 'He like book, I think.'"[71] No less than the Dadaists, Hemingway was a performance artist, self-consciously fashioning a persona that was at once deadly earnest and quixotically mocking. More than one critic has observed that he may not have been in complete control of the effects this had on his work. As Harold Bloom argues, the "distinction of Hemingway's [stoic, grave, eloquent, economical] prose style was astonishing, until it transmuted into self-parody, as in *The Old Man and the Sea*."[72] For Hemingway no less than for the rest of us, writing like Hemingway is necessarily to come under suspicion of writing too much like Hemingway.

The mainstays of writing classes, Hemingway's words of advice have become so familiar that their puzzling features tend to go overlooked. In his 1932 book on bullfighting, *Death in the Afternoon*, he declares that "if a writer of prose knows enough about what he is writing about, he may omit things that he knows and the reader, if the writer is writing truly enough, will have a feeling of those things as strongly as though the writer had stated them. The dignity of movement of an iceberg is due to only one-eighth of it being above water."[73] This so-called "Iceberg Theory"—present the "tip" of the matter correctly and the rest should be clear—is predicated on the notion that the reader processes a text like the spectators at a bullfight who "sense the meaning and end of the whole [event] even when they know nothing about it."[74] The doctrine itself is presented in such a compact form that one is tempted to say that it offers a vision of what writing might be more than it provides a guide for how to write. Even if we do not find ourselves puzzled by the claim that a good sentence need only say one-eighth of what it conveys because it can successfully gesture toward the seven-eighths of its message that remains implicit, it will be difficult to ignore the fact that the models at work are models of violence. Hemingway does not need to say in so many words that the bullfight concludes with the animal's slaughter (or more rarely, with the matador's injury or death), since we know this "as strongly as though" he had stated it outright. Unfortunately, this

71. Ian Crouch, "Hemingway Takes the Hemingway Test," *New Yorker*, February 13, 2014.

72. Harold Bloom, *Ernest Hemingway: Comprehensive Research and Study Guide (Bloom's Major Novelists)* (New York: Chelsea House, 2000), 9.

73. Ernest Hemingway, *Death in the Afternoon* (New York: Charles Scribner's Sons, 1950), 192.

74. Hemingway, *Death in the Afternoon,* 8.

leaves us with little or no information about why reading a successful sentence is like watching the ritualized execution of an animal. Precisely who is killing whom or what? Similarly, the claim that the iceberg is elegant because only a fraction of it sticks out above the surface of the water becomes something of a sore thumb, blithely inverting our customary association of this maritime phenomenon with catastrophe. Icebergs are notorious because what you do not see, the seven-eighths of their mass underwater, or in this case the seven-eighths of the sentence that is not there, is precisely what dooms you and your crew.

Perhaps Hemingway's imagery is not intended to be taken quite so seriously, not least since his stylistic reputation is based largely on the absence of poetic embellishments. But does he practice what he preaches? It is hard to read him for long without noticing that his prose is nowhere near as uniform as its popular image would suggest.[75] Hemingway's stories are populated by all sorts of different kinds of sentences, lengthy as well as brief, simple as well as complex. He pens numerous passages that walk a fine line between internal monologue and stream of consciousness, and he relies on anaphoric patterns as much as any verse poet.[76]

The real question, then, is why it is important for the myth of the homogeneity of Hemingway's work to persist. Reflecting on the stylistic diversity of the prose, Harry Levin cites the following passage from Hemingway's seven-page short story "After the Storm":

> I said "Who killed him?" and he said "I don't know who killed him but he's dead all right," and it was dark and there was water standing in the street and no lights and windows broke and boats all up in the town and trees blown down and everything all blown and I got a skiff and went out and found my

75. Selections from Hemingway's books do not score well when they are plugged into the online *Hemingway Editor*, which is designed to rate stylistic clarity and boldness on the basis of Hemingway's own pronouncements on the subject. See Crouch, "Hemingway Takes the Hemingway Test."

76. The following passage from *A Farewell to Arms* is frequently cited as an instance of Hemingway coming very close to writing stream-of-consciousness-prose: "Because we would not wear any clothes because it was so hot and the window open and the swallows flying over the roofs of the houses and when it was dark afterwards and you went to the window very small bats hunting over the houses and close down over the trees and we would drink the capri and the door locked and it hot and only a sheet and the whole night and we would both love each other all night in the hot night in Milan." Ernest Hemingway, *A Farewell to Arms: The Hemingway Library Edition* (New York: Scribner, 2014), 32.

> boat where I had her inside of Mango Key and she was all right only she was full of water.[77]

Levin observes that "Hemingway puts his emphasis on nouns because, among parts of speech, they come closest to things. Stringing them along by means of conjunctions, he approximates the actual flow of experience. For him, as for Marion Tweedy Bloom, the key-word is *and*, with its renewable promise of continuity, occasionally varied by *then* and *so*."[78] As they unfold, Levin's remarks turn against themselves to the point of self-negation, in the process betraying a very un-Hemingway-esque ambiguity. While he begins with the borderline trite observation that what matters in Hemingway are the nouns, by the end of Levin's three short sentences, we do not know whether he is claiming that it is nouns, adverbs, or conjunctions that are the most important elements for approximating "the actual flow of experience." Importantly, this exegetical imprecision has nothing to do with any assumptions about the inherent complexity of stream-of-consciousness prose. In fact, Levin wants to make the opposite case, proposing that "the [dominant] rhetorical scheme is polysyndeton—a large name for the childishly simple habit of linking sentences together."[79] So intent is he on confirming that there is nothing complicated taking place in Hemingway's writing that Levin has to make fun of his own fancy word for the habit of doing something simple with words. The result is a markedly equivocal judgment of Hemingway's work that is far from atypical. If he is widely celebrated for a style that allows us to readily grasp both what he is saying and everything that he is not saying, a number of commentators have come to the conclusion that the substance of what is imparted is not of great interest.

Perhaps for this reason, discussions of Hemingway tend to eschew extended considerations of content and focus on form, the critics prudently showcasing the strengths and marginalizing the weaknesses of an author Harold Bloom deemed a "minor novelist with a major style."[80] While reflections

77. Harry Levin, "Observations on the Style of Ernest Hemingway," *Kenyon Review* 13, no. 4 (Autumn 1951): 600.

78. Levin, "Observations," 600.

79. Levin, "Observations," 600.

80. Harold Bloom, *Genius: A Mosaic of One Hundred Exemplary Creative Minds* (New York: Warner Books, 2002), 573. In Bloom's judgment, Hemingway makes his readers think about how to write well, but he "cannot change the way you read" and "does not alter your entire relationship to language" (573). The problem with this pronouncement is that it goes beyond even

on this "major style" vary widely, they are remarkably consistent in proposing that its success or failure occurs at the level of the sentence. There is broad agreement that Hemingway was trying to write good sentences and that his achievements in this regard are why we still read him, the insubstantiality of his plots or the ideological limits of his worldview notwithstanding.[81] David Bromwich observes that "it is the sentences that first draw a reader in to Hemingway's writing"; Fredric Jameson pushes the argument a step further, declaring that "it is a mistake to think . . . that the books of Hemingway deal essentially with such things as courage, love, and death; in reality, their deepest subject is simply the writing of a certain type of sentence."[82] More specifically, Jameson insists that when we read Hemingway, we are less interested in what is happening than in whether the language will do the subject matter justice. In *Green Hills of Africa*, proposes Jameson, "*the shooting of the animal* in the content is but the pretext for the description of *the shooting in the form*. The reader is not so much interested in observing the kill as he is in whether Hemingway's language will be able to rise to the occasion."[83]

If reading Hemingway is primarily a matter of judging the success or failure of each sentence, where do the standards for success or failure come from, that is, how do we know when a given sentence is rising to the occasion? Jameson's unexpected answer is that Hemingway's sentences succeed because they accurately capture a reality that they themselves have constructed. He explains:

> For the immense and complex fabric of American social reality itself is clearly inaccessible to the careful and selective type of sentence which [Hemingway] practices: so it is useful to have to do with a reality thinned out, the reality of foreign cultures and of foreign languages, where the individual beings come before us not in the density of a concrete social situation in which we also are involved, but rather with the cleanness of objects which can be verbally circumscribed.[84]

---

a rigid form/content dichotomy and compartmentalizes this "major" style to such a degree that it can scarcely be accorded any power, almost to the point of erasing it entirely.

81. As Ron Silliman puts it bluntly: "Hemingway strives for an art of the sentence as the novel's determining language-unit." Ron Silliman, *The New Sentence* (New York: Roof, 2003), 15.

82. David Bromwich, "Hemingway's Valor," *Grand Street* 7, no. 2 (Winter 1988): 185; Fredric Jameson, *Marxism and Form: Twentieth-Century Theories of Dialectical Literature* (Princeton, NJ: Princeton University Press, 1971), 409.

83. Jameson, *Marxism and Form*, 411.

84. Jameson, *Marxism and Form*, 412.

In these terms, the entire persona of "Hemingway the expatriate" is designed to help produce a sanitized milieu that lends itself to representation in the author's unique style. If an Edgar Allan Poe short story may turn out to have been concocted for the sake of a single sentence, Hemingway invents an entire picture of reality within whose frame of reference his sentences cannot help but be judged satisfactory.[85]

Jameson may appear to be reproaching Hemingway for the limited, possibly impoverished vision of social existence in his work, but Jameson also acknowledges that it is because Hemingway focuses on prearranging the reality he describes that he is able to "return to the very sources of verbal productivity" in ways that other authors cannot.[86] Fleshing out this claim, Jameson cites a prototypical Hemingway sentence from the short story "Up in Michigan": "From Smith's back door Liz could see more barges way out in the lake going toward Boyne City. When she looked at them they didn't seem to be moving at all but if she went in and dried some more dishes and then came out again they would be out of sight beyond the point."[87] These two sentences make a case in miniature for the viability of Hemingway's Iceberg Theory by underscoring that the actual movement of the barges can be omitted from the description; yet the sentences do so hypothetically ("but if she went in"), in effect omitting the omission toward whose possibility they gesture. If Hemingway's sentences are ordinarily what Jameson calls a "neutral *compte rendu*," a formal report or review of external displacements, what we have here is a neutral report on this very neutrality that takes the form of a displacement of displacement.[88]

Are such simulations of simplicity in fact simple? Describing Hemingway's prose, Stanley Fish emphasizes the artificiality of its straightforwardness: "It doesn't seem to be doing much. It does not demand that attention be paid to it. It aspires to a self-effacement that allows the object to shine through as a master stonecutter allows the beauty of the stone to shine through by paring away layers of it."[89] On this account, Hemingway's sentences sound like Pound's

85. Jameson maintains that Hemingway understands his craft as a form of nonalienated labor, as if producing good sentences were a technical sport, on par with hunting or fishing. In this fashion, the writer can live up to the macho American ideal of the active outdoorsman, and writing can satisfy the Protestant work ethic "at the same time that it glorifies leisure" (Jameson, *Marxism and Form,* 412).

86. Jameson, *Marxism and Form,* 410.

87. Cited in Jameson, *Marxism and Form,* 410.

88. Jameson, *Marxism and Form,* 411.

89. Fish, *How to Write a Sentence,* 73.

fourteen-word poem taking shape through a protracted series of cuts. "There is no complication at all [in Hemingway's sentences]," Fish continues, "just (*or so is the claim*) the thing itself, limpidly presented."[90] The parenthetical remark is key. Each sentence in Hemingway seeks to create the impression that it is a lucid presentation while making sure that it gets credit for having achieved this effect. His writing trumpets the clarity of its own form so loudly that it is forever on the verge of drowning out its content.

To explore this tension further, Fish turns to the second sentence of *A Farewell to Arms*: "In the bed of the river there were pebbles and boulders, dry and white in the sun, and the water was clear and swiftly moving and blue in the channels."[91] Fish states with confidence: "The water in the second half [of the sentence] is a surrogate for the style's (unvoiced) claim to be making no claim for itself at all. Like the water, the style is 'clear' and 'swiftly moving'; it does not stop or take a turn or qualify something it has presented. In short, this 'simple' sentence is an allegory—one of the most complex of literary forms—of its own unfolding."[92] The doubly conflicted notion that this sentence mutely claims to be making no claim for itself reveals that its clarity has nothing to do with the immediacy Pound champions, nor even with straightforwardness. To the contrary, this sentence is a thoroughly artificial coordination of language and the external world that, as Jameson has suggested, sees the latter remade in the image of the former. Importantly, this does not occur in a self-reflexive gesture in which the text turns back on itself, an inverted Narcissus moment in which the water rather than the beautiful boy would encounter its own—transparent—image. Style represents style in an allegory, which, as Fish allows, is a complex form precisely because it is not easy to characterize the relationship between the two levels of presentation, one of which tells us about the water in the bed of the river, the other of which tells us—voicelessly—about telling us about the water in the bed of the river. Since the literal level of the text never fully gives way to a figural one, there is always a danger that we may miss this second level of signification, the transparency of the presentation becoming so convincing that to see through it is in effect not to see anything at all.

Jameson and Fish help us identify the complexities of a style that tries hard to be anything but complex. Walter Benjamin takes the argument a step further. Breaking with the prevailing wisdoms of Hemingway scholarship, he praises his contemporary not for the austerity or lucidity of his writing, but for helping

90. Fish, *How to Write a Sentence,* 73 (emphasis added).

91. Cited in Fish, *How to Write a Sentence,* 73.

92. Fish, *How to Write a Sentence,* 74.

us move beyond the notion that writers should aim to produce clear and simple sentences. According to Benjamin, we will never make progress in understanding style, much less good style, until we grasp that "there is no such thing as 'saying what you think.' "[93] Language does not represent preexisting thought so much as it makes a thought real through its expression, in the course of which the original conception is subject "to the profoundest modifications."[94] This is not just because in expressing an idea one realizes that it was not nearly as well formed as one had imagined. In the course of expressing itself, thinking changes itself. Working to get our ideas down on paper, we will find ourselves refining or even overhauling the very standards on the basis of which we judge ourselves to "have" ideas in the first place.

Benjamin argues that in the course of actualizing his intentions, a writer may "ennoble" the original aim, refine it, or "allow it to become too vague and general."[95] Success or failure depends "on the writer's training regimen. The more he disciplines his body, and the more he limits his body to running and avoids superfluous, uncoordinated, or slack movements, the more his gait will itself become a criterion of the goal of his wish, will refine it, or drop it if it is not worth the trouble."[96] Efficiency remains the defining feature of the writing process, and according to Benjamin, Hemingway's special genius lies in his ability to make visible in his style the refinements of his regimen, "these phenomena, which normally only the practiced eye can discern in a rigorously and intelligently trained body."[97] In other words, Hemingway's sentences show the reader what was done in order for them to take shape successfully. This is why, Benjamin concludes, "his prose presents us with the great drama of an education in right thinking through correct writing."[98] As Jameson and Fish suggest, the resulting style is a self-referential dynamic that blows its own horn so loudly that one wonders whether its triumphal formulations can perform the putatively pedestrian task of imparting content. Still, by making explicit the negations inherent in any model of "straightforward" prose, Hemingway exposes the limitations of "clear and simple" as a compositional mantra. His texts may never rival the experimental ventures of Mallarmé or Joyce, but they

93. Walter Benjamin, *Selected Writings*, Vol. 2, ed. Michael W. Jennings, Howard Eiland, and Gary Smith (Cambridge, MA: Harvard University Press, 1999), 471.

94. Benjamin, *Selected Writings,* 471.

95. Benjamin, *Selected Writings,* 471.

96. Benjamin, *Selected Writings,* 471–72.

97. Benjamin, *Selected Writings,* 472.

98. Benjamin, *Selected Writings,* 472.

are no less subversive in challenging our ideas about powerful writing from clause to clause.

If Hemingway is not actually a devotee of the "clear and simple" ethos for which he is celebrated, it may come as less of a surprise that Wyndham Lewis likened his style to the work of his contemporary Gertrude Stein, an author who is rarely accused of clarity and tends to be attacked rather than praised for her simplicity.[99] To say that Stein's corpus is a relentless interrogation of our compositional doctrines would be something of an understatement. At every turn, she reminds us that as much as we write in or with sentences, we also write against them. In an age of radical experimentation, she stands out for the relentless urgency with which she tests stylistic and grammatical norms. The result is a startling diversity of texts that not only subvert existing paradigms, but shake our fundamental ideas about representation, expression, and the politics of language.[100]

The results have often been regarded as less than user-friendly. As Catharine R. Stimpson observes, "Stein's texts have exemplified 'difficult' and 'unreadable' writing in English for the twentieth century."[101] An author who specializes in thwarting our expectations about what it means to read is presumably fated to endure a somewhat rocky reception, although it is far from obvious that Stein's writing is any more obscure or taxing than Joyce's or Beckett's.[102] At the

99. See Wyndham Lewis, "The Dumb Ox: A Study of Ernest Hemingway," *The American Review* 3, no. 3 (June 1934): 289–312.

100. On Stein's stylistic innovations as attempts to affectively reorganize the subject's relationship to language, see Sianne Ngai, *Ugly Feelings* (Cambridge, MA: Harvard University Press, 2005), esp. 249–61.

101. Catharine R. Stimpson, "Review: Positioning Stein," *NOVEL: A Forum on Fiction* 27 (1994): 318. Natalia Cecire emphasizes that "Stein's unreadable style has been taken as evidence of her genius and of fraud in equal measure. Indeed, it has been praised as innovative and condemned as nonsense on exactly the same formal grounds: a simple vocabulary, the elevation of sound-sense above semantic sense, and above all, repetition." Natalia Cecire, "Ways of Not Reading Gertrude Stein," *ELH* 82, no. 1 (Spring 2015): 284. Cecire's article offers an excellent discussion of the ironies that surround critics' inability to decide whether Stein's texts are best skimmed or read closely in extremely small doses.

102. Some of the condescension, not to mention vitriol, directed at Stein was undoubtedly fueled by gender bias. "Sentences so regularly rhythmical, so needlessly prolix, so many times repeated and ending so often in present participles," declared Edmund Wilson of Stein's writing, although one is tempted to rejoin that he could just as well have been talking about the poems of the endlessly celebrated Walt Whitman. Edmund Wilson, *Axel's Castle: A Study in the Imaginative Literature of 1870–1930* (New York: Charles Scribner's Sons, 1931), 240. In her lifetime, Stein was particularly notorious for her overreliance on repetition, to the point that her

same time, Stein was hardly a stranger to good press. A public intellectual whose notoriety extended well beyond avant-garde literary circles, she, no less than Hemingway, was a consummate engineer of her own cult of personality.[103] If "rose is a rose is a rose is a rose" continues to serve as the emblem of her oeuvre, a kind of shorthand for her entire corpus, this is in no small part due to her own—eminently successful—promotion of it as the quintessential Steinian slogan. As Empson was celebrating the potential revitalization of English grammar in British newspaper headlines, the American press was taking advantage of Stein's compositional proclivities for its own purposes, since as anyone in advertising knows, rhythm sells. As Alyson Tischler relates, "At the height of her fame in 1934, Steinian language appeared in newspaper headlines that announced her arrival in America. For example, when she landed in Chicago after lecturing in New York, a *Chicago Herald* headline, 'Understand Einstein? Just Try Stein-Stein,' was accompanied by the subhead: 'She Arrives—She Arrives—She Arrives—She Arrives—Arrives.'"[104] No less than Hemingway's "simple" style, Stein's language lent itself to appropriation. In New York City, her celebrity was further cemented when quotations from her writing as well as sentences modeled on it began to appear in department store windows, a foothold in popular culture that her oeuvre has never relinquished.[105]

If the real subject of Hemingway's texts is the ambition to write a certain kind of sentence, this is no less true of Stein, who if anything goes further in making her writerly training regimen visible, as Benjamin would have it, in her very style. The results can be unsettling, even vertiginous. While her texts repeatedly test our conceptions of grammar and representation by putting pressure on specific premises or conventions, Stein virtually never undertakes the same demonstration twice. Whereas Hemingway's work presents itself as a model for our own, Stein's challenges the very notion that a writer should ever submit herself to an external stylistic paradigm, because any composition worth its salt will in the final analysis ineluctably assert its own unique logic. Stein's readers thus find themselves forever renegotiating the terms of

---

style was pathologized in an unsigned editorial in the *Journal of the American Medical Association*, which diagnosed her with palilalia, a speech disorder that leads to the involuntary repeating of words, phrases, or sentences. See "Palilalia and Gertrude Stein," *Journal of the American Medical Association* 103 (1934): 1711.

103. See Cecire, "Ways of Not Reading," 485.

104. Alyson Tischler, "A Rose Is a Pose: Steinian Modernism and Mass Culture," *Journal of Modern Literature* 26, no. 3 (2003): 23.

105. See Tischler, "A Rose Is a Pose," 26–27.

the discussion, always slightly unsure which concepts or peculiarities of form and content will prove vital and which expendable. What is never in doubt is Stein's determination to evaluate theoretical hypotheses about language by trying to generate verbal formations that will contravene them. The resulting blend of speculative and experimental arguments is unique in modern letters.

If the sheer diversity of the linguistic experiments Stein pursues makes it difficult to speak in general terms of her "positions" or "doctrines," she does consistently work to unsettle the relationships between parts and whole that are normally thought to organize texts. Citing Flaubert and Paul Cézanne as influences, she writes that formerly "composition had consisted of a central idea to which everything else was an accompaniment and separate but was not an end in itself, and Cézanne conceived the idea that in composition one thing was as important as another thing."[106] Many of the peculiarities of Stein's works can be understood as an effort to realize such a parity between words, phrases, and clauses, if not between individual syllables. She explicitly associates this ambition with the notion that "one human being is as important as another human being," adding: "I was trying to get . . . this evenness of everybody having the vote."[107] The claim is not simply that each part is as valuable as any other. If Poe writes stories in which the entire narrative exists for the sake of one of its sentences, Stein suggests that a text exists for the sake of *each* of its sentences, phrases, or words, summarily declaring that "each part is as important as the whole."[108]

In line with Stein's invocation of Cézanne, her compositional tactics have frequently been paralleled with contemporaneous innovations in the visual arts. As Michael Kaufmann observes, many critics have responded to her 1914 *Tender Buttons* by claiming that she arranges words "in the same way that the cubists arranged bits of wood, metal filings, strings, and ersatz chair-caning in the collages, or they find her attempting Dadaist and surrealist absurdity."[109] In a similar vein, Charles Bernstein deems Stein to be the forerunner of the language poets of the 1960s and 1970s, describing *Tender Buttons* as "the most

106. Gertrude Stein, "A Transatlantic Interview—1946," in *A Primer for the Gradual Understanding of Gertrude Stein*, ed. Robert Bartlett Haas (Los Angeles: Black Sparrow Press, 1973), 15.

107. Stein, "A Transatlantic Interview," 16; Gertrude Stein, *What Are Masterpieces?* (New York: Pitman, 1970), 98.

108. Stein, "A Transatlantic Interview," 15.

109. Michael Kaufmann, *Textual Bodies: Modernism, Postmodernism, and Print* (Lewisburg, PA: Bucknell University Press, 1994), 52.

perfect realization of wordness, where word and object merge. No work from Europe or the Americas had gone so far in creating a work of textual autonomy, where the words do not represent something outside of the context in which they are performed and where the meanings are made in and through composition and arrangement. The sections of the work are not 'about' subjects that are discussed but are their own discrete word objects (verbal constellations)."[110] Such remarks typify the way in which scholars tend to approach a Stein text by seizing on its most provocative feature and generalizing it as the decisive organizing principle, a questionable approach given her insistence on treating all of the different dimensions of a composition equally. Reading Bernstein's account of *Tender Buttons*, one might well assume that the book was a series of word collages rather than sentences and sentence fragments demarcated by capital letters and full stops.

To a degree, *Tender Buttons* encourages this sort of interpretation. The first part of the book is called "Objects" and is divided into small sections ranging from a few lines to a page in length. Each consists of a title in all capital letters (A PLATE, A PIANO, A BLUE COAT) followed by a meditation on the designated item. As the book continues, however, the section titles cease to be exclusively nouns and begin to showcase other features of language, including comparison, negation, and the powers of conjunctions (MORE, NOTHING ELEGANT, DIRT AND NOT COPPER). Even if reference can be bracketed in the way Bernstein envisions, the linguistic dynamics under consideration here are as much volatile acts as stable "verbal constellations." In the end, Bernstein's interpretation of *Tender Buttons* must be regarded as symptomatic of an ambition to flee the vicissitudes of the sentence by reducing predication to a hermetic semiotics grounded in substantives, which is not Stein's ambition, or at least not one she pursued to the exclusion of all others.

Stein's wide-ranging reconceptualization of language was by no means unique among early twentieth-century intellectuals.[111] As Anne Lawton writes:

110. Charles Bernstein, *Pitch of Poetry* (Chicago: University of Chicago Press, 2016), 87–88.

111. Despite Stein's reputation as a provocatrice, her work was in many respects in step with the prevailing intellectual climate. Her meditations on grammar and on the relative authority of various parts of speech have affinities with the post-Fregean philosophies of language that were emerging in the work of Bertrand Russell and that of Ludwig Wittgenstein. Indeed, a number of passages in the latter's *Philosophical Investigations* read as if Stein might have authored them. Having studied with William James, Stein was familiar with the notion of "spontaneous automatic writing," and although she firmly rejected the suggestion that it characterized her own compositional praxis, her texts often comment on the problems that arise when a sentence tries to account for the intention that drives its production. Like many other modernist theorists,

"It hardly needs to be pointed out that in the 1910s and 1920s every avant-garde group in Europe and beyond engaged in the discussion of the nature and function of the poetic word."[112] From this perspective, some of Stein's more cryptic maneuvers turn out to be quite precise interventions in specific debates. Take, for example, F. T. Marinetti's campaign against classical sentence grammar and his account of the "raging need to liberate words, dragging them out from the prison of the Latin *periodus*."[113] Marinetti suggests that by producing "uninterrupted sequences" of nouns and unconjugated verbs devoid of punctuation, we can free language from the fetters of traditional predication.[114] "It is imperative," he argues, "to destroy syntax and scatter one's nouns at random, just as they are born."[115] Stein shares Marinetti's contempt for traditional punctuation, or at least for its effects, but despite her stated ambition to achieve true equality between all textual elements, she insists, against Marinetti, that there are distinct hierarchies among parts of speech. No less than Woolf, Stein believes that words must be approached in terms of their role—if only their potential role—in sentence grammar, as parts of phrases and clauses, and never as isolated stand-alone phenomena.

Stein praises words that engender dynamic, even unstable relationships and expose the contingency of the verbal formations in which they appear. Again in contradistinction to Marinetti, she celebrates verbs because they "can change to look like themselves or to look like something else; they, are, so to speak, on the move, and adverbs move with them."[116] Anything that smacks of a code or a stable one-to-one relationship between a word and a unit of sense strikes Stein as banal, leading her to dismiss nouns and adjectives as categorically boring. She does consider proper nouns livelier than common ones because they bear the traces of an original act of denomination and hence have a whiff of the

---

Stein was also preoccupied with problematizing the distinctions between traditional aesthetic forms and emergent media, particularly film.

112. Anne Lawton, "Šeršenevic, Marinetti, and the 'Chain of Images': From Futurism to Imaginism," *Slavic and East European Journal* 23, no. 2 (Summer 1979): 205.

113. F. T. Marinetti, "Technical Manifesto of Futurist Literature," in *Futurism: An Anthology*, ed. Lawrence Rainey et al. (New Haven, CT: Yale University Press, 2009), 119.

114. Marinetti, "Technical Manifesto," 123.

115. Marinetti, "Technical Manifesto," 123.

116. Gertrude Stein, "Poetry and Grammar," *Lectures in America* (New York: Random House, 1935), 212. On Marinetti and Stein, see Marjorie Perloff, *Wittgenstein's Ladder: Poetic Language and the Strangeness of the Ordinary* (Chicago: University of Chicago Press, 1996), esp. 83–90.

accidental about them, that is, the entity in question could have been named something else. Pronouns are better still, since they have a more general function and thus hold out the possibility of error, which Stein takes as a sign that language has not ossified.

Stein's campaign against nouns leads her to warn against prose becoming like poetry, which she characterizes as "a vocabulary entirely based on the noun as prose is essentially and determinately and vigorously not based on the noun."[117] Elaborating this claim, she writes that "poetry is doing nothing but using losing refusing and pleasing and betraying and caressing nouns," then adds:

> When I said.
> A rose is a rose is a rose is a rose.
> And then later made that into a ring I made poetry and what did I do I caressed completely caressed and addressed a noun.[118]

One should not conclude from these remarks that Stein regards poetry as an inherently ineffectual discourse. In caressing and addressing a noun, she produces a line whose exposition will prove as demanding as any philosophical pronouncement, the now iconic "A rose is a rose is a rose is a rose." The decisiveness of the period at the end of the sentence contrasts with the open-endedness of the grammar; the sequence looks as if it should have been punctuated with an ellipsis insofar as it appears to be well on the way to generating further iterations of "is a rose" ad infinitum. Uneasily balancing the finality of an adage with a suggestion of inherent incompleteness, the formulation ultimately offers neither the gnomic—or empty—wisdom of the tautological "a rose is a rose" nor the uncertainty that would have been effected by "a rose is a rose is . . ."

In the passage cited above, Stein invokes the rose sentence by referencing one of its earlier instantiations in her work, although the self-citation is imperfect. In its first appearance in her corpus, in a 1922 poem entitled "Sacred Emily," the line actually began with the noun rather than the article: "Rose is a rose is a rose is a rose."[119] Starting and ending with the same word, the original version bespeaks less open-endedness than circularity ("And then later made that into a ring"), a point that Stein makes even more explicit in a 1939 children's book in which a character is said to "carve on the tree Rose is a Rose is

117. Stein, "Poetry and Grammar," 231.
118. Stein, "Poetry and Grammar," 231.
119. Gertrude Stein, *Geography and Plays* (Boston: Four Seas Company, 1922), 187.

a Rose is a Rose is a Rose until it went all the way around."[120] The question is whether this is an example of a process elegantly coming full circle or something more akin to a snake eating its own tail. If it is a truly circular formation, we might just as well say that it begins with "is" ("Is a rose is a rose is a rose is a rose") as with "a" or "rose." With its operative unit oscillating between "A rose is," "Rose is a," and "Is a rose," Stein's formulation shows us words at once obeying and resisting the ordering logics of English syntax. If we deem the sentence "repetitive," we must acknowledge that each new piece of it "returns" as something that both is and is not identical with what came before. Stein writes: "Is there repetition or is there insistence. I am inclined to believe there is no such thing as repetition."[121] At first glance an exercise in tautological assertion, the "rose" line may permanently defer language's claim to articulate identity unmarked by difference. Rather than making some minimal semantic progress in passing from subject to predicate as from A to B, we find ourselves spinning in place as we go from "a" to "a," from "rose" to "rose," or from "is" to "is," all the while painfully aware that none of these connections constitutes more than a fragment of the sequence's "message."

In caressing and addressing a noun, Stein thoroughly compromises the self-identity of the substantive "rose," creating a sentence that is difficult if not impossible to assimilate to the standard logical and grammatical paradigms on which we typically rely when attempting to coordinate the formal and representational features of a text. This is not to say, as Marjorie Perloff has argued, that Stein's "verbal configurations are set up precisely to manifest the arbitrariness of discourse, the impossibility of arriving at 'the meaning' even as countless possible meanings present themselves to our attention."[122] There are certainly prominent ambiguities in many of Stein's sentences, which often appear to be designed to foreground the multiple semantic avenues down which given words or phrases may lead us. In the various texts in which the rose "formula" appears, we see that Stein plays on the ambiguity of "rose" (noun), "rose" (past participle), and the female name Rose, as well as on the possibility that any instance of "a rose" can be read as the past participle "arose." Nevertheless, she is not primarily interested in the arbitrary status of any given "option" on which the interpretation may settle, but in the systemic precariousness of all sentential structures. A construct such

120. Gertrude Stein, *The World Is Round* (New York: Harper Design, 2013), 53.

121. Gertrude Stein, "Portraits and Repetition," *Lectures in America* (New York: Random House, 1935), 166.

122. Marjorie Perloff, *The Poetics of Indeterminacy: Rimbaud to Cage* (Princeton, NJ: Princeton University Press, 1981), 76.

as "A rose is a rose is a rose is a rose" is less a clearly delimited example of a verbal act than a perpetually evolving, and devolving, dynamic.

In a notable passage in her 1931 book *How To Write*, Stein avers that "a sentence need not have a noun" and declares: "A noun should not remain. It is introduced. It should not remain. A noun should not remain in a sentence. With the a noun should not be in the partly seen hope that arises. A noun should not be in a sentence."[123] In an effort to dynamize the otherwise boring noun "noun," perhaps even forcing us to treat it as a verb, this series of propositions offers several different versions of the idea that if nouns are going to make an appearance in sentences at all, they should be there one moment and gone the next. Each time the word "noun" reappears in this passage, it is as an example of a term that is in the course of being driven out. This becomes most pronounced at the point at which two articles, one definite and one indefinite, follow a preposition that starts a sentence: "With the a noun." It is tempting to insert a comma ("With the, a noun . . ."), as if the relationship between nouns and definite articles were under discussion. Alternatively, "a noun" could be treated as a substantive in its own right that is introduced with the definite article ("With the 'a noun'"), or the two articles could be read together as one word ("With the-a noun"), as if every substantive were simultaneously indefinitely definite and definitely indefinite. In gesturing toward these various options without affirming one or more of them, the preposition "with" and the two words that follow it unsettle the authority of the subject of the sentence, the noun "noun," putting it on uncertain footing and making it, as Stein would say, "interesting."

At such moments, and there are many in Stein's work, the clash between the grammatical and lexical dimensions of the text forces us to question the viability of the most routine linguistic acts, be it making a noun into the object of a preposition or modifying a noun with a definite or indefinite article. When Stein declares, "A noun should not be in a sentence," we have to read this sentence as if "a noun" were *not* in it, which means we have to read it as if we can no longer take it for granted that we know what it means for any part of speech to "be in a sentence"—indeed, as if we can no longer take it for granted that something called "a sentence" exists. "I do want to know if there is a sentence," Stein wrote to the composer Virgil Thomson, "I thought perhaps there wasn't but I am almost beginning to be able to explain that there is."[124] What needs

123. Gertrude Stein, *How To Write* (New York: Dover, 1975), 145.

124. Cited in Steven Meyer, *Irresistible Dictation: Gertrude Stein and the Correlations of Writing and Science* (Stanford, CA: Stanford University Press, 2001), 272.

does the sentençe fulfill that we can scarcely imagine a discourse on reading and writing that would not invoke it in one form or another even as its very existence remains debatable?

In the course of the four hundred pages of *How To Write*, Stein asks more than fifty times: *What is a sentence?*[125] Or rather, in line with her stated aversion to question marks—"anybody can know that a question is a question and so why add to it the question mark when it is already there"—she writes over fifty times: *What is a sentence.*[126] Despite her assurance that we know a question when we see one, it is difficult not to read this as an ambiguous construction that is both a query about the identity of "a sentence" and a statement of fact: "The word *what* is a sentence."[127] Since an author who finds nouns boring is unlikely to be content with a definition of the term *sentence*, we must be clear in whatever account we give of it that we are not simply describing a word called *sentence*, but a verbal formation whose powers lie beyond the capacity of mere words, or at least mere nouns, to explain.

Stein's text highlights the multivalence of *what*, which can be an interrogative pronoun, determiner, or adverb, but is in every case a gesture toward greater specification rather than an instance of precision in its own right. In *How To Write*, each iteration of the refrain *What is a sentence* is complemented by one or more formulations that appear to answer the question—*A sentence is/does/can/must* . . .—but these seem less like definitions than one-off comments that by no means clarify whether any of the individual predications of a sentence being offered are necessary conditions, much less necessary and

125. On the unique challenges of *How To Write*, see Jacques Lezra, "How To Read *How To Write*," *Modernism/modernity* 5, no. 1 (January 1998): 117–29. Sharon J. Kirsch argues that *How To Write* was a satire of Edwin A. Abbott's *How To Write Clearly: Rules and Exercises on English Composition*, a reference work widely used at Harvard in the years before Stein's arrival at Radcliffe in 1893 and still in print as late as 1903. Sharon J. Kirsch, *Gertrude Stein and the Reinvention of Rhetoric* (Tuscaloosa: University of Alabama Press, 2014), 28. Abbott's book has been described as "one of the oddest and most complicated textbooks," its rules "totally arbitrary." John C. Brereton, *The Origins of Composition Studies in the American College, 1875–1925: A Documentary History* (Pittsburgh: University of Pittsburgh Press, 1979), 316. According to Kirsch, Stein has in her sights not just Abbott's text but the trend "to reduce writing to composition or rule-governed mechanics or to practice without theory" (*Reinvention of Rhetoric*, 30). In this vein, Kirsch maintains that "Stein's entire canon can be conceived as an extensive response to the changes taking place in the study of language and the shift from rhetoric to composition at the turn of the century when the institutional separation of rhetoric from literature took place" (22).

126. Stein, "Poetry and Grammar," 215.

127. On *what* as a sentence in *How To Write*, see Ngai, *Ugly Feelings*, 251–52.

sufficient conditions, for its existence. Ultimately, then, we may have no choice but to read the refrain as a claim that the word *what* is a sentence, although accepting this to be the case may not bring us any closer to knowing what a sentence is. In due course, we may find ourselves sputtering—What *what* are we talking about? Any *what*? Whatever *what*!—yet this moment at which language flounders may be precisely the point at which a sentence, whatever it is, puts words into play in distinctive ways that conventional subject-predicate schemas cannot capture.

Much of *How To Write* consists of similar efforts by Stein to open her language to the rhythms and logics that traditional understandings of grammar and representation are designed to sublimate. Beginning the section entitled "Sentences," she offers: "A sentence is made by coupling meanwhile ride around to be a couple there makes grateful dubeity named atlas coin in a loan."[128] At first blush, this is not so much a grammatically viable structure as an awkward fusing of disparate pieces of language. We may scan it and identify what appear to be functional phrases and a few gestures toward alignments of subjects and predicates, but when we reach the end, the relationships between the various parts never crystallize into a coherent formation composed of identifiably independent and dependent clauses. Many of the individual elements offer to do double duty, for instance, "a couple" can be the end of "meanwhile ride around to be a couple" or part of "to be a couple there makes grateful"; "grateful" can be aligned with "makes grateful" or "grateful dubeity." In this regard, the different parts of the sentence can "be a couple" or function "by coupling," which is precisely how the opening of the sentence avers that a sentence should be made.

To read Stein's maverick sentence appears to be less a matter of getting from A to B (perhaps guided by an atlas) than of aimlessly "riding around," or perhaps it is more a question of following the ebbs and flows of an internal economy such as the logic of circulation inherent "in a loan," be it a loan of "coin," of loan words, or of words that have yet to be coined. As couples couple, names name, and coins coin, the very distinction between nouns and verbs begins to seem unhelpful, if not outright misleading, and we may find that the most stable reference points in this verbal construction are the prepositions ("by," "around," "in") because they express the possibility of relationships independent of any assumptions about the individual relata. In Stein's view, every sentence is more like this one than we may wish to believe,

128. Stein, *How To Write*, 115.

and correspondingly less like the stable interplay of grammatical, logical, and rhetorical forces we typically imagine ourselves to be reading or writing. To those who balk in the face of such complexities and declare that whatever this collection of words framed between a capital letter and a period is, it is not a sentence, Stein has a ready answer: "A sentence says you know what I mean. Dear do I well I guess I do."[129]

In her relentless campaign to defamiliarize language, Stein has an uncanny knack for revealing just how few questions we generally ask about some of our most commonplace distinctions. A case in point is her focus on the relationship between sentences and paragraphs. Dictionaries will inform us that a paragraph is a clearly demarcated section of a piece of writing, usually a group of sentences, organized around a theme or topic. For her part, Stein is concerned to distinguish sharply between sentences and paragraphs: "Radically different, sentences and paragraphs cannot be reduced to a common denominator, for the paragraph is not the sum of the sentences in it. It is not an expanding sentence but something other than a sentence."[130] To declare that a paragraph is neither just an extended sentence nor the sum of the sentences it comprises is hardly an extraordinary position, although the more common observation is that the paragraph is a much less well defined unit than the sentence—to the point, some would say, that it can refer to virtually any section of text. Alternatively, it is maintained that the paragraph and the sentence share some features, for example, they are organized around a main idea, but differ in structure and development. Stein, however, wants to go further, rigorously demarcating a frontier between these two verbal formations. Her point is not that the whole is and is not greater than the sum of its parts, but that in this case the whole is not the sum of its parts at all. "A paragraph," she avers bluntly, "is not made of sentences."[131]

Stein's argument is grounded in an observation that she repeats in several different texts: "Sentences are not emotional but paragraphs are."[132] This claim rests on a notion of balance. "A sentence," she writes, "is inside itself by its internal balancing, think how a sentence is made by its parts of speech and you will see that it is not dependent upon a beginning a middle and an ending but by each part needing its own place to make its own balancing, and

129. Stein, *How To Write*, 34.

130. Cited in Ulla E. Dyod with William Rice, *Gertrude Stein: The Language That Rises 1923–1934* (Evanston, IL: Northwestern University Press, 2003), 398.

131. Cited in Dyod and Rice, *Gertrude Stein*, 398.

132. Stein, "Poetry and Grammar," 223.

because of this in a sentence there is no emotion, a sentence does not give off emotion."[133] The paragraph, in contrast, "exists not by a balance within but by a succession."[134] In stridently rejecting any conflation of grammatical structure and the linear appearance of words in space or time, Stein seems to be asking us to conceive of sentences in their most schematic form, as diagrams on a blackboard rather than as manifestations of sequences of sounds or marks on the page. Her argument flies in the face of most writing guides, whose prescriptions for producing good sentences almost invariably include recommendations for how their beginnings, middles, and ends can and should interact. Nonetheless, Stein insists that the sentence eschews the need for progression characteristic of the paragraph, because a sentence is an essentially ordered and hierarchical formation, and its first priority is always to maintain an equilibrium between its various subordinate and superordinate parts. It is in this sense that Stein argues that sentences do not move. Their forces counterbalanced, they are a-motional rather than e-motional.[135] In contrast, a paragraph, comprising a beginning, middle, and end, creates at least a semblance of sequence and is thus e-motive. It agitates, stirring things up by pushing against itself or away from its broader verbal environment, in any event betraying at least a minimal degree of instability.[136]

Having characterized this opposition between sentences and paragraphs, Stein tests its authority by attempting to produce verbal constructions that may not be governed by it. Describing the composition of her 925-page novel *The Making of Americans*, she explains that she sought to make her "sentences so long that they held within themselves the balance of both sentences and paragraphs," but the result was that what she produced "had neither the balance of a sentence nor the balance of a paragraph."[137] As she acknowledges, this might at first appear to be a setback: "I felt dimly that I had done some-

133. Gertrude Stein, *Narration: Four Lectures* (Chicago: University of Chicago Press, 2010), 22–23.

134. Stein, *Narration*, 22.

135. The English word "emotion" comes from the Latin *emovere*, "to move out" or "to agitate."

136. Ron Silliman argues that Stein's point is that "linguistic units integrate only up to the level of the sentence, but higher orders of meaning—such as emotion—integrate at higher levels than the sentence" (*The New Sentence*, 87). His notion that "emotion" is a "higher order of meaning" that cannot be expressed except at a level beyond the sentence clashes with most linguistic theory since the eighteenth century, in which brief utterances, often one-syllable interjections, are accorded the power to articulate, or create, affect.

137. Stein, "Poetry and Grammar," 224.

thing that was not leading to anything because after all you should not lose two things in order to have one thing because in doing so you make writing just that much less varied."[138] Stein's detractors would certainly agree. They complain that her simple lexicon and overreliance on repetition are a recipe for monotonous texts, and *The Making of Americans* has been expressly singled out for criticism on this score, to the point that Tanya E. Clement has recently argued, without irony, that the book is ripe for distant reading because it is "almost impossible to read [it] in a traditional, linear manner."[139]

What such criticisms miss is the fact that precisely what Stein is attacking is the foundational tenet of compositional instruction—an injunction found in nearly every style manual—that one vary one's word choice and sentence structure. In Stein's terms, stylistic diversity for the sake of diversity is itself bound to become monotonous, because it is premised on a false notion of difference, a difference won through unmotivated shifts that never actually challenge the integrity of the elements that are ostensibly undergoing modulation. In contrast, the power of *The Making of Americans* stems from its veritable onslaught of variations on phrases and clauses that creates a sense of the intimate—and intimately precarious—relationship between sameness and difference. Stein likens this to the way in which "in a cinema picture no two pictures are exactly alike each one is just that much different from the one before."[140] The result, she says, is "almost a thousand pages of a continuous present," but this is not a static or empty unbrokenness, but something "alive," "a movement lively enough to be a thing in itself moving, it does not have to move against anything to know that it is moving."[141]

In *The Making of Americans*, no word or sentence ever takes its own stability—or longevity—for granted. To cite a representative passage, permutations of which stretch across dozens of pages:

> Some are having angry feeling about some such thing about being certain about every one being a dead one sometime, about always being certain about this thing, about not often being certain about this thing, about never coming to themselves

138. Stein, "Poetry and Grammar," 224.

139. Tanya E. Clement, "'A Thing Not Beginning and Not Ending': Using Digital Tools to Distant-read Gertrude Stein's The Making of Americans," *Literary and Linguistic Computing* 23, no. 3 (2008): 361.

140. Stein, "Portraits and Repetition," 177.

141. Gertrude Stein, "Composition as Explanation," *Writings: 1903–1932* (New York: Literary Classics of the United States, 1998), 524; Stein, "Portraits and Repetition," 170–71.

> inside them being completely certain, completely not certain every minute about this thing, about not remembering this thing, about not listening about this thing, about other ones not saying they are certain about this thing, that they are not certain about this thing, about others listening, about others refusing to listen to this thing that each one sometime is a dead one, some are having angry feeling in them about such a thing sometime in their living and then in parts of their living they are having very little angry feeling about such things and part of their living they are having remembering having angry feeling about such a thing and part of their living they are not having at all angry feeling about such things.[142]

Neither exactly a sentence nor a paragraph, this sequence is quickly taken over by the word *about*, any of whose individual instantiations ostensibly confirms the power of language to concern itself with something or be apropos, even if only as a reference to itself. However, as "about" proliferates and mingles with the different forms of "some" ("sometime," "some such") that "somehow" make paradoxically vague claims to being specific, one begins to suspect that precisely what "some are having angry feeling about" is "about." Some are angry about the very demand that their feelings be about something, which in this passage is necessarily a demand that their language be about something. At once too specific and too vague, each manifestation of "about" does enough to articulate one more prepositional phrase, but not enough to dispel the impression that it is just another "certain some such" instance of a preposition whose very presence feels decidedly superfluous, since we are, after all, always talking or writing "about" what we are talking or writing about, aren't we?

In the first half of the passage, the sense that the various instances of the preposition "about" are never entirely free of the adverbial "about" ("approximately") is accentuated by multiple appearances of the word "certain," which gradually gives way in the second half to the authority of the determiner "such." Stein's language is angry "about always being certain about this thing, about not often being certain about this thing"; her language is angry about the talking and listening about different certainties that must go on; but most of all, her language is angry about the assumption that the aim of language, that what language is supposed to be "about," is certainty itself. Stein rejects the premise that words, phrases, and clauses strive for the reliability, stability, and constancy that are the hallmark of Cartesian thought. In this passage, to be certain "about some such thing about being certain about every one being a dead

142. Gertrude Stein, *The Making of Americans: Being a History of a Family's Progress* (New York: Something Else Press, 1966), 776.

one sometime" is to be angry about the claim that a standardized grammatical order secures the fixed identity of given words and phrases across repeated iterations and ensures that a given rhetorical or stylistic schema has one trustworthy, transparent significance.

One of Stein's names for the empty variation of word choice and sentence style that she is combating is "patriarchal poetry," which is also the title of a forty-page prose poem in which she ruthlessly critiques the patriarchal conception of identity. In one memorable passage, Stein writes: "Why while while why while why why identity identity why while while why. Why while while while while identity."[143] To interrogate these lines, one has no choice but to begin to write Steinese: Why "while"? Meanwhile what does "while" mean? Why "while" while [*besides, in addition to*] "why"? Are "while" and "why" erstwhile rivals? Is it worthwhile for us to while away the time parsing these iterations of "while" and "why"? Why, while the wiles of language are at work, does the uncertain "identity" of any instance of "why" or "while" threaten to while away—and why away—identity itself?

Patriarchal poetry relies on a static conception of language in which the predicative structure of a statement is never challenged, much less at risk of turning against itself. Yet while "while" is running loose, it is almost impossible even to pose the question *Why identity?* without first asking *Why "why"?* Predictably, patriarchal poetry's only "answer" to Stein's "question" is: "Patriarchal Poetry is the same as patriarchal poetry is the same as patriarchal poetry is the same as patriarchal poetry is the same as patriarchal poetry is the same."[144] In this consonance- and assonance-saturated discourse, patriarchal poetry—PP—is confronted with the uncomfortable truth that its claims to coherence rest on homophones rather than truth or logic: "Patriarchal Poetry or peace to return to Patriarchal Poetry or pieces of Patriarchal Poetry. / Very pretty very prettily very prettily very pretty very prettily."[145]

Certain aspects of Stein's political life, particularly her collaborationist activities under the Vichy government, sit uncomfortably with the notion that she was a radical author whose queering of the sentence should be unambiguously

143. Gertrude Stein, *Patriarchal Poetry, Writings: 1903–1932* (New York: Literary Classics of the United States, 1998), 577. Cary Nelson has declared *Patriarchal Poetry* to be "one of the great poems of the modern era." Cary Nelson, "The Fate of Gender in Modern American Poetry," in *Marketing Modernisms: Self-Promotion, Canonization, Rereading*, eds. Kevin J. H. Dettmar and Stephen Watt (Ann Arbor: University of Michigan Press, 1996), 353.

144. Stein, *Patriarchal Poetry*, 577.

145. Stein, *Patriarchal Poetry*, 594.

celebrated as a progressive aesthetic project. As *Patriarchal Poetry* indicates, however, it would be wrong to conclude that she did not explore the politics of language in provocative ways. One of her most sustained considerations of the ideological nature of the sentence takes place in a 1935 lecture called "What Is English Literature?" This piece sets out an expansive literary history that begins with Chaucer and builds to the apex of imperialism in the nineteenth century. From the outset, Stein writes as if the curious interplay of balance and imbalance that shapes sentences and paragraphs were reflected in or reflective of international relations. As she explains, one of the defining features of Imperial England—that it is an independent island whose daily existence is shaped by its exercise of sovereign autonomy—sits oddly with the equally salient fact that it owns a large part of the rest of the world. This is not the problem of the one and the many, but of the one and the everything else that is its own. In response, English writers strive to articulate a language that can account for the relationship between identity and possession, a discourse in which the relationship between *I am* and *I own* will be straightforward and stable.

The nineteenth century sees an intensification of England's paradoxical sense of itself as a whole that is also a part of the whole that is a part of it. The result is that what Stein calls a language of phrases gradually displaces the eighteenth-century discourse of sentences.[146] In the English literature of the period, she writes, "sentences and paragraphs were [still] divisions because they always are but they did not mean particularly much, but phrases became the thing," and this was true, she adds, as much for poetry as for prose.[147]

"If I were you"; "And I quote"; "All rights reserved." More than a single word but less than a full-fledged clause, a phrase is unmistakably a unit, but one whose status as an independent verbal formation is uncertain. Grammatically fragmentary, a phrase signifies or performs just well enough to make us wonder whether it is a drawback that it is not a sentence. Stein maintains that the discourse of phrases is soothing because it walks a fine line between the complete and the incomplete, offering some hope of accommodating the contradictory logic of imperial possession according to which England is

146. While she draws unique conclusions from the observation, Stein was neither the first nor the last to suggest that nineteenth-century English literature is shaped by reflections on the puzzles of property. Scholars have long maintained that the writers of this era were preoccupied with questions of inherited wealth and the changing nature of ownership in the age of empire.

147. Stein, "What Is English Literature?," *Lectures in America*, 43. In French, in whose zone of influence Stein spent the second half of her life, *la phrase* means "sentence."

simultaneously a part of the world and a world unto itself that makes the rest of the world its part.

As Stein's curious literary history continues and the twentieth century draws near, things change. "The daily island life," she writes, "was not sufficient any more as limiting the daily life of the English, and the owning everything outside was no longer actual or certain and so it was necessary that these things should be replaced by something and they were replaced by the paragraph."[148] With the decline of the empire and the weakening of the clash between national identity and ownership of the world, the paradoxical topology of parts containing the whole of parts becomes less disruptive, and the paragraph is embraced as a form of completeness that promises stability. In England, the paragraph's reign was brief, for authors did not prove adept in organizing what they wrote under its auspices and soon regressed back to the defunct language of phrases. In American literature, however, the paragraph blossomed, having, according to Stein, already begun to come into its own in the work of Henry James. James and his countrymen were able to develop a style unconcerned with explaining the mysteries of property, be it a question of owning oneself, parts of the world, or one's language. James wrote with such freedom, Stein argues, because the structure of his sentences and paragraphs never committed him to any particular understanding of the relationship between being and having. As David Bromwich characterizes her position: "American writing on this view is the reverse of imperial: rather it is unpropertied, and chiefly original in that it shows the difficulty even of owning itself."[149]

In an interview with her friend Donald Sutherland, Stein declared that in the nineteenth century "a sentence was part of a paragraph which was part of a chapter which was part of a book which was part of a shelf of books which was part of England or America or France and so on."[150] In contrast, she continued, "nothing now is really convincingly part of anything else."[151] This is perhaps her pithiest account of a language of radical equality, a vision of a discourse in

148. Stein, "What is English Literature?," 48. Jennifer Ashton argues that "to render the nineteenth century negligible, [Stein] figures its literary practices in terms of a cumulative progression toward a whole, a progression that can never achieve but only approximate the whole." Jennifer Ashton, "Gertrude Stein for Anyone," *ELH* 64, no. 1 (Spring 1997): 313.

149. David Bromwich, *Skeptical Music: Essays on Modern Poetry* (Chicago: University of Chicago Press, 2001), 226.

150. Donald Sutherland, "An Interview with Gertrude Stein," *Gertrude Stein: A Biography of Her Work* (New Haven, CT: Yale University Press, 1951), 194.

151. Sutherland, "An Interview with Gertrude Stein," 194.

which every part is just as important as every other part because nothing belongs to anything else. For Stein, imperialism wanes and modernism takes off when our most basic intuitions about the organizing principles of texts are replaced by a compositional field in which every putative part stands apart from the very notion of a part. Only by ceasing to treat words as parts of sentences, sentences as parts of paragraphs, and paragraphs as parts of essays or books will authors be free to articulate verbal forms that both break the old rules and establish new ones.

From Woolf to Pound, Hemingway, and Stein, early twentieth-century writers of all political and aesthetic allegiances answered Benjamin's call to fashion a sentence style in which their own distinctive compositional "training regimens" would be visible. Their writing itself became a kind of performance art, although it remains an open question what we can hope to learn from the performances. In different ways, Stein and Hemingway presented themselves as parodic paragons, mocking their status as exemplary wordsmiths and giving their would-be disciples fits, since it proved at once too easy and too difficult to emulate them. Nevertheless, the unique celebrity they attained as stylists—or antistylists—suggests that one of the key legacies of modernism is a curious fusion of avant-garde aesthetic dictates with practical compositional instruction. Henceforth, the rules by which famous writers claimed to practice their craft would quickly be disseminated to the rest of us. Changes in education, the rise of modern media conglomerates, and the expansion of celebrity culture undoubtedly played a role in this development, but the strident commitment of modernist authors to perfecting or radicalizing the sentence form was a necessary precondition.

The modernist text most likely to be found on a college syllabus today is not *The Old Man and the Sea*, *To The Lighthouse*, or *In Search of Lost Time*, but a pamphlet written in 1918 by a Cornell professor that in an expanded form would come to be known as William Strunk and E. B. White's *The Elements of Style*.[152]

152. Geoffrey Pullum explains the evolution of the text: "Strunk's first privately published version of *Elements* was dated 1918. There followed a little-known commercial version in 1920 [published by Harcourt, Brace and Company], two radically rewritten and now forgotten editions coauthored by Edward Tenney in 1934 and 1935, and six editions of the White revision (1959, 1972, 1979, 2000, 2004, and 2009, the last being just a 50th-anniversary reissue of the 2000 edition)." Geoffrey K. Pullum, "The Land of the Free and *The Elements of Style*," *English Today* 26, no. 2 (June 2010): 34. While White himself would champion the continuity between the later editions of *Elements* and Strunk's original pamphlet, he has on occasion been accused of corrupting the ethos of Strunk's text.

Strunk and White probably never dreamed that their work would enjoy such extraordinary success. As historian Richard H. Minear observes: "Few books have fared so well as *Elements of Style*. It has sold 10,000,000 copies. It was number 21 on a recent list of the 100 most important non-fiction books of the 20th century."[153] Sometimes read, more often purchased and then ignored, this text's staying power may indicate that the need for a how-to-write reference manual outweighs any theoretical or practical concerns about its dicta. Alternatively, it may be a sign that its core doctrines are not so easily put aside.

Strunk's 1918 pamphlet appeared at the end of a change in American writing instruction that saw a shift from classical rhetoric—with a focus on developing a personal style and finding something original to say—to "composition," where the emphasis was on "mechanical correctness," and grammar became a foundational part of the curriculum.[154] In due course, the pendulum would swing back in the other direction. By the 1940s, communications classes and a renewed stress on producing creative content were in vogue, and in the past seventy-five years, there have been several more such doctrinal oscillations.[155] The core edicts of Strunk and White's book have not only weathered these shifts but have thrived, seemingly immune to the vagaries of pedagogical fashion.

At the heart of *The Elements of Style* is a passage that has survived virtually unaltered from the document Strunk wrote for his students, one of whom was White. This is sometimes referred to as the DNA of the book's philosophy of composition:

> Vigorous writing is concise. A sentence should contain no unnecessary words, a paragraph no unnecessary sentences, for the same reason that a drawing should have no unnecessary lines and a machine no unnecessary parts. This

153. Richard H. Minear, "E. B. White Takes His Leave, or Does He? *The Elements of Style*, Six Editions (1918–2000)," *Massachusetts Review* 45, no. 1 (Spring 2004): 52.

154. As Robert J. Connors explains: "Between 1865–1895, such elements of mechanical correctness as grammar, punctuation, spelling, and capitalization, which would never have been found in textbooks before 1850, came to usurp much of the time devoted in class to rhetorical instruction and most of the marking of student writing." Robert J. Connors, "Mechanical Correctness as a Focus in Composition Instruction," *College Composition and Communication* 36, no. 1 (February 1985): 65.

155. See Robert J. Connors, "Handbooks: History of a Genre," *Rhetoric Society Quarterly* 13, no. 2 (Spring 1983): 87–98.

> requires not that the writer make all his sentences short, or that he avoid all detail and treat his subjects only in outline, but that every word tell.[156]

Almost forty years after he first read this paragraph, White wrote of it: "There you have a short, valuable essay on the nature and beauty of brevity—sixty-three words that could change the world."[157] Their notoriety notwithstanding, the most famous modernist manifestoes have been read by only a fraction of the number of people who have encountered this unassuming passage, which is anything but a fount of novelty. Some of the advice Strunk offers had been standard fare in English-language style manuals for centuries. That it should suddenly be ready for prime time had much to do with demographic factors, in particular the growth of college education in the United States, which led to an increasingly diverse population of students learning how to write, coupled with a newfound emphasis on communication skills in the workplace. As we shall see, the success of Strunk's core ideas may also have been a factor of the way in which he integrated older commonplaces about writing into newer aesthetic paradigms.

It would be an understatement to say that a host of different ideas are packed into Strunk's sixty-three words. This injunction to be concise is undoubtedly concise, although one wonders whether its density compromises the clarity of its message. White, who apparently could never pass up an opportunity to quantify pithiness, praised Strunk's original pamphlet as a "forty-three-page summation of the case for cleanliness, accuracy, and brevity in the use of English."[158] One might ask whether Strunk's embrace of the laconic went too far. Eighteenth- and nineteenth-century forerunners of *Elements* were often extremely long, preaching a compactness that they did

156. William Strunk Jr., *The Elements of Style: The Original Edition* (Mineola, NY: Dover, 2006), 24. The 1918 text is also available online at http://www.bartleby.com/141/. Mark Garvey characterizes this now canonical passage as Strunk and White's "Sermon on the Mount, the nugget that cradles the book's DNA." Mark Garvey, *Stylized: A Slightly Obsessive History of Strunk & White's "The Elements of Style"* (New York: Simon & Schuster, 2009), 15.

157. E. G. White, "Will Strunk," *New Yorker*, July 15, 1957, cited in Minear, "E. B. White Takes His Leave," 55. In the introduction to the third edition of *Elements* (1979), White reprinted these same remarks, but he referred to "fifty-nine words that could change the world," two instances of "his" and one of "that he" having been deleted, presumably to make the passage gender neutral. William Strunk Jr. and E. B. White, "Introduction," *The Elements of Style*, 3rd ed. (New York: MacMillan, 1979), xvi.

158. E. B. White, "Introduction," *The Elements of Style*, xiii.

not practice, but even White allowed that Strunk's book was sometimes "needlessly compressed," raising the question of whether brevity inherently begets accuracy.[159] In many contexts, precision is a factor of expansion—more detail—not succinctness. Similarly, the compatibility of concision and clarity is by no means self-evident, since intelligibility is often predicated on the degree to which things are spelled out rather than condensed, that is, one is expected to "show one's work," taking the reader through the steps that lead to one's conclusion.

In truth, White's emphasis on the value of brevity may not be an entirely faithful interpretation of the primal passage of Strunk's pamphlet. While concision is certainly one of its concerns, the central claim is that extraneous or idle words are a drag on composition and must be purged, a position reminiscent of Pound's injunction to avoid waste as well as of the Imagist manifesto that preceded *Elements* by five years, in which the writer is forbidden from using a single word that does not contribute to the presentation.[160] Strunk's version of this commandment has survived intact to this day and can be found in the publications of countless college writing labs, which offer prescriptions such as: "Like bad employees, words that don't accomplish enough should be fired."[161]

The no-frills, anti-ornamental bent of Strunk's doctrine has more than a hint of puritanical austerity—waste not, want not—suggesting that the protestant work ethic, not to mention the spirit of capitalism and its inexorable rationalization of modern life, are alive and well in this Fordist validation of the responsibility we have to actualize our labor power when expressing ourselves in print. *Elements* thus makes explicit what is already legible in Pound's philosophy, namely that style, morality, and political economy are intimately bound up with one another. Presumably this has always been the case, but in modernism, their interconnectedness is thematized as something of which writers may take advantage, as if by changing the language, one could change oneself or the world. Some admirers of Strunk and White have gone so far as to claim that their book is a guide to leading a balanced, grounded life as much as it is a collections of rules for fashioning good sentences. Various authors of contemporary writing manuals have followed suit and weighed in on the potential symbiosis of style and lifestyle, not infrequently with a moralistic bent. For example, in her recent *The Writer's Diet: A Guide to Fit Prose*, Helen

159. Cited in Minear, "E. B. White Takes His Leave," 56.

160. See F. S. Flint, "Imagisme," *Poetry* (Chicago) 1 (March 1913): 199.

161. Purdue Online Writing Lab, https://owl.english.purdue.edu/owl/resource/572/01/.

Sword warns us to "strengthen and tone [our] sentences," lest flabby writing make us vulnerable to body-shaming.[162]

According to Strunk, writing well is not actually good exercise, because the text is less a human worker than a machine.[163] With this motif, he extends the "mechanical" correctness of the grammatical rules governing sentences to encompass form and content in their entirety. A few decades later, the New Critics will speak of poems as organic systems of relationships, but Strunk's model is neither biologistic nor evolutionary; there are no vestigial organs at hand.[164] That this image of a well-functioning device is casually aligned with

162. Helen Sword, *The Writer's Diet: A Guide to Fit Prose* (Chicago: University of Chicago Press, 2016), 1.

163. Twenty-five years later, William Carlos Williams will sound very much like Strunk when he declares that "a poem is a small (or large) machine made of words. When I say there's nothing sentimental about a poem, I mean that there can be no part, as in any other machine, that is redundant." William Carlos Williams, "Introduction" to *The Wedge* (1944), in *The Collected Poems of William Carlos Williams*, ed. Christopher MacGowan, vol. 2 (New York: New Directions, 1988), 54. "Prose," continues Williams, "may carry a load of ill-defined matter like a ship. But poetry is the machine which drives it, pruned to a perfect economy" (54).

164. Modernist aesthetics and New Criticism can appear to be two sides of the same coin. The injunction to the author to ensure that every word is giving 110 percent is mirrored by the demand on the critic to treat the text as if any and every detail were crucial. A similar notion of exactitude informs both discourses, as when Cleanth Brooks writes that "if we are to speak *exactly* [italics added], the poem itself is the *only* [Brooks's italics] medium that communicates the particular 'what' that is communicated." Cleanth Brooks, *The Well-Wrought Urn: Studies in the Structure of Poetry* (New York: Houghton Mifflin Harcourt, 1947), 74. Even the evident clash between modernist machine aesthetics and the much-vaunted "organicism" of New Critical ideology may be less acute than it first appears. In *Understanding Poetry*, the text that would become as canonical for the teaching of literary analysis as Strunk and White's *Elements* would be for compositional instruction, Brooks and Robert Penn Warren begin by arguing that "a poem should always be treated as an organic system of relationships, and the poetic quality should never be understood as inhering in one or more factors taken in isolation." Cleanth Brooks and Robert Penn Warren, *Understanding Poetry: An Anthology for College Students* (New York: Henry Holt, 1950 [1938]), xv. The key term here is "system," because in fact "organic" serves primarily to emphasize the need to consider all the different elements of a poem together rather than in isolation, a demand that is perfectly compatible with the compositional dicta of Woolf or Stein. Similarly, both John Ransom's assertion that "the texture of poetry is one of incessant particularity" and Brooks's claim that "the general and the universal are not seized upon by abstraction, but got at through the concrete and the particular" recall the thinking of Pound and the Imagists. John Ransom, *The New Criticism* (Westport, CT: Greenwood Press, 1968), 25; Cleanth Brooks, "The Formalist Critics," *Kenyon Review* 13, no. 1 (Winter 1951): 72. In their "Introduction" to the *Modernism and the New Criticism* volume of *The Cambridge History of*

a drawing devoid of unnecessary lines indicates that the mechanical contrivance is not just a tool but an aesthetic object in its own right. The eminently functional text-machine is an artwork, an example of beauty without ornament. The longer we look at Strunk's sixty-three-word manifesto, the harder it becomes to disentangle his practical advice for writing from a host of modernist doctrines in which the beauty or sublimity of technology plays a central, and often politically problematic, role.

In Flaubert, Pound, or Strunk, the image of the writer as craftsman-engineer lends credence to the notion that if we cannot all be great poets, essayists, or novelists, we can nonetheless all benefit from being exposed to the right stylistic advice. The guiding principle is control. Word by word, the author is to be the master of her, or rather her writing's, fate. As in Poe's "The Philosophy of Composition," where the writer is enjoined to select every element of the text with an eye toward realizing an overarching goal, each piece of Strunk's text-machine is to play its part in producing the desired product or result, and if something is not helping the machine do its job, it must be purged. Lazy or idle words will not be countenanced.

No less than with the Imagist idea of the exact word, it is difficult to know if and when a given term is pulling its weight. Assessing whether a noun or adjective is actualizing its potential labor power is presumably not as straightforward as testing the amperage of an outlet. With the injunction against "unnecessary words," the idea of writing "by the rules" has been taken to such an extreme that it is as if the principle of spelling had been generalized to all aspects of composition, that is, just as one does not add extra h's to the word *the*, so one should never add extra words to one's sentences. Reminiscent of Pound's imaginary thermodynamics, this doctrine is informed by the fantasy of a frictionless world in which all the parts of the machine interact without resistance. Strunk never considers whether a given word's presence in a text, even a word that does exactly what it is supposed to do, may impact the way that other words do their jobs. Along the same lines, one might ask whether some words are able to do more in a sentence if other ones are doing less. Strunk follows Woolf and Stein in endorsing an equality between words, each of which is supposed to give 110 percent, but he strongly privileges activity

Literary Criticism, Louis Menand and Lawrence Rainey argue against the tendency to treat the New Critics and modernist aesthetics as two facets of a larger project. To a considerable degree, however, their argument is based on the observation that the New Critics themselves had little to say about writers such as Joyce, Stein, and Lewis, which hardly speaks to the potential similarities or differences between their respective aesthetic doctrines.

over passivity and actualization over potential, leaving no place for the semantic follies of "Passing Russell Square." According to *Elements*, a composition should not be driven by latent denotations or connotations. If a given term manifests itself in a sentence, it should come into its own now, not later.

The notion that the words of a text should fit together like the parts of a well-oiled machine also hints at an element of automation that lurks in Strunk's conception of good writing. He implies that the problems with our sentences stem from human error and that the solution is for us to get out of the way and let language do its work. Once a verbal process is safely up and running, we can sit back and admire its performance. A perpetual motion machine rather than a windup toy, an automated sentence should have unlimited staying power, and if all goes well, people should still be admiring it decades or centuries after it was written.

Several of the modernist authors we have considered reach a different conclusion. In Pound, Hemingway, and Stein, the power of the sentence lies in its caprice rather than its predictability, in its capacity to surprise, not its ability to perform reliably on command. Far from trying to perfect the sentence, these writers reveal that any sentence is both a celebration and a critique of the sentence form. For them, every sentence says, "This is what a sentence looks like," at the same time as it says, "This is not what a sentence has to look like." If what we want is advice on how to write well, the first lesson they offer is that we must learn to craft sentences that betray our uncertainty about whether we actually know how to do so. Even more challengingly, their second lesson is that sentences will never do exactly what is demanded of them and that in simultaneously falling short of and surpassing our expectations, they may be fated to leave us unsure as to precisely what we were hoping they would achieve in the first place.

Conclusion: The Sentence Fetish

Style is a word everybody uses, but almost no one can explain what it means.

FRANCIS-NOËL THOMAS AND MARK TURNER

One does not think words, one thinks only sentences.

PAUL VALÉRY

Almost a century after John Erskine and Mortimer Adler offered the first "great books" courses at Columbia University and the University of Chicago, these onetime cornerstones of the curriculum have come to be regarded as relics of an era in which the exclusionary dynamics of the literary canon were either ignored or actively embraced as a means of perpetuating cultural hegemony. Today, teaching a series of stand-alone texts on the premise that they are, in Matthew Arnold's famous phrase, "the best which has been thought and said" will invite skepticism if not outright disapprobation. This interrogation of the notion of great literature has conspicuously not extended to the notion of the great stylist, which has survived, if not thrived, with little scrutiny. Scholars who have dedicated their careers to identifying and disrupting the ruling ideologies show little interest in examining the assumptions about language, ethics, and culture on which our pronouncements about the power and elegance of sentences rely. Aesthetic judgment appears to become politically neutral when it is an elegant turn of phrase that is at issue.

This commitment to treating stylistic excellence as an unproblematic object of veneration means that the sentence is increasingly understood as something to be admired, like a painting or a sculpture. We live, as James Wood has said, in the "age of the sentence fetish."[1] Great writers write great sentences, ambitious writers aspire to do the same, and we all enjoy the results. In journalism or advertising, to focus on perfecting one's output sentence by sentence may

1. James Wood, "Unsuitable Boys: Novels about Americans looking for Love in Europe," *New Yorker*, February 8/15, 2016, www.newyorker.com/magazine/2016/02/08/unsuitable-boys.

seem reasonable, since success or failure often rests on one or two flashy formulations. If the goal is to produce a longer text, we may not be well served by the conviction that each piece of the puzzle should be a miniature artwork. Giving full rein to the aphoristic aesthetic can see a short story turn into something resembling a pompous collection of would-be maxims. In the case of the novel, the romance of the first line often weighs particularly heavily on the writer. Anything short of "A screaming comes across the sky" feels as if it dooms the work from the start, even as we are aware of the pitfalls of trying too hard to begin with a bang.

If the practical downsides to striving for perfection in every sentence are clear, there may still be value in attempting to do so. One author who thought that any phrase or clause should be the *ne plus ultra* version of itself was the Viennese critic Karl Kraus, who never tired of boasting about the unparalleled standards to which he held himself and his journal *Die Fackel*, which he single-handedly wrote and edited. "I have often stopped the press and destroyed a print run," he declared, "just because the milligram scales of my stylistic sense rejected a word."[2] Kraus expected nothing less of others, and he famously savaged his contemporaries for what seemed like miniscule errors of grammar or diction, in one instance accusing the Austrian novelist Stefan Zweig of being complicit in the destruction of *Bildung* ("education") because of a single misconjugated verb. This radical perfectionism was informed by Kraus's conviction that the smallest feature of a text could, as Walter Benjamin put it, betray "the intellectual universe of an author."[3] For Kraus, to write was to attempt to write flawlessly; there simply was no other mode of production. By contrast, Percy Bysshe Shelley proposed that intermittent success with one's sentences is more than respectable: "A single sentence may be considered as a whole, though it may be found in the midst of a series of unassimilated portions."[4]

Would we be pleased with the results if we somehow did succeed in stringing together one stellar sentence after another across pages or even chapters? Gary Lutz describes taking inspiration from novels "in which almost every sentence was a vivid extremity of language, an abruption, a definitive inquietude. These were books written by writers who recognized the sentence as

2. Karl Kraus, *Dicta and Contradicta*, trans. Jonathan McVity (Urbana: University of Illinois Press, 2001), 95.

3. Walter Benjamin, "Karl Kraus," *Selected Writings*, Vol. 2: *1927–1934*, ed. Michael W. Jennings et al. (Cambridge, MA: Harvard University Press, 1999), 439.

4. Percy Bysshe Shelley, "A Defense of Poetry," *Major British Poets of the Romantic Period*, ed. William Heath (New York: Macmillan, 1973), 978.

the one true theater of endeavor, as the place where writing comes to a point and attains its ultimacy."[5] For Lutz, an author cannot rest on her compositional laurels for even a moment; with each subsequent sentence, she puts her reputation on the line. The resulting text may be distinctive, but even under optimal circumstances, it is bound to be taxing. As one vivid construction after another threatens to tear free of the whole, the "definitive inquietude" may be something of a shock to the reader, who can only be stopped in her tracks so many times. Harold Bloom describes this problem in the work of Gabriel García Márquez: "My primary impression, in the act of rereading *One Hundred Years of Solitude*," he relates, "is a kind of aesthetic battle fatigue, since every page is crammed full of life beyond the capacity of any single reader to absorb. . . . There are no wasted sentences, no mere transitions, in this novel, and you must notice everything at the moment you read it."[6]

Putting aside such reservations, Lutz insists that it is possible to write sentences that are extraordinary verbal gestures in their own right yet still move the text in which they appear forward. As he describes it, each sentence can be "an outcry combining the acoustical elegance of the aphorism with the force and utility of the load-bearing, tractional sentence of more or less conventional narrative."[7] The key is not to rush things out of fear of becoming stuck on a given phrase or clause. While a writer necessarily desires "to get out of one sentence as soon as possible and get going on the next," Lutz urges us to linger over each one, even as it becomes "claustrophobic, inhospitable, even hellish," because "our habitual and hasty breaking away from one sentence to another results in sentences that remain undeveloped parcels of literary real estate."[8] In the course of being written, a sentence momentarily becomes the entirety of one's project, its be-all and end-all; yet the moment a sentence is finished, this

5. Gary Lutz, "The Sentence Is a Lonely Place," *Believer*, January 2009, http://www.believermag.com/issues/200901/?read=article_lutz. Lutz leaves no doubt that he is describing an almost impossible brand of perfectionism. As he explains, he used to favor sentences that "had about them an air of having been foreordained—as if this combination of words could not be improved upon and had finished readying itself for infinity."

6. Harold Bloom, "Introduction," *Bloom's Modern Critical Views: Gabriel García Márquez* (updated edition), ed. Harold Bloom (New York: Chelsea House, 2007), 2. Wood notes that the question of "where we make a fetish of the perfect sentence, or a more relaxed religion of the appropriate form" is a perennial problem for the novel. James Wood, "A Novel Brings Israel's Conflicts to New York," *New Yorker*, July 24, 2017, www.newyorker.com/magazine/2017/07/24/a-novel-brings-israels-conflicts-to-new-york.

7. Lutz, "The Sentence Is a Lonely Place."

8. Lutz, "The Sentence Is a Lonely Place."

status is transferred to the next one. As the ultimate arena of writerly achievement, each sentence is at once a potential triumph and a self-imposed prison from which we may not soon emerge. As daunting as this sounds, Lutz is adamant that true excellence is won not by persuading oneself that the whole is greater than the sum of the parts, but by making each part a tiny masterpiece.

A different but no less impassioned argument for taking pleasure in great sentences is made by Stanley Fish in *How to Write a Sentence: And How to Read One*. To explain how we can produce the kinds of sentences we so fervently admire in the work of others, Fish has to intervene in a long-standing debate among writing teachers at all levels of instruction. On one view, students learn how to craft fine sentences when they are given opportunities to discuss topics that engage and inspire them. In the terms of classical rhetoric, they should embrace *inventio* (invention and discovery) and let their enthusiasm and imagination run wild, trusting that inspired forms will follow. Opponents of this position maintain that students will be able to write effectively only once they have familiarized themselves with rigorous stylistics, which may include the canons of grammar, logic, and rhetoric as well as a dose of narratology.[9]

These two pedagogical strategies need not be mutually exclusive—individual instructors can and do avail themselves of both. For his part, Fish has no patience for the notion that students will make progress simply by being given opportunities to write about what interests them, insisting that at least in the first instance good form can be learned with almost no concern for content.[10] In taking this stance, he is not calling for the adoption of one or more style guides or for the revitalization of classical manuals of rhetoric, as if he believed that young people should spend their time memorizing lists of tropes and figures. His thesis is that we learn by example. Insofar as any sentence implicitly makes a claim that it is acceptable to speak or write in *this* way, it is potentially imitable. While there may be an unlimited variety of sentences to be written, there is no reason not to take advantage of structures, patterns, and rhythms with a proven track record and reuse them in other contexts. In this regard, canonical works of all kinds can serve as models for our own writing, but we need not restrict our search for exemplary sentences to the texts of famous authors. Great writing, Fish insists, can be found anywhere, be it in

9. For a more recent discussion of this debate, see Dana Goldstein, "Why Kids Can't Write," *New York Times*, August 2, 2017.

10. Several years earlier, Fish made this point more succinctly in an op-ed piece. See Stanley Fish, "Devoid of Content," *New York Times*, May 31, 2005.

newspapers and legal briefs, on billboards and graffiti-covered walls, or even occasionally in a fourth-grader's paper.

Having enjoined us to look for sentences that captivate us with their elegance, creativity, or precision, Fish is quick to dismiss the wealth of writing guides available for today's high school and college students. Taking William Strunk Jr. and E. B. White's *The Elements of Style* as his prime example, Fish observes that such books tell us how to produce sentences without ever explaining what a sentence is, although Amazon notes that people who buy Fish's book also buy Strunk and White. More than almost anyone writing on the topic of sentences, Fish is willing, even eager, to tackle the question of what one is, offering: "(1) a sentence is an organization of items in the world; and (2) a sentence is a structure of logical relationships."[11] As straightforward as these statements may appear, they represent a philosophical position with far-reaching implications. Fish treats them less as two different definitions of the concept of the sentence than as two ways of saying the same thing. For him, coherence, clarity, and meaning rest on the possibility of affirming that anything to which we want to refer can be incorporated into a system of logical connections. Like Ernest Hemingway, who fashions an entire world so that a particular kind of sentence will excel, Fish, a latter-day rationalist, ties the success or failure of any sentence to a worldview in which individual phenomena and processes can and must be understood in terms of formal patterns of reasoning with clear parameters of validity.

Fish proposes that "the logical forms that link actor, action, and the object of action" in a sentence constitute "finite and learnable" relationships, whereas the wealth of content that can be expressed by them is "infinite and incapable of being catalogued."[12] His description recalls Noam Chomsky's account of how the grammar of a language, a finite set of rules, allows for the production of an infinite number of sentences. There is, however, one important difference. As a literary critic, Fish is well aware of the irrepressible twists and turns of language that resist formalization and classification; but his goal is to do something that Chomsky does not, namely to conflate grammar and logic to such an extent that language becomes an orderly machine that gives shape to all possible meaningful relationships, in our minds or in the world. In these terms, vagueness, uncertainty, or confusion are nothing more than symptoms

11. Stanley Fish, *How to Write a Sentence: And How to Read One* (New York: HarperCollins, 2011), 16.

12. Fish, *How to Write a Sentence,* 133.

of poorly constructed clauses and can be dispelled with a few well-placed line edits.

In according near absolute authority to this logico-grammatical paradigm, Fish presents the sentence as a controlled dynamic. Correspondingly, a sentence that is "out of control or was never under control in the first place" is not actually a sentence at all, but "a random list" or "just a collection of unrelated words."[13] We can compose sentences that create the impression of "speech and writing just haphazardly tumbling out of the mouth" or seem to be expressing "the thoughts of [someone] who is not worrying about getting every particular just right," but these are stylistic ruses that are no less ordered than a sentence that overtly "ranks, orders, and sequences things, events, and persons in a way that strongly suggests a world where control is the imperative and everything is in its proper place."[14]

For Fish, the sentence is fundamentally a defense against the random, the irrational, and the chaotic. He writes as if Leibniz's fantasy of a truly logical language had been perfected to the point that as long as we follow the rules, our writing and thinking, not to mention our world, cannot go astray. To be fair, Fish is well aware of the fact that his doctrine may rest on shaky ground. Having arranged his book as a taxonomy of different types of sentences, he finds himself spending much of his time discussing the exceptions, and many of the sentences he seems to regard as the most powerful or provocative prove to be formations that according to his models have no business existing at all. Moreover, the longer he continues, the less clear it becomes exactly who is in control of these splendid formulations. As much as savoring an excellent sentence means appreciating someone else's cleverness or creativity, Fish admits that it is also an opportunity to watch language doing its work without us. Channeling Gertrude Stein's account of how much she enjoyed "feeling the everlasting feeling of sentences as they diagram themselves," he writes: "The reason diagramming sentences is completing is because the completing is being performed by the sentences themselves; they do it; all we have to do is attend. And if we attend faithfully, surrendering to the unfolding logic of predication, not only the completing, but the excitement of its having been done, will be ours by proxy."[15] Sentences are invigorating because they stand alone as autonomous processes. Like theatrical performances, their magic enthralls

13. Fish, *How to Write a Sentence,* 21.

14. Fish, *How to Write a Sentence,* 134.

15. Gertrude Stein, *Writings and Lectures 1911–1945* (London: Peter Owen, 1967), 124; Fish, *How to Write a Sentence*, 160.

us, but as much as we take vicarious pleasure in their accomplishments, part of what is exhilarating about them is the fact that they confront us with incontrovertible evidence of the ways in which language is not beholden to our aims and whims. If sentences can do countless things for us, they can also do things, many things, that we cannot dream of doing for ourselves.

Fish insists that "the reward for the effacing of ourselves before the altar of sentences will be that . . . we will possess a better self than the self we would have possessed had we not put ourselves in service. Sentences can save us. Who could ask for anything more?"[16] If the religious tone of these claims is somewhat tongue-in-cheek, Fish is quite earnest in his desire to show that we surrender control to the sentence only to regain it at a higher level by confirming that it was within our power to cede control in the first place. Whether this recuperation is as effortless or successful as he implies may be less than obvious to any writer who has ever grappled with the potentially ungovernable character of his or her sentences, which is arguably everyone. Far from reaffirming our status as the ultimate masters of the verbal arena, watching sentences do their thing is liable to make us realize that we were never nearly as much in charge as we imagined.

For Fish, the defense against this conclusion is an aesthetic one. Confronted with self-sovereign sentences that resist becoming tools with which we can exert control over our thoughts or the world, we respond by treating them as "stand-alone monuments."[17] In designating them as beautiful objects on which we can gaze admiringly, we hope that the pleasure we take in them will dissimulate the fact that they could just as well be regarded as products of an artificial intelligence whose abilities we do not fully understand, much less direct. In any event, Fish betrays no fear that in analyzing the marvelous sentences we unearth, we may somehow detract from our enjoyment of them, maintaining that the more precisely one can explain the "technical achievement" of a sentence, the more one will like it.[18]

In *Reading Style: A Life in Sentences*, Jenny Davidson encourages us to give our sentence fetish free rein. Based on an undergraduate course she taught at Columbia, her book makes a case for what is to be learned, and what enjoyment is to be had, from "reading for the sentence."[19] Davidson begins by taking

16. Fish, *How to Write a Sentence*, 160.

17. Fish, *How to Write a Sentence*, 134.

18. Fish, *How to Write a Sentence*, 7.

19. Jenny Davidson, *Reading Style: A Life in Sentences* (New York: Columbia University Press, 2014), 11 (hereafter cited in text as *RS*).

us on a tour of some of her favorite sentences, which are primarily drawn from canonical works of literature. Observing that the New Critical object of study was almost exclusively the lyric poem, she invites us to bring close reading to bear on longer prose works, where "the aspects of meaning contributed by word choice, by diction, [and] by syntax" are just as crucial as in other genres (*RS*, 11). While scholars of the novel may object that they have been doing this for some time, the spirit of the gesture is commendable, Davidson's selection of admirable sentences is unimpeachable, and she offers elegant analyses of them.

Despite all of this, Davidson feels that there is something objectionable about what she is doing, as if the pleasure she takes in analyzing sentences were immoderate. "By stripping literary language down to its constituent parts," she writes, "I perversely gain a sense of transcendence, an emotional as well as intellectual liberation that comes by way of the most precise consideration of details of language" (*RS*, 2). The word "perversely" stands out, since it is not obvious why she feels the need to excuse the fact that rigorous analysis can be an empowering experience. The adverb returns when she emphasizes the degree to which her reading practice is characterized by modal and tonal antitheses, claiming that it is "at once perversely unworldly and profoundly practical, at one and the same time supremely playful and deadly in earnest" (*RS*, 9). Whatever else it achieves, investigating questions of sentence style stirs up strong affects, reminding us that fetishism is an inherently volatile dynamic.

In a close reading of a novel, questions of economy inevitably arise, since one cannot discuss every line in equal detail. Davidson insists, however, that selecting particular sentences on which to focus is not simply a matter of bowing to the realities of finite time and energy, because "all sentences are not created equal" and should not be treated as such (*RS*, 2). Some sentences, she adds, "are more interesting, more intricate, more attractive or repellent than others" (*RS*, 2). Once again, her vocabulary bespeaks a charged dynamic, for the pleasure of reading good sentences is now paralleled by a sense of revolt or disgust when unappetizing sentences present themselves, suggesting that what is really at stake is the right to have such feelings, the right to pursue an ethics of aesthetic experience. Averring that she is allowed to "loathe" a book when "her passionate contempt is colored partly by my conviction that it's morally as well as aesthetically pernicious," Davidson makes it clear that in the age of the sentence fetish, the prerogative, if not the obligation, to lavish our attention on some sentences is complemented by a responsibility to condemn others (*RS*, 10).

Like Kraus, Davidson maintains that the microcosm contains the macrocosm and that individual sentences reveal nothing less than "the complex set of intellectual, emotional, political and cultural traits that make up a given [writer's] identity" (*RS*, 12). "The sentence," she declares, "is the key to the heart," and moreover, "style may itself serve as a kind of morality" (*RS*, 13). For Davidson, style is not just the manner in which a particular ethical posture or worldview is expressed in speech or writing. Style *is* morality, because in giving shape to relationships, values, and judgments, it articulates standards of right and wrong, privileging one sort of behavior and denigrating another by establishing the means by which specific types of actions can and should be applauded or disparaged.

As a result, Davidson's call for us to read "for the sentence" ends up bifurcating form and content. Focusing on George Eliot's *Middlemarch*, she deems it to be "both unparalleled in its greatness and full of sentences that make me cringe, not because of the insights they express but because of the words in which those thoughts are couched. At such times, Eliot's style has about it something graceless or embarrassing" (*RS*, 24). Eliot's tone is pretentious and sanctimonious, her diction "smug," but Davidson insists that the psychological content on offer is so strong that it excuses "the blocky embarrassments of the language" (*RS*, 23). If anything, it is the divergence between the quality of Eliot's style and the content of her insights that makes the writing memorable. *Middlemarch*, Davidson concludes, "would not be nearly so brilliant if it were not so frequently and grotesquely ponderous in its locutions" (*RS*, 25). The sentences are "ugly," but their aesthetic failure intensifies our sense of the importance of what is being said. The ultimate consequence of fetishizing sentences is that the distinction between moral and aesthetic judgments collapses, an event with complex if not dangerous political implications. In this regard, Davidson's celebration of sentences contrasts sharply with that of Fish, who makes a concerted effort to keep the aesthetic experience of good and bad sentences separate from any ethical calculus.

Fish and Davidson both accord the individual reader considerable autonomy in judging sentences superior or inferior. When it comes to the choices we make in crafting our own sentences, most writers do not enjoy a similar degree of freedom. Depending on our age and stage, it is easy to feel overwhelmed by the sheer number—and evident arbitrariness—of the compositional mores and taboos with which we must contend. In some cases, stylistic dos and don'ts are contingent on the whims of instructors or editors; in others, we must respect the conventions of our institution or industry. In this context, style manuals play a peculiar role, serving more as abiding figures of authority—the specter of a code—than as something we consult in a systematic effort to follow the letter of the law. Infamously capricious in their pronouncements on split infinitives, the passive voice, or the use of contractions, such texts' influence is far from clear, even as they continue to sell by the tens of thousands.

While they have the reputation of purveying rules grounded in little more than a single "expert" opinion, style manuals do speak with one voice when it comes to their core dicta. Helen Sword recently took stock of a hundred contemporary books on writing marketed to American college students and instructors. Her survey revealed them to be "virtually unanimous" on several points, most notably in their call for "sentences that are clear, coherent, and concise."[20] The corresponding injunction to avoid vagueness and imprecision was nearly as common. If this consensus is intriguing, the length of its pedigree is no less so. "Style to be good must be clear, as is proved by the fact that speech which fails to convey a plain meaning will fail to do just what speech has to do. Clearness is secured by using the words (nouns and verbs alike) that are current and ordinary." These remarks sound as if they were drawn from a writing guide from the 1920s, although in fact they are taken from a two-thousand-year-old text by Aristotle.[21] Working within a narrower frame of reference, Andrew Elfenbein has argued that "the eighteenth-century [conception of the] well-formed sentence has been passed down, almost unchanged, to the twenty-first century."[22] This lineage becomes explicit in the scholarly work of William Strunk Jr., co-author of *The Elements of Style*. In an edition of essays he edited on Boswell's *Life of Johnson*, Strunk celebrates the prose style of Whig historian and politician Thomas Macaulay (1800–1859), praising him for writing "short sentences" that were "admirably clear," and adding that Macaulay's "professed aim was to write no sentence that did not disclose its meaning on first reading."[23] As Elfenbein notes, "It is only a small step from this praise to [Strunk's] later, more famous advice in his monumentally successful *Elements of Style*: 'Vigorous writing is concise. A sentence should contain no unnecessary words, a paragraph no unnecessary sentences.'"[24]

20. Helen Sword, *Stylish Academic Writing* (Cambridge, MA: Harvard University Press, 2012), 26.

21. Aristotle, *The Rhetoric and Poetics of Aristotle* (New York: Modern Library, 1984), 167 (1404b).

22. Andrew Elfenbein, *Romanticism and the Rise of English* (Stanford, CA: Stanford University Press, 2009), 209–10.

23. Cited in Elfenbein, *Romanticism and the Rise of English*, 209.

24. Elfenbein, *Romanticism and the Rise of English*, 209.

Clarity, coherence, and concision. While one hesitates to speak of universal standards of compositional excellence, we rarely set out to write something confused, incoherent, or unnecessarily long, unless our intention is to dissimulate, confuse, or simply test our audience's patience. On what basis, however, does any member of this trio of writerly ideals permit of systematic evaluation? Surely clarity or coherence are in the eye of the beholder, or in this case the reader. In assessing the lucidity and consistency of a text, academics are notoriously partisan, in the same breath denouncing the obscurantism or impenetrability of an adversary's writing while lauding the similar prose of an ally for offering a pellucid window onto the truth. Apparently, suspicions must be raised any time an ostensibly objective standard for clarity or coherence is put forward. This does not, however, change the fact that a text's reception is always in part a factor of how it is written.

Combine the Cartesian privileging of clear and distinct perceptions with the philosophical tradition of favoring simplicity over complexity, and it is only a short step to the conclusion that bad writing is a symptom of a weak mind.[25] Small wonder that the condemnation of a text's style is frequently a thinly veiled attack on its content, if not an insinuation that we are contending with muddled thinking. At the same time, as much as a rigid form/content dichotomy seems impossible to sustain, whether at the level of the sentence, the paragraph, or an entire text, we may not want to find ourselves in the position of being unable to distinguish between judgments about style and judgments about the truth or falsehood of arguments.

Theodor W. Adorno argues that compositional standards such as "lucidity, objectivity, and concise precision" are the inventions of writers and editors seeking to accommodate those who prefer not to be taxed while reading.[26] Although this claim may be insufficiently attentive to the long history of such compositional criteria, Jean-Pierre Mileur cautions against assuming that one

25. "So I now seem to be able to lay it down as a general rule," writes Descartes at the beginning of his *Third Meditation*, "that whatever I perceive very clearly and distinctly is true." René Descartes, *Meditations on First Philosophy*, trans. and ed. John Cottingham (London: Cambridge University Press, 1996), 24. The conviction that simplicity is a virtue has a long pedigree in philosophy. Already in evidence in Aristotle's *Posterior Analytics* but perhaps best known from Occam's Razor, the concept of simplicity is itself far from simple, uneasily conjoining a prejudice for the argument that makes fewer hypotheses with a prejudice for the argument that postulates fewer entities in or features of the world.

26. Theodor W. Adorno, *Notes to Literature*, vol. 1, trans. Shierry Weber Nicholson (New York: Columbia University Press, 1991), 95.

generation's call for clarity and simplicity is the same as another's. What if, he asks,

> ideals of clarity and simplicity have come to serve a different ideological purpose, in our present context, from the one Descartes had in mind? What if, in this period of the overproduction of printed matter and the proliferation of methods of quick reading, they were intended to speed the reader across a sentence in such a way that he can salute a readymade idea effortlessly in passing, without suspecting that real thought demands a descent into the materiality of language and a consent to time itself in the form of the sentence?[27]

Mileur's remarks were made well before digital telecommunications had profoundly intensified and magnified the tendencies he describes. In the past quarter-century, we have heard many versions of his prescient remarks, but there has also been considerable pushback against the premise that slower reading is necessarily better reading. The assumption that sentences that are written to be read quickly are inherently less substantive than those that are not has also been called into question. Such debates have not, however, blunted the enthusiasm for clarity. The more convincingly we demonstrate it to be a contingent or dated standard, the more entrenched it seems to become.

In *The Sense of Style*, the linguist Steven Pinker offers an account of what it would mean to make clear writing a paramount principle. He begins by endorsing the "classic style" championed in Francis-Noël Thomas and Mark Turner's *Clear and Simple as the Truth*. As Pinker summarizes the doctrine: "Prose is a window onto the world. The writer knows the truth before putting it into words; he is not using the occasion of writing to argue for the truth; he just needs to present it."[28] This model of representation relies on a series of dichotomies that may be difficult to sustain: truth/the language that reveals it, knowing something/expressing it in words, arguing/presenting. A

27. Jean-Pierre Mileur, *The Critical Romance: The Critic as Reader, Writer, Hero* (Madison: University of Wisconsin Press, 1990), 18.

28. Steven Pinker, *The Sense of Style: The Thinking Person's Guide to Writing in the 21st Century* (New York: Penguin, 2014), 29. One of the virtues of Thomas and Turner's book is that in contradistinction to Pinker, they call attention to the degree to which style is predicated on a host of philosophical—and inherently ideological—assumptions about the nature of individuality and community, the hierarchies that obtain between different peoples and groups, and, perhaps most obviously, truth and language. To defend a style is necessarily to defend an entire worldview. See Francis-Noël Thomas and Mark Turner, *Clear and Simple as the Truth* (Princeton, NJ: Princeton University Press, 1994), esp. 19–27.

counterpoint to such advice is offered by Eric Hayot in *The Elements of Academic Style*. Hayot opens with a paean to "active writing," which "should not involve saying things you already understand and know, but instead let you think new things."[29] "You cannot know what your ideas are, mean, or do," he argues, "until you set them down in sentences, whether on paper or on screen."[30] In contrast to Pinker, Hayot is unwilling to distinguish even provisionally between thinking and writing or thoughts and their expression.

Pinker is aware of the potential criticism. The "classic style," he acknowledges, "remains a pretense, an imposture, a stance."[31] The goal is to write as if one knew the truth before putting it down on paper, to make it "*seem* as if the writer's thoughts were fully formed before he clothed them in words," while in fact "the messy work has been done beforehand and behind the scenes."[32] Pinker does not object to the notion that writing is a productive process rather than a transcription of what has already been conceptualized, providing that the final copy doesn't betray the traces of hesitancy, doubt, or confusion that so often characterize an argument in its incipient form. Our goal should be to share polished products and to avoid airing the dirty laundry of earlier drafts, rife with all the halting steps and missteps they contain.

Pinker has no difficulty explaining why he thinks the pretense and posture that ground this "classic style" are necessary: "The purpose of writing is presentation, and its motive is disinterested truth. It succeeds when it aligns language with the truth, the proof of success being clarity and simplicity."[33] The claim is that the appearance of clarity and simplicity in a sentence is evidence of an alignment between language and truth. The confidence with which Pinker asserts this is odd, since he has just acknowledged that such clear and simple presentations are carefully engineered simulations that actively suppress any trace of a disjunction between writing process and product, that is, they are overtly dishonest about how they got to be what they are.

Pinker maintains that writing that is not clear and simple cannot be a disinterested presentation of truth and is probably infected by methodological or ideological bias. To express doubt about what one is saying—in many contexts a sine qua non for argumentative integrity—is not the way to win his

29. Eric Hayot, *The Elements of Academic Style: Writing for the Humanities* (New York: Columbia University Press, 2014), 1.

30. Hayot, *Elements*, 1.

31. Pinker, *The Sense of Style*, 37.

32. Pinker, *The Sense of Style*, 38 (emphasis in original).

33. Pinker, *The Sense of Style*, 29.

confidence. He condemns those who "flaunt" such concerns, averring that "good writers" simply do not spend time and energy undercutting their own claims, at least not in front of their readers.[34] For Pinker, an honest acknowledgment of the limits of one's project is a symptom of frivolity or self-indulgence rather than of rigor. His clear and simple truth has the clarity and simplicity of dogmatism.

Hayot takes a different position, arguing that the products of active writing "belong . . . to the means that made them. They emerge from a process; they represent their becoming, and that emergence, in their final form."[35] A rigid opposition between first draft and final copy betrays a misunderstanding of what will be lost when we assume that the goal of inquiry is the definitive revelation of a pristine truth. The simulation advocated by Pinker is thus to be avoided: "Writing *as though* you already know what you have to say hinders it as a medium for research and discovery; it blocks the possibilities—the openings—that appear at the intersection of an intention and an audience, and constitute themselves, there, as a larger, complete performance."[36] If we set out from the assumption that our goal is to move from messy uncertainties to well-organized certainties, or at least a semblance thereof, we predetermine the relationship between form and content or method and result and thereby risk predetermining the answers we seek, as well. For Pinker, the point is to write something that appears as if it fell fully formed from the heavens, whereas for Hayot, good writing should never pit process against product.

Hayot and Pinker take diametrically opposed positions on a foundational issue in the philosophy of style. The practical advice they offer for crafting sentences differs as well, although perhaps not in the way one might anticipate. For his recommendations, Hayot relies extensively on Joseph M. Williams's 1985 *Style: Ten Lessons in Clarity and Grace*. Williams's two basic rules for a good sentence are "whenever possible, express at the beginning of a sentence ideas already stated, referred to, implied, safely assumed, familiar, predictable, less important, readily accessible information"; and "express at

34. Pinker, *The Sense of Style,* 37. In *Clear and Simple as the Truth*, Thomas and Turner stress that their "classic style" is not a "reflexive" style and that writing itself is not the subject. "The classic writer," they maintain, "assumes that his subject can be known and can be expressed without distortion," and "classic style acknowledges nothing that does not fit its model of elegance" (79, 105). In this regard, they want to distinguish the classic style, which "presents something," from the contemplative style, which "presents an interpretation of something" (89).

35. Hayot, *Elements*, 1.

36. Hayot, *Elements,* 1 (emphasis added).

the end of a sentence the least predictable, the newest, the most important, the most significant information, the information you almost certainly want to emphasize."[37] If these guidelines are followed, the relationships between one's sentences should be crystal clear, because the beginning of each will point back to what preceded it, while the end will present new material that will subsequently be reinvoked and reinforced in the following sentence. The most important thing is not to produce a string of isolated aphorisms. When in doubt, we should err on the side of giving "priority to emphasis and cohesion, to what fuses sentences into cohesive discourse."[38]

The writing guidelines Hayot takes from Williams are themselves inspired by *The Elements of Style*, where Strunk and White enjoin that "the proper place in the sentence for the word or group of words that the writer desires to make most prominent is usually the end," and add that "the word or group of words entitled to this position of prominence is usually the logical predicate—that is, the *new* element in the sentence."[39] Crucially, Strunk and White extend this argument to any unit of discourse: "The principle that the proper place for what is to be made most prominent is the end applies equally to the words of a sentence, to the sentences of a paragraph, and to the paragraphs of a composition."[40] This move is echoed by Williams and in turn by Hayot, who writes: "Material at the *end* of any unit of prose (clause, sentence, paragraph, essay, chapter, book) will have more structural weight than the material before it."[41]

One can think of countless stories, anecdotes, or arguments in which information acquires a privileged status by virtue of appearing at the end. As an account of how individual sentences work, however, this doctrine privileges the linear succession of words over the hierarchical organization of syntax. In this regard, Hayot's term "*structural* weight" is misleading, since sequence is only one of the many factors that help highlight or downplay a given sentence element, and in any case, the structure in question is not linear. Hayot's point is ultimately more psychological or experiential than grammatical. Even Williams seems to acknowledge that sequence is only one of several issues to

37. Joseph M. Williams, *Style: Ten Lessons in Clarity and Grace*, 2nd ed. (New York: Scott, Foresman, 1985), 33, 34.

38. Williams, *Style*, 33.

39. William Strunk Jr. and E. B. White, *The Elements of Style*, 4th ed. (New York: Pearson, 1979), 32.

40. Strunk and White, *Elements of Style*, 33.

41. Hayot, *Elements*, 196–97.

consider when he argues that "if you begin a sentence well, the end will almost take care of itself."[42]

Pinker takes a different approach. As a linguist, he is highly attuned to the potentially misleading assumptions that people, in particular authors of style manuals, make when they privilege the linear unfolding of a sentence in time or space over its structural hierarchy or casually parallel the presentation of information in sentences with its presentation in other discursive units. He is also concerned to avoid the unexamined assumptions about human perception or cognitive psychology that ground many of the stylistic pronouncements that are commonly purveyed. In this respect, his book offers a breath of fresh air by providing an unusually broad, thoughtful vision of what writing well involves. Rather than repeating commonplaces, he reflects in detail on the different forms of clauses and paragraphs without ever taking for granted that what lends clarity and coherence to one kind of textual unit is necessarily helpful with others.

While Hayot's active writing may offer a more dynamic mode of inquiry than Pinker's classic style, Pinker's stylistic prescriptions at the level of the sentence are richer, although ironically the sections of his book that discuss these issues look more like the kind of exploratory inquiry Hayot advocates than the lucid window onto the truth that Pinker himself endorses. Hayot and Pinker also seem to share common ground when it comes to citing specific examples of good writing—much of the academic prose Hayot praises would almost certainly meet with Pinker's approval as well. Any sense that their conceptions of style may be obliquely compatible vanishes, however, when Pinker discusses sentences of which he does not approve. The archenemy of his classic style is "the worldview of relativist academic ideologies such as postmodernism, poststructuralism, and literary Marxism," a grab bag of doctrines to which he would almost certainly relegate Hayot.[43] No less than for Fish, style is for Pinker a worldview, with all the far-reaching implications this entails.

If relativism is one of Pinker's principal bugbears, there is much more at issue. In illustrating what he condemns, Pinker avails himself of some sentences collected by Denis Dutton, an American philosopher best known as the founder of the website Arts & Letters Daily. In the late 1990s, Dutton staged an annual publicity stunt, a Bad Writing Contest, which received considerable media attention. As an archetypal piece of flawed writing, Pinker selects the

42. Williams, *Style*, 53.
43. Pinker, *The Sense of Style*, 35.

1997 "winner" of Dutton's contest, the opening sentence of a collection of essays on film by Fredric Jameson:

> The visual is essentially pornographic, which is to say that it has its end in rapt, mindless fascination; thinking about its attributes becomes an adjunct to that, if it is unwilling to betray its object; while the most austere films necessarily draw their energy from the attempt to repress their own excess (rather than from the more thankless efforts to discipline the viewer).[44]

Pinker begins his exposition of this passage thus: "The assertion that 'the visual is essentially pornographic' is not, to put it mildly, a fact about the world that anyone can see."[45] The assumption that a fact about the world is something that one can "see" suggests, "to put it mildly," a limited understanding of the concept of a fact, not least since it will be less than obvious whether most of the "facts" on which Pinker himself relies are truths that can be seen. Can we, for instance, "see" that the facts about the world are necessarily things that can be seen? A scientist of language, Pinker pays far too little attention to the ways in which the metaphorics of vision have underwritten the discourse on insight since antiquity.

As best as one can see, Pinker's stated desire is to be able to see everything, and in this respect, he proves Jameson's point, that is, he desires to be raptly gripped by a pornographic world of facts. Perhaps aware of the trap into which he is stumbling, he asks rhetorically: "Can't something have 'its end in rapt, mindless fascination' without being pornographic?"[46] In attacking Jameson for being insufficiently concrete, Pinker appeals to vague commonplaces about the pornographic. He does not want to think about what the word "pornographic" means any more than he wants to think about the implications of his commitment to a particular understanding of the relationship between seeing with the eye and seeing with the mind's eye. Confronted with a specific understanding of a term, he can spare no more time than is required for him to see that what is being said is unfamiliar to him, at which point he dismisses the matter.

Offended at being presented with an idea that does not conform to his worldview, Pinker declares that the ultimate effect of Jameson's sentence is "that the puzzled reader is put on notice that *her* ability to understand the world counts for nothing; her role is to behold the enigmatic pronouncements

44. Fredric Jameson, *Signatures of the Visible* (New York: Routledge, 1990), 1.
45. Pinker, *The Sense of Style,* 35.
46. Pinker, *The Sense of Style,* 35–36.

of the great scholar."[47] Jameson's crime is to have written a sentence that does not state something that the reader, in this case Pinker, already thinks. With his conclusion that "bad writing" of this sort "makes the reader feel like a dunce," Pinker intimates that a sentence is supposed to make us feel smart by confirming that we already have a command of whatever is under discussion.[48] "Good" writing is "clear and simple" because it tells us what we believe to be the case before we read it. In other words, we do not understand the propositions of a well-written sentence so much as we understand that we have already understood them. To the extent that this is not what happens, we are within our rights to condemn the sentence as muddled or obscure and move on.

Pinker's argument foregrounds just how threatening other people's sentences can be. On his view, reading anything that we did not write ourselves exposes us to the possibility of humiliation. In a widely cited *Wall Street Journal* article in which Dutton boasted about his writing contest and disparaged numerous academics for their stylistic sins, he said of another of his prize sentences, written by Judith Butler: "To ask what this means is to miss the point. This sentence beats readers into submission and instructs them that they are in the presence of a great and deep mind. Actual communication has nothing to do with it."[49] Like Pinker, Dutton wants to read sentences that mirror his own views back to him. Anything less amounts to being brought to heel by force.

In the end, Pinker does not bother to hide the solipsism he endorses: "Writing is above all an act of pretense. We have to visualize ourselves in some kind of conversation, or correspondence, or oration, or soliloquy, and put words into the mouth of the little avatar who represents us in this simulated world."[50] In the slide from "conversation" to "soliloquy," it becomes evident that the model of writing being envisioned involves a dialogue between oneself and the

47. Pinker, *The Sense of Style*, 36 (emphasis in original).

48. Pinker, *The Sense of Style*, 36.

49. Denis Dutton, "Language Crimes: A Lesson in How Not to Write, Courtesy of the Professoriate," *Wall Street Journal*, February 5, 1999. Dutton's full citation of Butler's sentence reads:

> The move from a structuralist account in which capital is understood to structure social relations in relatively homologous ways to a view of hegemony in which power relations are subject to repetition, convergence, and rearticulation brought the question of temporality into the thinking of structure, and marked a shift from a form of Althusserian theory that takes structural totalities as theoretical objects to one in which the insights into the contingent possibility of structure inaugurate a renewed conception of hegemony as bound up with the contingent sites and strategies of the rearticulation of power. ("Language Crimes")

50. Pinker, *The Sense of Style*, 28.

avatar into whose mouth one puts one's own words. As in Hemingway's oeuvre, where a world is constructed for the sake of a particular kind of sentence, Pinker imagines the simulation of an entire realm in which one can speak safely, with no danger of saying something that will not be understood, because one speaks only to and for oneself. Perfect sentences are the product of an active imagination, but the creativity required to produce them is less an ability to fashion unique syntactic patterns or coin particular turns of phrase than the capacity to construct a sort of ideal sentence situation in which one's compositions cannot help but thrive.

What is a sentence? On the face of it, it is a formation of language that has been put to work in one fashion or another, successfully or unsuccessfully. When the objective parameters of its grammar and logic are complemented by subjective flourishes that allow something distinctive or even unique to take shape, this utilitarian verbal construct may prove to be elegant or beautiful. Despite what Pinker may wish, however, style is never simply a private affair. Every sentence is about what every other sentence is or should be, because every sentence presents itself as a potential model for all other sentences, whether as a standard by which existing sentences can be measured or as an ideal form toward which future sentences should strive. In this respect, every sentence, no matter how modest or grandiose, casts every other sentence in a new light.

Numerous modern authors have been influenced by the idea that every time we write a sentence, we are in some sense assuming responsibility for every sentence that has ever existed or could exist. This conviction can foster an almost unimaginable level of perfectionism, as if not only the fate of one's own work but of composition in general rested on one's ability to get every phrase and clause just right. Alternatively, the result may be an endless series of experiments as we strive to change the forms and standards that define the sentence, albeit at the risk of losing sight of what we supposed it to be in the first place. For writers caught in the grips of this dilemma, there is no way to be sure whether anyone has ever truly finished a sentence, finished with a sentence, or seen one of their own sentences finish with them—assuming, as Stein cautions us, that there is such a thing as a sentence at all.

Given the immense anxiety that surrounds the sentence and our perceived need to write clear, precise, or beautiful ones, it is small wonder that the most common pieces of stylistic advice all amount to some version of "play it safe." The tacit injunction to write responsible, law-abiding prose may be part of a larger program of social control, on par with keeping one's yard neat, paying one's taxes, and not driving too fast on the highway. Speaking and writing well, a sine qua non for participating in almost any communal activity, can quickly switch from being one's best means of influencing other people to a means of keeping us in our place. Of course, these coercive dynamics capture only one dimension of the politics of the sentence. Our discussion has repeatedly illustrated the difficulty of disentangling the sentence's representational and performative powers from different forms of individual or collective agency. Reviewing the archetypal speech acts of human or divine authority—*I am who I am*, *I sentence you to death*, *I think therefore I am*—we are reminded that the notion that a particular paradigm of subjective authority is grounded in a specific verbal form is far from novel.

What would it mean, however, to review modern political thought from the perspective of a self understood first and foremost as a relative of the sentence? There is a striking parallel between the liberal subject, an ostensibly self-determining agent whose capacity to be counted as complete or autonomous often derives from without rather than within, and the sentence, customarily defined as self-standing yet constitutively open to combination with and revision by the other putatively self-standing formations around it. The alignment of the liberal subject and the sentence—call it an association, resemblance, or analogy—becomes even more compelling when we consider that both may be ideals that exist more in theory than in practice, or at least they are both concepts on which so many competing demands are placed that they can never fully meet our expectations.

Well aware of the sentence's status as a hinge between individual autonomy and collective control, both the artistic and the political avant-gardes have frequently challenged the hegemony of subject-predicate schemas. The reigning paradigm, however, has proven to be quite resilient. Success tends to be fleeting when it comes to developing alternative signifying fields driven by more than just the shock value they acquire by virtue of being "different." Revolutions in or of the sentence invariably find themselves affirming its ineluctability, which should arguably come as no surprise given that linguists assure us that the sentence is a feature of every human language.

Perhaps the key to radicalizing the kinds of politics underwritten by the sentence is to move away from the notion of the sentence as a *unit* of discourse. "A sentence has wishes as an event," writes Stein.[51] In her terms, the ultimate aspiration of any sentence is to transcend its status as a stable piece of a text—a known commodity—and become a genuine transformation of language.

51. Gertrude Stein, "Saving the Sentence," *American Poetry Review* 36, no. 1 (January/February 2007): 33.

Hegel's speculative sentence, the Marxist slogan, and Stein's own unique verbal formations all expose us to grammatical, logical, or rhythmic dynamics that have little or no place in the traditional sentence. Considerably complicating our sense of what it means for a group of words to stand alone, such linguistic phenomena serve to remind us that we are far from formalizing and codifying everything that language can say or do.

In *The Prisonhouse of Language*, Fredric Jameson invokes Jacques Lacan's famous adage "the unconscious is the discourse of the other" and comments: "This seems to me to be a sentence rather than an idea, by which I mean that it marks out the place of meditation and offers itself as an object of exegesis, instead of serving as the expression of a single concept."[52] Etymologically a verdict or judgment, a sentence invariably presents itself as complete, but it is never reducible to a mere equation or definition. Far from a docile medium for a content that is indifferently related to it, a sentence is both creative and destructive in its own right. We want our sentences to have an air of consequentiality, and we aspire to finish each and every one of them with a flourish. Sentences are powerful, however, because they are by nature sites of ongoing reflection and analysis and are thus permanently marked by an air of the provisional. As definitive as it may claim to be, a sentence cannot help but confirm that there is more to say or do, if only about the way in which it is saying and doing things. In this respect, every age is the age of the sentence fetish, since we can no more stop celebrating the sentence's magical powers than we can be confident of our ability to control them or steadfast in our resolve to do without them. Long or short, incisive or convoluted, *a* sentence always has a message about *the* sentence, which is why Stein helps us recognize that whatever else it is doing, a sentence is almost certainly asking the question: What is a sentence?

52. Fredric Jameson, *The Prisonhouse of Language: A Critical Account of Structuralism and Russian Formalism* (Princeton, NJ: Princeton University Press, 1972), 170–71.

INDEX